The West and China since 1500

The West and China since 1500

John S. Gregory

First published 2002 by
PALGRAVE MACMILLAN
Houndmills, Basingstoke, Hampshire RG21 6XS and
175 Fifth Avenue, New York, N.Y. 10010
Companies and representatives throughout the world

PALGRAVE MACMILLAN is the global academic imprint of the Palgrave
Macmillan division of St. Martin's Press, LLC and of Palgrave Macmillan Ltd.
Macmillan® is a registered trademark in the United States, United Kingdom
and other countries. Palgrave is a registered trademark in the European
Union and other countries.

ISBN 0–333–99744–1 hardback

This book is printed on paper suitable for recycling and made from fully
managed and sustained forest sources.

A catalogue record for this book is available from the British Library.

Library of Congress Cataloging-in-Publication Data
Gregory, J.S. (John Stradbroke), 1923–
    The West and China since 1500 / John S. Gregory.
        p.   cm.
    Includes bibliographical references and index.
    ISBN 0–333–99744–1 (cloth) — ISBN 1–4039–0280–1 (pbk.)
    1. China—Relations—Foreign countries.   I. Title.

DS740.4 .G74 2002
327.510182′1′09—dc21
                                                             2002072338

Printed and bound in Great Britain by
Antony Rowe Ltd, Chippenham and Eastbourne

To Nancy

Contents

Preface

This survey of Western civilization's relationship to the once very distant civilization of China has been prompted by my talking, after my retirement from university teaching, to other retirees attending University of the Third Age (U3A) classes. Encouraged by the evident eagerness of these mature age students to know more about China, including the history of its relations with the West, I set about writing what was intended to be a relatively brief account of the fluctuating relationship of these two great but very different cultural traditions for the kind of intelligent, general interest rather than specialist audience which makes up U3A classes. Chapter I reflects that approach and intent. However, as the writing proceeded more detail crept in, so that the later chapters, especially the third and fourth, thickened. Without forgetting or, I hope, altogether losing my University of the Third Age audience, I moved gradually towards writing for the student of modern Chinese history and politics pursuing more formal courses of study, offering them some details and interpretations – on the opium trade, the treaty system, the missionary movement, the status of Taiwan, for example – which may stimulate debate in the classroom.

This is not a history of China, of which there are many, but simply a survey of the West's approach to that country since the time when regular contact with it was established. My title is *The West and China*, putting 'the West' first to emphasize that, although something of what was happening in China during these five centuries of contact must necessarily be included, the essential focus is upon Western culture – how it has approached and sought to understand China; how it has reacted to it; what it has gained from it, what demanded from it; how it has treated it; how it has adjusted to the great changes which have taken place within modern China, changes prompted in large part by the West's very presence. There are some authoritative studies entitled *China and the West*, notably by Wolfgang Franke and Jerome Chen, and my bibliography lists many other relevant and specialized studies, while any general history of China will refer to many of the issues raised in this study. Thus the serious student may read much else to set against what is recounted here.

Though necessarily sweeping rapidly over five centuries, I have endeavoured to maintain a balance between the very general and the fairly specific, a balance which I hope will satisfy both the kind of reader who attends, or may one day attend, U3A classes, and the younger student attending other kinds of classes. Having been 15 years in retirement I am no longer as close to the cutting edge of scholarship on modern Chinese history as I endeavoured to be when a university lecturer, but in preparing for my U3A classes, and in setting out to write this survey text, I have made considerable efforts to catch up with at least some of the relevant scholarly literature. However, the subject is vast, so the indulgence of the reader is sought for any serious oversight of recent scholarship. I have set out to write a reflection, a summing up of my nearly half a century of studying and teaching about China, with the object of encouraging further reflection by my fellow Westerners, old and young, about their relationship to a great alternative tradition.

The pinyin system of romanization is used, save for some geographic names well known in older forms (Canton, Hong Kong, Kowloon), and for Sun Yat-sen and Chiang Kai-shek, whom I suspect many readers would not readily recognize in their pinyin personas of Sun Zhongshan and Jiang Jieshi. One piece of pedantry I have persisted in is to refer to Chinese emperors as 'the such-and-such emperor', since the 'names' by which they are usually identified are in fact reign titles, their personal names being taboo. It is rather as if in English history we referred to Elizabeth I only as 'the Virgin Queen', never presuming to refer to her by her actual name.

I am indebted to the U3A organization of my home city, Melbourne, for providing me with the audiences which stimulated me to set about writing down something of what I was saying to them. I am grateful to my academic colleagues, Dr Tom Fisher and Dr Paul Rule, for their comments on sections of the manuscript, especially to Paul Rule for his help on aspects of the missionary presence. My son Martin and daughter Janet have between them made up for my lack of computer skills and have provided constant love and support, as has my dear wife Mary who prepared the map and has made many constructive comments on the text. Most of all I am indebted to my friend Dr Nancy Renfree, but for whose unfailing interest, encouragement, and practical skills, I doubt these ideas would have been turned into words on the printed page.

J.S. Gregory
Melbourne, February 2002

Doing history means building bridges between the past and the present, observing both banks of the river, taking an active part on both sides.

Bernhard Schlink – *The Reader*

Every history is a map: it leaves out some features of reality and singles out others which are thought to display its essential structure . . . The process of mapping becomes the surveyor's process of triangulation, and the reference points are important less in themselves than as marks for triangulation – that is, as points from which to take a bearing.

J. Bronowski and B. Mazlich – *The Western Intellectual Tradition*

Historians are bound by right to be exact, truthful, and absolutely unprejudiced, so that neither interest nor fear, dislike nor affection, should make them turn from the path of truth, whose mother is history, rival of time, storehouse of great deeds, witness of the past, example and lesson to the present, warning to the future. In this history I know that you will find all the entertainment you can desire; and if any good quality is missing, I am certain that it is the fault of its dog of an author rather than any default in the subject.

Cervantes – *Don Quixote* (Part I, Ch. 9)

The conquered always submit to the stronger; but their submission is merely provisional when civilizations clash. Long periods of enforced co-existence may include concessions or agreements and important, often fruitful, cultural exchange. But the process always has its limits . . . The vanquished surrender, but preserve themselves too.

Fernand Braudel – *A History of Civilizations*

Map   Major rivers, regions, treaty ports etc. referred to in the text.

Introduction

Co-existing with China will be one of the great challenges facing the West in the twenty-first century. Indeed some see it as likely to be the greatest challenge, with China having the potential to develop as a super power capable of matching the West, in particular the United States, economically, politically, militarily. Whether or not that happens, there seems no doubt that, given the collapse of the Soviet empire, China is likely to emerge as the main counterweight to any continuing Western dominance in world affairs.

After an introductory chapter outlining some of the major differences between the two great cultural traditions, this book reviews the changing relationship of the West with China since the early sixteenth century, when Westerners first came to the great empire of East Asia by sea, and thereafter persisted in doing so. There had been earlier contacts by land, but of only a limited and occasional character, leaving a residue of stories and ideas about 'Cathay', which were as much mythological as factual. It was not until the sixteenth century that China began truly to enter the Western consciousness – a consciousness by then beginning to be overwhelmed by a heightened awareness of the great diversity of cultures on this globe. Among those cultures was China's which, by the end of the century, was recognized as being also the Cathay of the mediaeval travellers. By then Western traders and missionaries had made firm contacts in both the north and south of this great empire, contacts which over the succeeding centuries were to expand immensely, though not always evenly or peaceably. That is the process surveyed here, from a Western perspective, with the focus upon the actions and perceptions of the West rather than upon China's.

This coming together of the West and China on a regular and sustained basis since about 1500 has been one of the major cultural

1

confrontations of modern history. It has been part of that process we now call globalization, which has involved many such confrontations between different cultures, great and small, with the West always and everywhere an active participant – in the Americas, in Africa, throughout Asia, to the remotest island of the Pacific. The scale and character of those confrontations has varied considerably, and that simple sounding entity 'the West' has by no means been uniform in its approach to and dealings with other cultures. But it is an underlying assumption of this book that there was an entity one can call 'the West' which, whatever its internal variations and rivalries, has displayed a recognizably distinct and consistent set of values and assumptions in its relations with other traditions. These have included, first, that extensive trade between the peoples of our world is a universal good, and should be promoted by governments; second, that the Christian faith and, in its modern secularized form, individual human rights, is also such a good, and should be at least tolerated, ideally promoted, by governments; and third, that relations between governments, especially of major societies, should be on the basis of theoretical diplomatic equality, and be regulated in detail through negotiated treaties enforceable under a system of international law. Trade, religion and diplomacy were the three main prongs of the Western thrust into the world beyond Europe that by the sixteenth century was under way so energetically, and so ominously, for the rest of the world.

China, a quarter of mankind, was naturally one of the major targets of that thrust. It was also one of the most formidable. No European state came near to matching it in size or population, nor could the quality and achievements of its culture be gainsaid. In the seventeenth and eighteenth centuries very many Westerners saw China as at least the equal of Western civilization in important respects. For nearly three centuries of limited but steadily growing contact the West was the learner, the suppliant, seeking more and more contact with this vast but integrated civilization which promised great riches, both cultural and economic. The flow of ideas and trade was, during these centuries, overwhelmingly from east to west, in part because the Chinese, although by no means as closed off to the world beyond their borders as their neighbours, the Japanese and Koreans, were then attempting to be, were conditioned by their geography and history to be less receptive to external influences and opportunities than was the West; in part because the West then had, in material terms, little of value to offer China. But by the late eighteenth century the great advances in technology being achieved by the West, plus the growing capacity of its nation states to organize their resources, both human and material, efficiently, meant that it had become capable of challenging seriously the values and assumptions, and the power, of the great alternative civilization on the far eastern limits of the Eurasian continent they shared. The Macartney mission of 1792–3 defined the main terms of that challenge.

After looking fairly closely at the Macartney mission, which was the point in time when the mounting Western challenge to the then prevailing Chinese view of trade and diplomacy became quite explicit, the book proceeds to review, sometimes in very broad-brush terms, sometimes in a little detail, the means and stages by which Western power and values were imposed on China. The process was complex – often (some would say always) brutally aggressive, one-sided and exploitative, but also, in my view, having some genuinely well-intentioned aspects which, though often curtailed and overshadowed, should be part of the record. The missionaries demonstrate this double-sided nature of Western imperialism in China very clearly, and accordingly they receive as much attention as the traders and diplomats. In addition, some attempt is made to survey changing Western opinion about, and perceptions of, China and the Chinese over the centuries. The general argument of the book may be summed up as being that the balance of control, influence and dominance moved from being for several centuries China-centred, to being Western-centred in the nineteenth and for much of the twentieth centuries, but is now more even than at any time previously. This is a hopeful, healthy basis for the future of the relationship, but will need skill and understanding to sustain it. The record of the West's relations with China, though marred by much incomprehension, aggression and injustice, seems to me overall a record of mutual gain – but the record is certainly mixed, as this overview history endeavours to make plain.

1
A Wide World Apart, with Differing Views of Heaven and Earth

China and Western Europe lie at opposite ends of the great Eurasian land mass that stretches half way round the northern hemisphere of our globe. Although connected by land these two regions, roughly equal in size and both heartlands of major civilizations, are about as far apart as two places on Earth can be. The lands between stretch for many thousands of miles across snowbound mountains and high plateaus, arid deserts, deep forests and wide steppes. Travel across them has never been easy and still is not, save relatively in the north, through Manchuria and Siberia on the longest railway in the world. No trans-continental highway links them even yet, while the rivers, those natural highways of pre-modern times, run mostly northwards to the Arctic Circle or south into inland seas, rarely facilitating east–west travel. Geography, though providing a land connection, has not made regular contact between China and Europe easy.

Nor has politics. Before the eastward expansion of Russia, itself only marginally a European or Western power, into Siberia and Turkestan during the eighteenth and nineteenth centuries, plus a comparable extension and consolidation of Chinese power westwards into regions such as Mongolia and Tibet during the same centuries, the vast lands of central Asia were rarely under the effective control of any major power. Only during the thirteenth and fourteenth centuries was an empire of the steppes created by Mongol tribes led by Genghis Khan, and a rough kind of 'pax Tartarica' created which prompted a few European mission-aries and traders, of whom Marco Polo was allegedly one,[1] to travel to the country that became known to mediaeval Europe as Cathay. Had it lasted this Mongol empire might have been the channel for a much earlier and very different saga of sustained contact between China and the West than that which actually developed. But although it rapidly conquered the great empires that ringed central Asia and even threatened to reach, via Muscovy and the Ukraine, into distant Europe, this Mongol empire was short lived, not lasting beyond the fourteenth century. Contact by land between the far east and the far west of Eurasia remained rare and indirect.

There was always some trade, of course, along the exotic sounding but lengthy and tenuous Silk Road, conducted in many stages and through many intermediaries, and over the centuries there was also some diffusion of ideas and techniques, mainly from China to the West, as the great historian of Chinese technology, Joseph Needham has extensively illustrated. But, except for the Mongol interlude, direct contact was almost non-existent before the sixteenth century. By the fourteenth century of the Western calendar Europe was certainly well aware that there was a great empire and an advanced civilization far to its east, and had shown some eagerness to seek it out for missionary and trading purposes. But China, seeing itself as the central kingdom at the very hub of civilization, showed little disposition to explore the possibility of desirable contact with regions to its far west, although then technologically as capable as Europe to attempt to do so. If there was ever to be any significant and sustained contact between China and Europe it seemed that the initiative would have to come from the West, and the route be by sea rather than land.

That in fact is how it happened, with the Portuguese sailing to India in 1498 and on to China by 1520, acquiring a permanent base there at Macao by 1557. Thereafter a succession of Europeans – traders, missionaries, diplomats, armies and navies, and eventually tourists – came in increasing numbers, so that by the nineteenth century relations with the West became a major problem for the Chinese, as for many others also. The expansion of Europe – of the West – across the great oceans to every continent and virtually every island of the world is the dominant feature of modern world history. Not just great and populous empires such as India or China, but more remote and sparsely populated lands such as Australia were all caught up in this explosion of Western power and enterprise. Part of the process was permanent settlement by Europeans in many of the places to which they sailed, so that the term 'the West' came to include much more than just the European peninsula of the Eurasian continent. Heavily populated China was never subject to such settlement, nor to direct colonization, but it was exposed to many other aspects of Europe's expansion. Her experience of it, and adaptation to it, is one theme of this book, though the main emphasis is on the West's shifting relationship with and reaction to this great alternative tradition. But first we should look at the possibility that history might have taken a very different course, that instead of Europeans discovering and exploiting the sea route to Asia the Chinese might have preceded them, and sailed first to Europe.

China sails but fails to 'discover' Europe

Such speculation is justified by the fact that, at the beginning of the very century during which the Portuguese probed their way down the west coast of Africa until they eventually rounded its southern cape and entered the Indian Ocean, the Chinese had several times sailed, in strength, to India, on to Arabia and the Persian Gulf and a considerable way down the east coast of Africa. Why, in contrast to the Portuguese, did they not persevere and sail further on around Africa into the Atlantic and, conceivably, to Europe or the Americas? History is full of great 'what-might-have-been' question marks, but this is surely one of the greatest and most intriguing.

Between 1405 and 1433 seven government-sponsored large Chinese fleets sailed through the island-studded waters of South East Asia to such ports as Calicut and Cochin in southern India, ports already well known to Chinese traders, and several times they sailed further on – to Hormuz at the mouth of the Persian Gulf, to Aden at the mouth of the Red Sea, and to Mogadishu on the north east African coast. A giraffe was among the local specialities shipped back to China, and on the last of the voyages several Chinese reached Mecca, presumably as pilgrims, since the commander of most of these fleets was a Muslim, Zheng He (Cheng Ho). The fleets consisted of 60 or more vessels, many of them of a size (over 2000 tons, 120 metres in length and 50 in beam) which would have dwarfed the vessels on which the Portuguese later sailed, and the total complement of some of the fleets was well over 20 000. They set out from southern China at approximately three to four year intervals, the last in 1430, and the voyages took on average two to three years. The world had surely never seen such large-scale feats of seamanship. Yet after 1433 the voyages ceased, the government withdrew entirely from the enterprise, and some years later much of the detailed naval record was destroyed. By the end of the century, with the Portuguese just over the horizon, China was no longer a significant naval power.

Why were these voyages undertaken? Why were they so completely abandoned? And, more broadly, did these voyages demonstrate, as a recent text on world history suggests, that in the early fifteenth century China had a capacity 'to become one of the great global powers of the coming age ... a major countervailing force to check the expansive drive and rise to global dominance of Western Europe'?[2] How different would the course of world history, including the history of Sino-Western relations have been, if only China had maintained the capacities it had shown by these voyages?

It is easier for the historian to pose than to answer such questions, but some pursuit of them seems warranted. On the question why these voyages were undertaken, it is relevant that they were prompted and supported by the Yong Luo emperor of the only recently established Ming dynasty. In 1402, this emperor had usurped the throne from a nephew who escaped, possibly to Southern Asia. Determination to pursue him and to assert the authority and prestige of a new and controversial emperor among tributary states, in some of which a good many Chinese, potential supporters of the deposed nephew, had settled, seems to have been a major reason behind the voyages, at least initially. Chinese forces from the fleets were in fact used at several times to ensure that rulers were in place who would be reliable tributaries to the Chinese court. Commercial advantage, though probably among the objectives, appears to have been secondary to diplomatic, 'showing the flag' motivation. With the death of the Yong Luo emperor in 1424 only one more voyage was undertaken, and that after a longer than usual interval. The cost of such voyages, plus the fact that their commander was a Muslim, a eunuch and a favourite of the emperor, aroused strong hostility among Confucian-trained officials, traditionally the main advisers on court policy. For them the security of China's inner Asian frontiers against possibly resurgent Mongol forces was far more important than asserting and extending Chinese power across the seas. Furthermore, foreign trade was never seen as a vital national interest by such officials. So, with a less committed emperor on the dragon throne, not only were the voyages stopped but some of the basic records destroyed, 'by administrative thugs in the service of the Confucian anti-maritime party', as Needham bitterly comments.[3]

Needham saw Chinese naval strength in the early fifteenth century as outclassing that of any other Asian nation, and as being more than a match for that of any contemporary European state. Given the size of the Chinese vessels, and the numbers on board them, this seems an acceptable judgment, at least for the fifteenth century. But it has still to be asked, even had the Chinese preserved their fleets and persisted with their voyages, might they really have navigated their way into the Atlantic and on to Europe and constituted, as the just quoted world history text puts it, 'a major countervailing force' to the emerging power of Europe? There is no answer to this question that can approach even the tentative degree of certainty historians can offer as to why the voyages were undertaken and eventually so thoroughly stopped. All one can say is that such a turn around of history seems conceivable provided, first, that the Chinese, like the Portuguese, persisted in their enterprise and, second, that they learned new skills, such as navigating successfully across, and not just around, great oceans. Equally, if not more important, they would have needed to mount strong guns on their vessels, armament without which they would have been very vulnerable, despite their size, to the kind of fire power European ocean-going vessels had acquired by the sixteenth century.

'One generalization is certain', says a leading historian of the European voyages of discovery, 'throughout the Age of Reconnaissance European ships and fleets were greatly superior, as fighting units, to any non-European ships and fleets which they encountered in the Atlantic, the Indian Ocean or the Pacific. Despite their small numbers, no non-European power on those ocean shores was strong enough to dispute their passage on the high seas.'[4] As another historian of the early phases of European expansion put it, with the Chinese comparison specifically in mind:

> It has been fashionable in the last few decades to sing the virtues of the Chinese junk, and there is no doubt that, as far as seaworthiness and navigational qualities in general go, these laudatory songs are deserved. The Chinese junk could compare honourably with Western sailing vessels for mercantile endeavours or voyages of discovery, and the successful explorations of admiral Cheng Ho in the early fifteenth century are excellent proof of this, if proof is needed. The problem however is that the junk never developed into a man of war. Like the Mediterranean galley the Chinese junk remained essentially a vessel suited for ramming and boarding . . . the war junk was fit only for the traditional way of fighting, and such it remained.[5]

Gunnery was the key to European naval supremacy in Asian including Chinese waters, a supremacy not absolutely total to begin with, but by the eighteenth and nineteenth centuries virtually so, and naval strength underpinned the great growth of Western economic and political power.

A recent detailed study of the fifteenth-century Chinese fleets indicates that their main fighting ships, called *fuchuan*, were about 50 metres in length, carrying crews of about 250 and, with planks and raised platforms, were designed for close combat and boarding.[6] The larger ships, although carrying some light bronze cannon, were not considered fighting ships, and were designed primarily for prestige and comfortable travel. With their bulkhead construction they might not have been easy for the European vessels of the sixteenth century to sink, but that they could have turned back those vessels is not self-evident. Size should not be equated with power or efficiency. The Portuguese ships, and those of other Europeans who followed them, may have been far smaller than Zheng He's, but they were far more lethal. Of course one cannot doubt that the Chinese were capable of learning additional skills in navigation and gunnery. But the fact that they had built and sailed large fleets, carrying many men but not heavy cannon, through the coastal waters of southern Asia and as far as Africa is not in itself clear proof either that they could, within a few more decades, have navigated their way to the Atlantic and to the continents that border it, or that with such fleets as these they could have provided a successful countervailing force to European vessels once these arrived in Asian waters. It is possible, but the Chinese would have had to persist and to learn a great deal more to achieve such results.

Both persistence and successful learning require motivation. The Chinese had such motivation for certain things, such as building a great wall across the northern reaches of their land, which they did in addition to sailing as far as Africa during the fifteenth century. But their motivation for exploring the world beyond the seas, for expanding their share of international trade, and for seeking to convert other people to their faith – all objectives that drove the Portuguese and other European nations to persist relentlessly with their voyages – was far weaker. Behind motivation lie basic values, assumptions about Heaven and Earth, attitudes to the world at large, to what is regarded as important for the state to promote. These are the crucial keys to understanding the intriguing contrast between the outcome of the Chinese and European voyaging around Africa in the fifteenth century. It is to the different world views of these widely separated but, by the sixteenth century, inexorably coming together civilizations that I now turn, leaving a large question mark hanging over what might have been the results of the Ming voyages if persisted in by the Chinese.

Geographies compared

First, some consideration of the geography of the two regions can help towards understanding their different attitudes towards foreign trade, and to relations generally with other peoples. Geography is basic to the history of any people, be they tribe, nation or great empire. Where a country lies in relation to others; whether it is well defined by natural features such as seas, mountains and rivers; the character of its neighbouring regions; its climate; its internal topography – how far landlocked, how well served by internal waterways, the extent of its mountains, plains, marshlands or forests – all these, as well as other less obvious geographical features, will profoundly influence the development of any region and the outlook on the world of its inhabitants. Of course other forces than the physical and material constraints imposed by geography also operate, and in our modern, highly mobile and globalized world many of these constraints have in fact been greatly diminished. Geography does not condition our history to the degree it once did, but it remains an important influence on any society. The Chinese view of the world was certainly strongly shaped by its geography, as was Europe's by its very different geography.

Europe's civilization emerged around the shores of a sizeable but manageable sea ringed by a great diversity of cultures. Western Europe's location relative to the other major civilizations which, like it, originated around or close to the shores of the Mediterranean Sea, helped condition its peoples, or at any rate a significant proportion of its peoples, to look outwards to a rich and varied world beyond. It was a world of constant challenge and frequent danger (the Turks were besieging Vienna as late as 1683) but also one of great stimulus and potential profit. The economic development and intellectual orientation of early western Europe's civilization are incomprehensible without constant reference to the world of the Mediterranean and the variety of cultures that developed around it. China's civilization originated on a wide plain along the middle reaches of the long, silt-saturated and flood-prone Yellow River, a plain beyond which lay only non-literate tribal peoples – pastoral nomads to the north and west, slash and burn agriculturalists to the south. To the east lay a vast ocean offering no navigable inland seas and no near neighbours for profitable commerce and cultural exchange. The nearest civilization comparable to China's, India, lay far to the south, beyond thick forests, jungles and high mountains. The south China coast did become, later in China's historical development, a base for some contact with the smaller island states of South East Asia, but the core area of China's civilization, between the Yangzi and Yellow rivers, remained very remote from any such contacts. China's civilization developed in a much more contained and separated part of the world than did its western counterpart. It was not as isolated as the civilizations of central America, but was significantly more isolated than the other great civilizations of Eurasia – India, the Middle East and Europe, both east and west.

Literature and religion may serve to illustrate the kind of basic difference between China and western Europe that geography helped create. Traditional Chinese literature, written in its distinctive ideographic script and preserving a long and rich corpus of writing, a corpus more than comparable to that which early modern Europe inherited from its classical and mediaeval sources, was, however, not so exposed to the rich variety of works, images and stories that Europe received from its neighbouring civilizations of the Middle East, especially after the Crusades of the eleventh and twelfth centuries. Although in the early period of Tang dynasty rule (618–907) China was in its 'international age, the age of imports, the age of mingling, the golden age' that Edward Schafer explores in his great book *The Golden Peaches of Samarkand*, this open attitude began to pass away by the ninth century, after prolonged internal rebellions had ravaged much of the land. Soon 'fewer rarities from overseas and overland could be found in the stricken country', writes Schafer, '[and] the great persecution of foreign religions tended to remove from the sight of the average Chinese not only the foreign priests and worshippers but also foreign books and the images of foreign gods.'[7] Despite some renewal of wider contact during the Song dynasty (960–1260), late traditional China, in contrast to late mediaeval and early modern Europe (that is twelfth to sixteenth centuries), became a far more closed off world than, for a time during the Tang and Song dynasties, it seemed it would be. Far off cities such as Samarkand dropped from the Chinese consciousness and did not stir the imagination of Chinese story tellers, as not only Samarkand but Byzantium, Damascus, Persepolis, (through which Marlowe in remote, insular England could dream of riding in triumph) and most of all Baghdad, (where Aladdin, Ali Baba and Scheherazade could cast their spells over a thousand and one nights) did for Europeans. It was not that the Chinese lacked imaginative stories, but theirs were set either somewhere in the central kingdom itself or, like the popular tales recounting the fabulous deeds of Monkey and his associates, in a landscape of dreams, not in exotic sounding yet actually existing foreign lands and cities. No Confucian essayist created imaginary, sharp-eyed visitors from some other sophisticated civilization to comment on the foibles of China and the Chinese, as writers such as Montesquieu, Voltaire and Goldsmith did for eighteenth-century Europeans. More prosaically, the great number of words and concepts that have entered everyday European languages from Middle Eastern and Asian sources cannot be matched in Chinese before modern times. Traditional Chinese literature is rich and various, and the classical form of the language is a particularly taut, supple instrument for the nuances of lyrical poetry; but the strong strand of external inspiration and stimulus present over many centuries in European literature is relatively absent from China's until quite recent times.

In the case of religion, on the other hand, long before the arrival of Europeans, China was profoundly influenced from beyond its borders by the entry of Buddhism in the early centuries of the Christian era. That faith did bring with it many foreign words and concepts of a religious connotation, and prompted the famous stories of the travels of Monkey. But despite the deep penetration of Buddhism into Chinese culture its holy places never entered the Chinese consciousness in the way that the holy places of Palestine entered the European. Great numbers of devout Chinese did not journey to India as pilgrims or crusaders, nor did Buddhist texts, prayers and sutras ever become the dominant sacred books of the ruling elite, even though at times some members of that elite were deeply influenced by Buddhist ideas and concepts. The basic texts of Confucian orthodoxy remained purely Chinese, and the honoured, quasi-holy places of Confucianism were all firmly within the borders of the central kingdom. China certainly accepted Buddhism, the greatest pre-Western influence on Chinese culture, but Sinicized it thoroughly, almost forgetting its Indian origins.[8] Like the rest of the world, that country remained remote, in intellectual terms hardly at all an actual place. Thus religion, like literature though in different ways, demonstrates the essential separateness of the Chinese tradition. Throughout most of its history China looked only inwards or, if outwards, mainly towards the sparse deserts and grasslands of Central Asia, where only non-literate, nomadic and often troublesome tribesmen roamed.

China 'the central kingdom' of East Asia

Late traditional China, that is the China of the Ming (1368–1644) and Qing (1644–1911) dynasties which had, from the early sixteenth century on, actually to deal with Westerners, of course knew of the existence of some non-Chinese peoples with cultures developed well beyond the level of its near tribal neighbours, peoples such as the Koreans, Vietnamese, Cambodians and, intermittently, the Japanese. But these cultures were seen as, and to a significant degree were, off-shoots of China's own civilization, not as radical, enticing or challenging alternatives, as Europe saw the cultures of the Middle East. The smaller east Asian cultures did indeed, in their quite distinctive ways and to varying degrees, reflect a great deal of China – in their systems of writing; of government and administration; in the layout of their capitals; in dress and rituals of courts; in absorbing something of the Confucian ethic and value system. Traditional China was like a great sun around which these satellite cultures circled. It dominated a cultural and political universe very different from that within which mediaeval Europe gravitated. For many centuries Europe was in fact a peripheral culture, overshadowed by the distinctive cultures of the Middle East, which were in many ways more brilliant and advanced than its own.

The Chinese name for their empire at the centre of the world they knew was, logically enough *zhong guo*, meaning the central state or middle kingdom. It seems worth reflecting briefly on this name in comparison to the European word 'Mediterranean'. It is natural enough for any culture, great or small, to think of its part of the world as somehow central, so neither China nor Europe is peculiar in having place names expressing such an idea in its lexicon. The Chinese and Latin words seem nearly identical in meaning, though 'Mediterranean' is more properly translated as 'in the middle of, surrounded by, land' rather than as 'at the centre of the world'. Nevertheless it seems clear, from the evidence of mediaeval maps, that Europeans did commonly think of that sea as being at the centre of their world, the hub being often placed devoutly at Jerusalem. In its formative periods, both in classical and mediaeval times, European civilization developed around an enclosed sea which functioned as a highway – a highway by no means always safe but at least manageable for galleys and small ships, which facilitated contacts not only between various parts of Europe but, most significantly, also between Western Europe and other great cultures. The centre of ancient mediaeval and early modern Europe's world was a place of travel and trade, of cultural contacts both hostile and profitable. The centre of traditional China's world was a great plain of yellow Earth which, adequately watered, irrigated and protected within the wall, supported a productive agriculture and many great cities, across which it was certainly possible to trade and travel, as the Chinese did. But such trade and travel did not bring them to any Byzantium, Levant, Persia or Egypt, only to more centres of Chinese culture or to tribal peoples, who might have some useful commodities to exchange but who had no high culture or great cities which might stimulate and challenge.

By the later Middle Ages, of course, the main centre of European civilization was shifting from the Mediterranean to the Atlantic seaboard, but this did not diminish, rather it enhanced and extended, the outward looking orientation which had been inherent in Europe's culture from its origins. In China also, over the centuries, there was some shift of focus, so that other regions – such as the lower Yangzi valley, the rich and well-watered plateau of Szechuan, and the diverse river and coastal valleys of the south – came to match and even outstrip the north China plain in wealth and culture. But, as with Europe, this shift in 'key economic areas' did not alter the original and fundamental orientation of the civilization since, mainly for reasons of defence and military strategy, north China remained the crucial political region. The whole great extent of late traditional China, expanded by the sixteenth century from its northern yellow Earth origins to encompass the eighteen provinces of 'China proper', continued with only rare and short interruptions to be ruled from the north. It was there that the inward-looking view of the world, which was to so inhibit and complicate China's efforts to adapt to the European dominated world it would have to face by the nineteenth century, had originated and was tenaciously preserved.

Certain other features of the geographies of China and Western Europe help explain and reinforce this difference in outlook to the wider world that was such a crucial contrast between the two traditions. Neither region is landlocked, but Europe has a much longer and more heavily indented coastline, embracing several enclosed seas, the Mediterranean chief among them. It is a coastline which, even on its Atlantic and North Sea ocean fronts, provides many protected harbours with deep river estuaries. The many navigable rivers of Europe flow in all directions, radiating out rather like the spokes of a wheel from a broad central hub formed by the Alps and other mountains. These rivers and the long, indented coastline to which they flow provide a 'structure', a natural scaffolding for extensive trade which, in pre-modern times, required water transport, whether coastal, riverine or canal, for any bulk transport. To this continental coastal and river framework we may add the great estuary of the Thames, only a few miles across the sea from that great centre of mediaeval commerce, Antwerp, so that even insular England was drawn deeply into the great circle of late mediaeval international and intra-regional European trade.

In contrast, China's rivers, far greater in size though they are than most of Europe's, flow predominantly in one direction, from west to east, towards a curving coastline that provides no protected internal seas and relatively few good harbours, especially in its northern reaches. In China the flow of the great rivers cuts across the southward frontier push of the culture of the north China plain, a push that ate steadily, like a silkworm devouring a mulberry leaf, as the Chinese metaphor put it, into lands that, by a centuries-long process of clearing, terracing, irrigating, occupation and ethnic assimilation, were gradually made as thoroughly Chinese as the northern plain. As these regions became richer and more heavily populated the northern-based government naturally sought to tap their wealth, but to do so efficiently it had to construct a special north – south waterway, the Grand Canal. The great Yangzi river remained unbridged until the middle of the twentieth century, and the riches of Szechuan continued to lie, far up beyond the narrow gorges of the middle Yangzi, largely out of the reach of the central government. China's other great, long river, the Yellow, is a kind of liquid mud, a constant problem to contain within its silted bed high above the plain through which it flows finally to the sea. The ocean into which both it and the Yangzi flow often belied the name Europeans were to give it as they began to sail across it in the sixteenth century, pirates as well as typhoons making it frequently far from pacific. Only in the south were there extensive internal waterways or many ports leading to some external trade. In general, China's topography did not facilitate economic activity beyond its own borders and coastline nearly as much as did Europe's.

Economies compared

This is not to suggest that China was economically backward compared to late mediaeval or early modern Europe. China's great size and productivity, especially of such desirable commodities as tea, silk and porcelain, plus the reasonable accessibility of its southern ports to South East Asia, ensured that there was considerable trade both within and to this biggest of all domestic markets. For its time traditional China's was a quite sophisticated economy, in advance of Europe's in the development of such techniques as paper money and credit transfers – 'flying money' as the Chinese called such transactions. Under the later Song dynasty, China's whole economy, including trade with South East Asia, was particularly vigorous, one historian of cross-cultural trade judging that China then led the world in per capita productivity.[9] But the Mongol conquest, completed by 1260, and the century of occupation that followed seem to have curbed growth in a manner as severe as, and more long lasting than, the impact of the Black Death on fourteenth-century Europe. Whereas Europe's economy soon recovered and expanded, China's settled into what has been aptly called a high equilibrium trap. The inner Asian frontier reasserted itself as the crucial one for China, and there was a shift away from the new southern maritime frontier, which had been developing strongly under the later Song. This shift is massively reflected by the Great Wall, built by the Ming dynasty after it had expelled the Mongols in 1368. With the remarkable exception of the voyages already discussed, China by the late fifteenth century returned decisively to inward-looking policies and orientations. The Song, and the preceding Tang dynasty, had shown that the Chinese were capable of shifting, of taking notice and advantage of the outer world but, after the trauma of Mongol conquest and occupation, a new and purely Chinese dynasty, the Ming (1368–1644), retreated and made China a more closed off kingdom than it had been. Chinese were prohibited from travelling abroad, although some communities of overseas Chinese remained, in Thailand and Manila for example, and some foreign trading continued. But such trade was restricted to at most a very few ports, and for Westerners ultimately to only one, Canton. Theoretically such trade was tied to a system of tribute bearing as a condition for even limited access to China's great internal market. That market remained very tempting to interested outsiders, but after the Song dynasty the considerable commercial energies and capacities of the Chinese were overwhelmingly directed to the regions within, rather than beyond, the central kingdom.

Underlying all was the simple, basic fact that China with a population of some 200 million by late Ming times, that is the early seventeenth century, was very self-sufficient in the essentials its peoples needed in those times of far more modest consumer expectations. As one Western observer was later ruefully to observe, the Chinese produced 'the best food in the world – rice; the best drink – tea; best clothing – cotton, silk and fur. Possessing these staples they do not need to buy a pennyworth elsewhere.'[10] Europeans, always prone to think of foreign trade as a highly desirable, normal and necessary activity, were indeed to find it difficult to persuade the Chinese to spend a penny on much that they offered other than opium. The China market, with its many millions of potential customers, never proved to be the bonanza Westerners anticipated, and may not be that much easier, even if more accessible, in the future.

Traditional China should not be seen as somehow peculiar and abnormal in this inward orientation. It would be as near the truth to suggest that it was Europe that was peculiar in its outward thrust and obsessive pursuit of trade and wealth to the furthest corners of the world. Neither civilization should be judged irrational in its contrasting behaviour, for each was, I have been arguing, conditioned to act as it did by the nature of the region in which it developed. Furthermore, neither was stuck for all its history in some rigid, immutable mould. Neither was, on the one hand, consistently innovative and exploratory, nor on the other consistently conservative and self-centred. Early modern

Europe was certainly exceptionally expansive and experimental, in intellectual as well as physical fields, but the European capacity for rigidities, stereotypes, prejudices and arrogant presumptions of pre-eminence in culture and civilization was not notably less than the Chinese. Any overall assessment of predominant characteristics depends a good deal on which periods of the history, which parts of the whole tradition, one takes as the basis for judgment. An inter-galactic visitor to planet Earth, arriving sometime between the seventh and twelfth centuries of the Christian era, would have been likely to judge Tang–Song China as more dynamic and expansive in every way than the Western Europe of that period. Over the very long perspectives of their separate histories, and especially for several centuries after the fifteenth, European civilization has generally been more aware of and therefore, partly of necessity, more geared to and ready to be involved with other civilizations than has the Chinese. But it is not a simple straightforward contrast over the whole of recorded history, and now, as we are very well aware, the times are changing fast.

China, it should also be added, was not exceptional among the great Asian empires in its relative lack of interest in international trade. The major historian of early Asian-European cultural contact, D.F. Lach, noted a certain indifference towards such trade as characteristic of several Asian states, and concluded that Europeans came to dominate the trade in Asian waters

> not only because the great nations of Asia had no navies able to challenge them effectively, but in part because the Chinese and Japanese remained officially unconcerned about overseas commerce. Passivity about international trade likewise characterized the Mughal Empire and Siam. In fact the great Asian empires...were all land empires, boasting powerful armies rather than navies. Their govern-ments seemed more concerned to regulate seaborne commerce than to profit from it.[11]

Other historians also have discerned a degree of ambiguity in Asian societies towards the sea.[12] It was the European drive to expand across the great oceans of the world to trade and to proselytize that was exceptional, peculiar, disruptive.

Here it is necessary to take note of the argument of Joanna Waley-Cohen in her recent book *The Sextants of Beijing: Global Currents in Chinese History*.[13] She argues that traditional China, far from being closed to the outside world was always engaged with it and actively sought foreign goods and ideas. Insofar as there was any tendency to limit foreign influences and ideology, she suggests, this sprang only from a concern to maintain Chinese values and traditions, rather than from any ingrained hostility to techniques or ideas of foreign origin. This is a salutary reminder that China was never a 'hermit kingdom' as Korea attempted to be (save towards China), nor as restrictive towards external contact as Japan was under Tokugawa rule (1603–1868). Certainly, as I have just suggested, during Tang and Song times China was more rather than less expansive, economically and in other ways, than was Europe for most of those centuries. But the proposition that Ming–Qing China was energetically and enthusiastically engaged with the outside world seems to be open to at least some question by virtue of such decisions as to abandon the voyages of the early fifteenth century, and to dismiss so comprehensively the missions of both Macartney at the end of the eighteenth century and of Amherst at the beginning of the nineteenth (see Chapter 2). The reasons behind such decisions were doubtless various, as Waley-Cohen argues, but that they were made at all suggests that for the rulers of China during the first centuries of the Western advance on China, commitment to foreign contact and trade was not a high priority. While conceding that traditional China was always to some degree open to the world beyond – its very size and geographic position made anything like total closure impossible – it will remain a central proposition of this book that for several centuries after 1500 China's rulers (its populace less so) had far greater reservations about the importance and worth of foreign trade and contacts than did the rulers of Western nations.

Polities compared

There is one other important difference between the Chinese and European traditions to which geography seems relevant. Early in their histories both civilizations were united into extensive empires, the Han (221 BCE–220 CE) in the case of China, and the far more multi-cultural Roman in the case of Europe. There is a possibility that there was some brief direct contact between these two great empires, and a taste for luxuries such as silk from the East has been counted as one of the reasons for the decline of the Roman. Eventually both empires broke up, and long periods of political disunity within their former domains followed. But by the early seventh century China was reunited under a strong and dynamic dynasty, the Tang, with its capital at Chang-an on the western edge of the northern yellow plain. Despite some further relatively brief periods of disunity and some shifting of capitals, China has maintained this tradition of political unity ever since. In contrast Europe never regained political unity, though it still gropes towards it. By the seventeenth century the pattern we still know of a Europe divided into many states of varying and shifting strength, was becoming well defined. These states all developed an imagined, unified community on 'national principles', composed of a volatile mix of religion, race, language, plus a consciousness of some kind of shared cultural heritage, including heroic wars. Nationalism, a sense of national identity, became a distinctive feature of Western political life which, in due course the rest of the world, including China, had also to adopt, in greater or lesser measure.

The European nation states were commonly deeply suspicious of one another, and the biggest among them competed for dominance. None was able to create any long-lasting hegemony, much less a unified empire, although Napoleon made a powerful attempt. To contain their chronic rivalry and the worst of its consequences a system of diplomacy based on the principle of a balance of power between roughly equal states and their allies evolved, and by the seventeenth century a code of what Europeans called 'international' law began to be defined under which all sovereign states were of theoretically equal diplomatic status. Any agreements or treaties made between these various states, whether negotiated under duress or not, were to be seen as binding. Thus was created within European civilization a complicated, fragile, multi-centred world of international politics and diplomacy, very different from the single-centred pattern which had evolved within the Chinese tradition.

In China, under a weak or declining dynasty, control from the centre, from the one and only Son of Heaven on the great dragon throne, might become very loose. But generally the centre did hold, and the principle that there was but one ultimate sovereign, one legitimate source of authority under Heaven, remained firm. Ideally that authority ruled lightly, 'driving the chariot of state with a loose rein' in the Confucian–Daoist phrase. Its agents within the central kingdom itself and the rulers of the tributary satellite states around, all exercised considerable autonomy. But the right of the ruler of China, under the mandate of Heaven, to direct, control and to call to account all under Heaven was theoretically absolute, not to be constrained by any man-made system of law. Only the will of Heaven, expressed through successful rebellion, might transfer the mandate to a new and worthier dynasty. In practice, the highly centralized authority of the emperor was greatly constrained by circumstance, by the practical realities inherent in administering so vast an empire, not to mention influencing distant tributaries. But in principle there was no limit, no check or balance, to the will of the emperor or to the pre-eminence of the central kingdom. When Europeans arrived in force and insisted upon the superiority of their system of relations between states, and on the legal sanctity of treaties negotiated between theoretically sovereign equals, there was naturally much conflict and confusion, as these two very different political traditions clashed.

How important was geography in creating these contrasting political traditions? One historian who has argued that it was a decisive influence is C.P. Fitzgerald. In a lecture comparing the Han with the Roman empire he stated firmly that 'the geography of China tended to impose unity, that of the Roman empire to bring it into jeopardy.'[14] The Roman world, he suggested, was 'deeply severed', with the Adriatic separating the Balkans from Italy, which had no easy land communication with France (Gaul), which was in turn separated from Spain by the Pyrenees, while the Swiss alps shut off the Danube valley from the rest of Europe. By contrast, he continued,

> it is not possible to divide China between north and south by a secure natural frontier. . . . There is no clear cut barrier and consequently no obstacle to the passage of armies. . . . The lack of distinct and difficult barriers between north and south prevented the rise of different cultures and hence the emergence of new nation states, even after long periods of political disunity.

Fitzgerald recognized that there were what he called 'lesser differences' also at work which reinforced this basic difference in geography and helped explain the continuing unity of the Chinese empire. One of these is an ideographic system of writing which, for the literate ruling elite, meant that regional or national literatures of the kind that characterized modern Europe did not develop in China. Further, the Chinese empire was not invaded, as the Roman was, by very large numbers of diverse barbarians within a relatively short span of time, overwhelming and often displacing the settled population. China's invaders, whether they conquered the whole or, more usually, only part of the central kingdom were small in number compared to the native Chinese population, and were either soon assimilated into the dominant culture or, like the Mongols, expelled. Finally, one should note that the southward moving frontier of Chinese settlement moved steadily but relatively slowly, so that the ethnically not so dissimilar peoples south of the Yangzi were either thoroughly Sinicized or gradually pushed to the outer fringes of the empire. Several factors other than geography therefore help explain the contrast in the political patterns that developed in Europe and China. For Fitzgerald though, geography seemed the most important, creating the mould within which long-lasting political forms were shaped for both Europe and China.

While accepting that geography had something to do with these contrasting political traditions, I think it easy to exaggerate its importance in this regard. Even if we agree that China 'within the wall' was more of a geographical unity than Fitzgerald's 'deeply severed' Europe (and not everybody does), we should not assume that the political units into which Europe became divided were defined by geography above everything else. Nor should we exaggerate the degree of unity, political and cultural as well as geographic, of China. The contrast, though real, is less clear cut, the impact of geography less decisive in creating it, than Fitzgerald's presentation suggests.

To look at the European case first, although a good many of the national units into which that region became divided seem natural, that is to say dictated by mountains, coastlines and major rivers, this is to a considerable extent illusory. Historically Europe's political frontiers have by no means matched the 'natural', and still do not, even where these seem very obvious. Spain spilled over the Pyrenees until well into the seventeenth century; the French fought for centuries to achieve what they claimed as their natural frontiers – Rhine, Alps, Pyrenees – and have only quite recently given up the struggle; Italy, culturally and economically advanced though it was, remained for centuries a political checkerboard, a mere geographical expression, as Metternich put it; Germany was not united politically until the late nineteenth century, and its eastern frontiers have remained very indeterminate, as its neighbour Poland can most tragically testify. Even the British islands constituted no natural united kingdom for Scots and Welsh, not to mention Irish. There is, perhaps, a rough sort of congruence between the major geographical features and the modern political map of Europe, but much of the geographical mould is decidedly floppy, especially around the 'Low Countries'. Geography never seemed to discourage one or other of the great continental powers – Spain, France, Germany – from trying to impose their own kind of unity upon the whole, whatever the supposed 'natural' frontiers.

Conversely China, although perhaps not as 'deeply severed' geographically as Europe, is certainly divisible into regions that could easily have become the base areas for separate states – the isolated rich, high plateau province of Szechuan for example. The Yangzi might surely have been as 'natural' a frontier as ever the Rhine has been for Europe. 'Were it not for China's comparative isolation in South Eastern Asia there might be but little common culture and even less political coherence', wrote Cressey, the leading Western student of China's geography sixty years ago, while a contemporary scholar claims, in sharp contrast to Fitzgerald, that 'In geographic terms China was far less unified than the base area of Western civilization or even the subcontinent of India.'[15] I am inclined to the view that there is a little more geographical coherence about China 'within the wall' than there is about Europe, and so to some extent follow Fitzgerald rather than the just quoted R.J. Smith. But if China's history had developed in such a way as to produce a sustained pattern of separate states, I am sure historians would have little difficulty in using geography to help explain such a development. It is certainly an exaggeration to say, as Fitzgerald does, that geography 'imposed unity' on China. At least as important were the other factors summarized above.

In any case one should not exaggerate the unity of China. It was real but imperfect. Although the peculiar form of the written language ensured that all who were literate understood it, however they might speak it, the differences in regional dialects were, and remain, substantial. Although the provincial and local officials appointed by the emperor reported to him in their special literary language, they normally exercised a good deal of autonomy, especially financial, within their jurisdiction. To become an official and get rich was the ideal career path for any literate, ambitious young man in China. True, traditional China's administrative system was very impressive, holding together a single state of far greater extent than any in Europe. But as those much smaller European states achieved their varying brands of national unity they became much more organized, far better able to mobilize and concentrate their resources than the vast but loosely held together bulk of the great central kingdom to their far east. Great size and apparent political unity were not signs of real strength for China once it was faced with those smaller but more highly integrated, assertive nation states of modern Europe, states that became increasingly intent on imposing their ideas on trade and diplomacy upon China, as upon many other parts of the world.

Religion and law compared

In addition to trade and diplomacy there was a considerable religious dimension to this coming confrontation. When the Portuguese arrived in India in 1498 one of them stated that they came 'in search of

Christians and spices', a phrase which well reflects the importance of the religious as well as the trading impulse behind the European drive to explore and expand overseas. Religion alone, without the prospect of profitable trade, would probably not have been enough to sustain the enterprise, even for the devoutly persistent Portuguese, conditioned as they were by their long struggles to advance the Cross against Islam within their own region. But the prospect of finding religious allies, such as Prester John, and of making converts among the peoples of Africa and Asia helped greatly to stimulate and to justify the effort that the search for a sea route to the east required. China, like India and Africa, became a major field of enterprise for the Christian missionary, as it was for the trader. The challenge of a very different tradition of belief and behaviour was, if anything, even greater for the missionary than for the merchant or the diplomat. Having looked so far at differences in basic geographic, economic, and political orientations, I conclude this introductory chapter with a brief examination of differences in religious and legal ideas, which are also very important to an understanding of the reasons for the tensions that were to develop between these two great traditions once they came together in sustained contact.

In contrast to virtually every other major cultural tradition, China's cannot be closely identified with a religious faith in the way that the West's can be with Christianity. Traditional China is generally labelled Confucian, but Confucian thought and precepts, although strongly emphasizing moral principles and values, are not obviously religious in the commonly understood Western sense of that word. Neither Confucius nor most other leading teachers of that intellectually rich period of early Chinese history known as the Hundred Schools made any claim to divine inspiration or to special knowledge of any spiritual after-world. In their search for the Dao, for 'the Way' to both personal fulfilment and social harmony, to the good life and the good society (comparable to Plato's roughly contemporary search for 'justice') these thinkers defined an ethical code and value system for China that was broadly Confucian, though mixed with Daoist and other teachings, including pre-Confucian. It was a code defined not by prophets claiming to be, and accepted as being, in touch with some extraterrestrial authority, but by sages or philosophers claiming only to know this world, and concerned only with life on it. In contrast to the West, and to the world of Islam, revealed religion did not provide the main ethical basis of Chinese civilization.

It is true, as already noted, that from about the third century onwards, that is many centuries after Confucius and the intellectual ferment of the Hundred Schools, a great world religion, Buddhism, did enter China and had wide appeal and lasting influence. But in certain major respects Buddhism may be said to be closer to Confucianism than it is to Christianity or Islam, for example in its emphasis on the achievement of enlightenment, or salvation, via the conscious discipline of the noble eight-fold path rather than by the efficacy of some divinely inspired revelation and text. Buddhism, though a powerful influence, especially on the popular mind, became a supplement rather than an alternative to the pre-existing secular-oriented, family-centred code of Confucianism which remained, albeit in a later much embellished and ritualized 'Neo-Confucian' form, the dominant orthodoxy, especially for the ruling elite. Elite and populace alike developed a decidedly eclectic attitude towards matters of faith and belief, not just tolerating but participating in all the 'San Jiao', the three great teachings of Confucianism, Daoism and Buddhism. The phrase 'a Confucian in office and a Daoist in retirement' reflected this flexible approach, so different from the intense and exclusivist attitude towards religious belief common in the West, especially in the early-modern West of the Reformation era. 'It may be said not only of China's unfocussed, diffused religion but of its institutional faiths as well (that is Buddhism) that . . . they were in general far more relaxed, more tolerant and less self demanding than have been the major monotheistic religions', is the summary of Derk Bodde, a major scholar of Chinese thought.[16]

There were plenty of particular gods and spirits in the Chinese pantheon, but no overriding, anthropomorphic personal God. Encompassing all was *tien*, Heaven, a remote, impersonal but essentially beneficent force, concerned with the maintenance of general social harmony and balance for all under Heaven rather than with the faith or salvation of individual souls. The main responsibility for maintaining a good balance between Heaven and Earth devolved upon the emperor, the Son of Heaven, who held its mandate to rule. But he held that mandate only provisionally, for so long as his theoretically superior virtue manifested itself in a well-ordered empire. Though the emperor had a quasi-divine status while he held the mandate, in the last resort practical, mundane criteria determined whether or not Heaven, and his subjects, continued to accord him and his dynasty that status. The Chinese sense of Heaven, of the divine, was decidedly pragmatic, even prosaic. Indeed some Western observers concluded that China virtually had no religion, no clear sense of the divine as separate from the profane day to day world. The same might be said to be true of our modern, post-Enlightenment and secularized West, but for the greater part of their centuries of contact since about 1500 China and the West have represented very different traditions of belief about the religious dimension of the human condition. Very many concepts, ideas and practices which are basic to Christianity – of a personal God; of a sense of sin as distinct from crime; of the efficacy and dignity of blood sacrifice; of a divinely established Church in which regular congregational worship led by an honoured priesthood was a norm; of a strong missionary impulse, indeed duty, to convert the heathen – all these distinctive features of the Western religious tradition, plus a good many more, were either quite alien to or much weaker within the far more diffused and relaxed religious tradition of China. Heaven and Earth were fused in the Chinese mind, whereas Christianity emphasized their separateness, their different state of being. Both China and the West conceived, as probably all mankind has, a Heaven that influenced, and in some way ordered, life on Earth, but they saw its role and its relationship to the world of men very differently.

In law, as in religion, Chinese concepts, practices and institutions differed markedly from those of the West. In Confucian China the basis for good government was seen to be administration by good men rather than dependence on good law. Law had its place, and very detailed codes of criminal law were drawn up by several dynasties. But more important was the appointment to office of men thoroughly versed in the principles of upright moral behaviour as set out in the great Confucian canon of writings, a canon consisting not simply of the classic texts, such as the Analects of Confucius and the book of Mencius, but of commentaries, philosophical and reflective essays, of histories (where the important precedents were to be found) and other writings compiled over the centuries by a succession of scholars and officials. Those who gained public office, who became 'mandarins', proved their fitness not by birth, not by any process as crude as popular election or as arbitrary as inherited status, but by passing an exacting series of public examinations which tested their command of this great canon. Most failed, or at best got only part way through the process, but final graduation as a *jinshi*, an 'advanced scholar' guaranteed appointment either as a district magistrate, responsible for a region often comparable in size to, and greater in population than, an English county, or as an assistant within a department of government in a provincial or the imperial capital. A district magistrate was known as the *fu-mu guan*, the father–mother official, a description which reflects the idea that the family was the model for good government and the basis of social order. Reality of course fell well short of the ideal, so codes of law were necessary to curb the *xiao-ren*, the small and misguided people who did not always readily submit to the natural moral order as it was embodied in the family and which extended outwards and upwards to the heads of clan, to magistrates and other officials, and to the emperor above all. Rather than prescribed law, natural morality, as defined in the classic Confucian texts, should guide and govern all social relationships and behaviour. Legal rules were at best just a reflection of this morality, and the letter of the law should never be allowed to override it. As Confucius put it, 'Govern the people by regulations, keep order among them by chastisements, and they will flee from you, and lose all self respect. Govern them by moral force, keep order among them by ritual and they will keep their self respect and come to you of their own accord.' (Analects II, 3).

Whereas the West thought in terms of a natural or divine law, which human law should reflect and in which it finds its ultimate justification, in China codified law, even if necessary to some degree, was not seen as embodying a basic principle of nature, still less as something of divine origin or authority. The Chinese Heaven did not lay down laws nor dictate precise rules of belief and behaviour, as in the Ten Commandments or the Koran. Within the long and complex Chinese tradition there was certainly a significant 'legalist' position, and something of the view that precise and strictly applied laws were essential for good government certainly found its way into the general practice of government in Confucian China. But in Confucian thought the written law never came to be seen as the ultimate authority or source of justice in society or government. The moral dimension, as spelled out in the Confucian canon and as interpreted by the responsible person, be they head of family, clan, guild, magistrate or emperor, was always greater, more fundamental, more authoritative than the merely legal. One should not make the contrast between the two traditions too absolute and stark. Western law too is based to a large degree on moral values, but when the two are in conflict, or appear to be so, the letter of the law is likely to prevail. In the Western tradition to 'uphold the law' has been a principle generally accepted as necessary to social order and good government, but the Chinese tradition has never given such primacy or autonomy to its legal institutions.

Further, the legal system and practices that developed in China lacked many of the features seen as normal in the West, whatever the variations that existed within Western national codes. The Chinese had no courts separate from the district magistrate's yamen or office, nor any specialized profession of lawyers accessible to individual litigants and trained to argue cases before judge and jury. There were no specially designated judges, and certainly no juries. Within his jurisdiction the magistrate acted as judge, policeman, tax collector, administrator of public works and much else. He employed assistants, of course, to help in the performance of all these functions, and some of these became expert in the administration of laws. But they did not become 'lawyers'. Civil disputes were expected to be settled elsewhere – within the family, the clan, the guild, among the village elders – and to bring such disputes to the yamen was prima facie evidence of moral failure. There were no extensive codes of civil law comparable to the criminal codes. Unless of some status, the best proof of which was to hold a degree of some sort – though wealth helped, since some of these degrees became purchasable – it was always unwise to come before the magistrate. Punishments, as well as costs, could be very severe, but varied with status, including status within the family. The primary concern was to restore the balance between Heaven and Earth, between the moral and social order, rather than to assess cases according to strict rules of evidence, probability or reasonable doubt. If the individual responsible for a crime, for a disturbance to social harmony, could not be identified or apprehended then it was considered appropriate to punish someone else who could be held morally even if not directly responsible. Justice to the individual, concern for any rights for the accused, was subordinate to the concern to carry through some ritual retribution for violation of the social order. Western legal systems, it should be said, could also operate in very arbitrary and unpredictable ways and, before the modern post-French and American revolutionary emphasis on human rights and equality before the law, Westerners caught up in the Chinese legal system were not necessarily worse off than they would have been under their own legal systems. But by the nineteenth century Westerners became very concerned over a system of law and institutions based on so different a logic from that which underlay their own system. A system in which 'an accused person might be arrested arbitrarily and detained indefinitely, was presumed guilty, might be forced to incriminate himself through confession and had no advice of counsel, nor much chance to make a defence',[17] came to be seen by modern Westerners as unacceptable, and led to an insistence on extraterritorial rights as part of the treaty system imposed by the West on China in the nineteenth century.

But there were to be three centuries of sustained, gradually increasing contact between these two great civilizations before they came into sharp conflict in the nineteenth century over trade, diplomacy, religion and law. It is time now to turn to survey the nature of this pre-nineteenth-century contact, a contact sought solely by the West and accepted less than enthusiastically, and only within distinct limitations, by the ruling elite of China. Westerners had to cross a wide world, conceptually as well as physically, to make and sustain that contact, but eventually it was China that had to make the greatest adjustments, had to move furthest and reassess most radically its place on Earth and under Heaven. The West forced this process on China, in stages and by a variety of means, some well-intentioned enough, others decidedly harsh, arrogant, even evil. The interplay of these two great traditions, based at opposite ends of the world's largest continent, constitutes a long and very complex story. The next three chapters survey the main outlines of that story while offering interpretations and judgments that are certainly open to debate. But informed debate is the way to get beyond myths and stereotypes, comfortable though those may be. There are certainly plenty in the generally accepted story of the West's relations with China. Some of them are examined and tested in the following pages.

2
Coming Together, Rather Slowly and on China's Terms (1500–1800)

The arrival of Europeans in Asian waters at the beginning of the sixteenth century was far from meaning that they quickly became a dominant force, controlling economies and establishing extensive colonial empires. Fifty years ago the Indian diplomat and historian K.M. Pannikar published a lively and influential book, entitled *Asia and Western Dominance*, in which he argued that the centuries which began with the arrival of Vasco da Gama in Calicut and ended with the withdrawal of British forces from India in 1947 and of the European navies from China in 1949 constituted a clearly marked epoch of history. What he defined as 'the da Gama epoch' was characterized above all by 'the dominance of maritime power over the land masses of Asia and by the domination of the peoples of Europe, who held the mastery of the seas, over the affairs of Asia.' In the first, though not the second, edition of his book Pannikar went on to claim that this dominance model was 'true not only in respect of areas like India, Ceylon and Indonesia, where along the coasts the European powers had trading settlements and some political power, but also in respect of China and Japan. . . . In fact from the beginning of the sixteenth century China may be said to have been subjected to an effective naval blockade.'[1]

Pannikar presented an attractive but decidedly distorted view, seeing this long span of history too much through the prism of the nineteenth and early twentieth centuries, when European imperialism was rampant and most parts of Asia were indeed deeply affected, though very unequally, by the Western presence. A more accurate long term overview of the matter seems to be that suggested by B.B. Kling and M.N. Pearson in their introduction to a 1979 collection of essays on aspects of the European presence in Asia entitled, very differently from Pannikar's book, *The Age of Partnership: Europeans in Asia before Dominion*. They wrote:

> in broad terms the degree of European influence is best depicted by a curve which rises slowly (the sixteenth century), then declining a little (the seventeenth century) then rises again, but slowly (the eighteenth century) and finally rises increasingly steeply (the 19th century). This variation apparently has contributed to faulty assessments of the European impact.[2]

In this chapter I will survey the contacts – commercial, religious, cultural and diplomatic – made between China and the West down to the nineteenth century in terms of this curving rather than Pannikar's straight out 'dominance' model.

The Traders

Having found the sea route from Europe to Asia the Portuguese wasted little time in pushing on beyond India towards China. A mere ten years after da Gama's arrival at Calicut one of their commanders was instructed by his king:

> You shall ask after the Chijns, from what part they come and from how far, and at what times they come to Malacca... and if they are wealthy merchants, weak men or warriors... if they are Christians or heathens, if their country is a great one, and if they have more than one king amongst them... and, if they are not Christians in what do they believe and what they adore, and what customs they observe, and towards what part does their country extend.[3]

There was much to learn, including the basic point that the country the Portuguese were now approaching by sea was the Cathay a few mediaeval missionaries and other travellers had reached by land and described for Western readers several centuries earlier.

The Portuguese under Albuquerque gained control of the strategic Malacca Straits in 1511, and by 1514 one of their traders had reached Canton, though not in a Portuguese vessel. Within a few more years, however, several of these had arrived, some carrying an embassy led by Tomé Pires seeking to establish a permanent base for trade. That embassy had a most unfortunate time of it, first facing long delays before being permitted to go on to Beijing, then meeting hostility from the court officials there, who saw it as a tribute-bearing mission and so instructed it, in response to complaints from other tributaries, to restore Malacca to its recently displaced sultan. When Pires refused to pass on these instructions to his king in Portugal he and his companions were unceremoniously sent back to Canton in 1521, where they were imprisoned and, within a few years, died.[4] Together with other nasty incidents it was not a good beginning, but it demonstrated clearly that, even though the Chinese could not prevent the Portuguese and other Westerners from coming to their shores, they could limit, and to a considerable degree control, even dominate, their activities.

About thirty years after Pires' disastrous embassy local officials did grant the Portuguese a permanent base at Macao, a small peninsula well away from Canton, in recognition of their help in checking piracy in the region. But this base was subject to still considerable Chinese supervision, including control of land access to the area. It was as much a confinement as a concession to these often troublesome, but also profitable and sometimes useful, barbarians. For a time trade with them developed at various ports on the south China coast, but became confined to fewer and fewer, eventually to only Canton. By the later sixteenth century the Spaniards, coming across the Pacific from the Americas via the Philippine islands, shared in this trade but, with a base well away in Manila, from whence most of the trade was carried in Chinese junks, they had fewer contacts and confrontations with the Chinese. Their main contribution was to ship in silver from their mines in Mexico to pay for the exports. Spanish silver dollars became the favoured international currency of the region.

This early European trade into Asia was for long basically a carrying trade, transporting Asian products to markets both within Asia as well as to Europe – mainly spices originally, but over the centuries many other products – textiles such as muslin, cotton, silk; porcelain; timber; tea; and ultimately opium shipped from India to China. Better armed against the all too prevalent pirates, European vessels could play a key role in this carrying trade both within and beyond Asia, but they brought in few goods which could find ready or large markets there. Spanish silver was always acceptable, to help lubricate the intra-Asian trade, but supplies of that were uncertain, and by the eighteenth century inadequate to help much in balancing the rapidly growing trade in tea from China, then still the only source of that beverage. During the period 1710–59 the East India Company, to pay for its growing exports from Asia, shipped in £27 million worth of bullion, but only £9 million worth of goods. It was not until it was found that opium, produced in

India, could be readily sold in China that this balance of trade problem was solved, creating other problems in the process. But this is to run ahead, beyond 1800. Until the nineteenth century European traders, first the Portuguese, followed by the Spanish and, by the seventeenth century, the Dutch, English and French, were basically intermediaries, carriers of desirable Asian products within Asia and around the world.

As carriers and intermediaries European traders were fitted easily enough into the margins of the Chinese world. As we shall see later in this chapter, a Chinese emperor at the very end of the eighteenth century could still airily dismiss the idea that Europeans had anything of great value or interest to bring to the central kingdom, which in Confucian eyes already enjoyed the full bounty of Heaven. Mindful of the responsibilities that its favoured position under Heaven imposed, China would allow any reasonably submissive outer barbarian, European or other, to share in its riches by permitting some trade. But such trade was seen as in no way a necessity for China itself, just as an act of favour to 'lesser breeds without the law', as an English poet, looking down the other end of the telescope, was later to put it. This, it should be emphasized, was very much the official Confucian view. Plenty of Chinese outside the bureaucratic elite saw foreign trade as very desirable, and were keen to participate in it as fully as possible, even when the main commodity was illegal opium. But the official view, which set the conditions for Westerners, was that foreign trade was hardly even incidental to the health of the Chinese economy and could therefore be confined to a few places, where control could be most effectively exercised. The foreign traders admitted to those places should behave as, and be treated as, tributaries to China. They were certainly not to be free to come and go on their own terms.

This theory and system was not devised just to handle the Europeans who began arriving in the sixteenth century at various ports in southern China. The Chinese had already had long experience in dealing with foreign traders coming both by land and sea. Arab traders had come to China as far back as Tang times, but by late Song times (twelfth–thirteenth centuries) a sophisticated control system, based on further experience with traders from South East Asia, was well in place. This system continued through to the Ming, (fourteenth–seventeenth centuries) which was the ruling dynasty when the Portuguese reached China. It has been summarized by the great American sinologist, J.K. Fairbank, in his study *Trade and Diplomacy on the China Coast*, as involving 'the supervision and taxation of trade by officials responsible directly to the capital; the confinement of trade to certain ports; the confinement of foreigners at these ports to their own quarter, where they were under the authority of one of their own number.'[5] Elements of this system carried through to the system laid down for Canton by Qing officials in the eighteenth century and indeed, Fairbank argues, even into the treaty system created in the mid-nineteenth century. More of that later, but the point to emphasize here is that there was considerable continuity of ideas and practices, that European trade with China developed within the framework of an already well-established pattern of Chinese trade with South East Asia.

By the later eighteenth century those small beginnings had grown considerably. The volume of tea exported from Canton grew from about 1½ million pounds in 1720 to 45 million a century later, an *'ascension la plus vertigineuse'*, as the French historian who has examined Western trade at Canton during the eighteenth century in greatest detail aptly comments.[6] It became, before the growth of the opium trade, probably the biggest single commodity trade in the world. Many countries participated in this trade at Canton, with the English East India Company, a kind of early multi-national corporation, the dominant but by no means sole player on the Western side. By 1760 the Chinese decided it was time to define even more precisely the conditions under which they would allow this rapidly growing trade to continue.

The Canton system of control

A summary of the main features of this 'Canton system of trade' is desirable here, both to provide some detail to illustrate the main proposition of this chapter, that is that the Chinese set the terms for these early relations with the seaborne Europeans, and to provide background for understanding some of the issues and outcomes to be looked at in the next chapter. Under this system merchants could now trade only at Canton, but were permitted to reside there only during the few monsoon months when trade was at its peak. For the rest of the year they had to retreat to Macao, paying hefty entry and exit fees as they did so. At Canton the merchants were confined to an island in the river, outside the city limits, on which the various nations engaged in the trade built their 'factories' or agencies. In these there were to be no women, wives or otherwise; no guns, or other arms, and no more than a small number of Chinese servants. The merchants were not to row on the river for pleasure – a mystifying practice then to the Chinese, for whom physical effort should always have some practical purpose. But they might take the air on the 8th, 18th and 28th day of each month, in the flower gardens across the river, in groups of not more than ten guided by an interpreter. They were permitted only to walk, not to take sedan chairs, however ready to pay for these, and were not to spend the night outside the factories. They could not make direct representation to Chinese government officials, but might petition them through one of the dozen or so Chinese merchants licensed to deal with them, a group known as the Co-hong. These Co-hong merchants were responsible for ensuring that all these rules were observed.

One other very reasonable rule the Chinese imposed was that no foreign naval vessels should enter the river on which Canton stands, some 60 miles upstream. Macao is well outside the entrance known in Chinese as Hu Men or Tiger's Gate and in Portuguese as 'Bocca Tigris' or the Bogue. Chinese forts guarded it, but by the eighteenth century the fire power of European warships was such as to make these land defences quite inadequate. The vastly superior power of the West at sea, which was the basis of its expanding influence and power around the world, had become overwhelming by then. It was not only size and gunnery but advanced navigational skills, the capacity to sail across the widest oceans and calculate exactly where they were, that by the mid-eighteenth century made these ships so formidable. The authorities at Canton had had some uncomfortable moments in 1743 when Commodore Anson insisted on bringing his 1000 ton 60 gun *Centurion*, much battered and depleted on its long voyage around the world, up the river to rest and resupply. The sight of a foreign vessel of that size and power anchored in the river and overlooking the city, though it was something that later generations of Chinese would become familiar with, was very disturbing. In fact, Anson and his crew behaved reasonably well, helping fight a fire in the city, though he was not impressed by much of what he saw of the government and the society, condemning 'the timidity, dissimulation and dishonesty of the Chinese', and he roundly cursed their merchants when, as he finally sailed away, he found many of the supplies he had been given were, to put it mildly, of inferior quality.[7] Adequate resupply facilities constituted an ongoing problem for large Western ships on long voyages, even for the steam ships of the next century, which needed regular coal depots if nothing else. This was one of the reasons why, just over a century later, another naval commodore from a newly emerged Western power, the USA, sailed into Tokyo bay in 1853 to the great discomfort and alarm of the Japanese. That famous encounter led to a formal treaty guaranteeing access to Japanese ports and supplies, as China by then had also been forced to agree to, after the first of the Opium Wars. The compromise worked out after Anson's earlier show of force at Canton was that supply facilities would be provided at the mouth of the river.

Through the eighteenth century then, Confucian China could still feel that it was controlling the conditions of trade and keeping unwelcome Western naval power at a reasonably safe distance. The formalization of the Canton Co-hong system about 1760 underlined all this. But by the end of the eighteenth century significant changes had developed – a widening discrepancy of naval strength; a rapidly growing volume of trade, centred more and more around a controversial product, opium; and a shift in Western ideas about trade, away from mercantilist toward free trade principles. By the early nineteenth century the combination of these changes – naval, economic and intellectual – created the conditions for a radical alteration in the pattern of relations, in essence a Chinese pattern, that had emerged since the early sixteenth century.

It is worth adding here that before the nineteenth century the Chinese imposed pattern for trade was by no means disagreeable to most of the Western traders who resided at Macao and spent a few months each year in the factories at Canton. Life in both places was comfortable, despite the restrictions, and the profits were large, despite the exorbitant Chinese charges imposed. These pre-free trade European merchants were well used to government regulation and controls, for that was the norm in that mercantilist age. The main trader at Canton by the eighteenth century, the English East India Company, was itself a monopolist company, and whatever the difficulties and minor irritations – personal, commercial or bureaucratic – was not disposed to protest too much. 'Nations in general must be admitted to possess the right of regulating their commerce according to their separate views of policy,' their directors wrote as late as 1817, though they did go on to insist that the Chinese should be consistent and even-handed in the application of their policies.[8] But by then Adam Smith had written his *Wealth of Nations* and Western lawyers were arguing that there was 'a general obligation upon Nations to promote mutual commerce', and that freedom rather than regulation of trade was the natural order for all mankind. Thus it was stated by the Swiss theorist of international law, Vattel, even before Smith's influential book was published in 1776, that:

> Nature rarely produces in one district all the various things men will have need of ... If all districts trade with one another, as nature intended, none will be without what is necessary and useful to them, and the intentions of nature, the common mother of mankind will be fulfilled [and] each Nation will be assured of satisfying its wants ... so that mankind as a whole will gain thereby.[9]

This was the new view of trade coming to prevail, not without some hiccups and resistance, in the West. China would eventually accommodate itself to it, but it would take a couple of centuries.

The Missionaries

The traders fit the curve model suggested at the beginning of this chapter fairly well. Their influence, at least as measured by the numbers of their ships coming to China and the volume of trade they carried, did rise slowly but fairly steadily during the sixteenth century, hit something of a plateau during the seventeenth but rose steeply during the eighteenth century. The missionaries, however, fit the model much less well, their curve only beginning late in the sixteenth century, rising to encouraging heights by the end of the seventeenth and the early eighteenth centuries, but then declining very steeply, not to rise again until the mid-nineteenth century. Furthermore, their influence, as measured by the sustained acceptance of their ideas, was greater on Europe than on China, for they – or at least the Jesuits among them – became the first scholarly informants on China to the West, and through them China became a focus of interest and debate for the educated classes of Europe. We still use the Latinized word Confucian, derived from the name that the Jesuits gave to the master Kung, as our portmanteau word to label Chinese civilization, and until quite recently the largest multi-volumed history of China in a Western language was one written in French in the eighteenth century by a Jesuit.

Sustained Western missionary activity in China, as distinct from the short-lived forays made by a few mediaeval priests, began in 1581 when the Jesuits, that intellectually elite, highly disciplined order of the Catholic Church, founded only forty years earlier by Ignatius Loyola, entered the south of the country in the persons of Michele Ruggieri and the brilliant Matteo Ricci. The Jesuit order was dedicated not just to winning back those parts of Europe being lost to Protestantism but also to carrying the faith into the wider world brought within European reach by the voyages of discovery. The China mission was part of a global enterprise, and the Jesuits have been aptly described as 'the first planetary men, the first in whom the world network became, to some degree, a world system.'[10] Not that the China mission of the seventeenth and eighteenth centuries was a purely Jesuit exercise. Other Catholic orders also became involved, but their presence so complicated and compromised the Jesuit initiative that by the end of the eighteenth century the whole Western missionary push into China was badly stalled. The Jesuit order itself was by then in limbo in Europe, and although other Catholic missionaries retained some small presence in China this was slight and tenuous. The entry of Protestant missionaries into the field by the early nineteenth century, plus the treaties imposed on China by the middle decades of that century, led to another great revival of missionary activity and influence, Catholic and Protestant alike, though that revival was also to go into steep decline in the mid-twentieth century, just as had happened in the eighteenth century. More than the traders, more even than the diplomats, the missionaries demonstrate the sometimes roller-coaster character of the history of Sino-Western relations.

The Jesuit approach to China

The Jesuit approach to the immense challenge of converting a sophisticated, highly literate culture such as China's was to present their Christian message in terms as far as possible consistent with the dominant beliefs and practices of that culture. This led them to seek to understand fully not just its language but its rich and complex literature, its philosophy and religion, its system of government and its social structure, in order to make themselves as acceptable as possible to those in power. They sought to promote a Constantinian conversion, one led from above by the ruling elite, and in order to win over that elite they strove to make themselves not just acceptable but useful to it, to serve it with whatever other specialized knowledge in addition to their Christian message they could provide. Thus they functioned not simply as men of religion, but as mathematicians and astronomers, able to draw up more reliable calendars than the Mahommedan astronomers then used by the court; as interpreters and diplomats able to help negotiate a satisfactory border agreement with the Russians beginning to expand into Siberia; as architects who could help plan and construct a Summer Palace complex in Beijing, to be later destroyed by other Westerners; as physicians who could help keep the emperor in good health; and as metallurgists were even able to cast cannons. They spoke, dressed and as far as they could lived and behaved as literati, many of them (though not all) working as minor bureaucrats who served the Confucian court while they sought also to convert it. It was a highly intelligent, non-confrontational approach, developed in part out of earlier Jesuit experience in the missions to India and Japan, which had begun a few decades before that to China. Thus Matteo Ricci, or Li Ma-tou as he became, having won his way gradually from South China to the capital, where he was permitted to reside after 1601, wrote that:

The ultimate purpose and the general intention of this sect, the Literati, is public peace and order in the kingdom. They likewise look towards the economic security of the family and the virtuous training of the individual. The precepts they formulate are certainly directive to such ends and quite in conformity with the light of conscience and with Christian truth...One might say in truth that the teachings of this academy, save in some few instances, are so far from contrary to Christian principles that such an institution could derive great benefit from Christianity and might be developed and perfected by it.[11]

Ricci had criticisms to make of the way in which the original Confucian texts were interpreted by contemporary scholars, and also of the readiness of the Chinese to follow Buddhist and Daoist along with Confucian ideas. He complained later in his journal that 'In believing that they can honour all three laws at the same time they find themselves without any law at all, because they do not sincerely follow any one of them.' Clearly there was much work to do for the dedicated missionary, but in that work Confucianism, as understood by Ricci and his successors, was seen more as an ally than as an obstacle. For the Jesuits Confucianism was a highly moral, socially responsible creed, requiring only some additional Christian insights to be a perfectly acceptable basis of the social and moral order. In the Jesuit plan it would appear that China could remain Confucian, with added Christian characteristics – or should that equation be reversed? When adopting ideas of foreign origin, be they Buddhist, Christian, Communist or Capitalist, the Chinese have always displayed a capacity to give them strong Chinese characteristics. The Jesuits seem to have recognized this, and were prepared to adapt to it.

Ricci died in 1610, saying famously to the companions who had joined him by then, 'I leave you at a door opened up to great rewards, but fraught with peril and labour.'[12] Indeed it was so, and the path beyond that door was often made very difficult by the hostility shown not only by some Chinese but also many Catholic critics. In the end these criticisms were to overwhelm this early Jesuit mission to China, so that it must be counted as one of history's magnificent failures. But before that became evident, after proving their superiority as astronomers and their value as linguists and diplomats, the order won the respect of the great Kangxi emperor of the new Qing dynasty. In 1692 he issued an edict which effectively granted toleration to Christianity, removing from it any suspicion of being a false sect likely to lead the people astray and cause disturbances. This was to put it among the accepted official cults, and converts were won even among high-ranking officials. The building of a church within the imperial city itself was permitted after the Jesuits had helped cure the emperor of an attack of malaria by using a new drug, quinine. The door then seemed to be opening so wide that a newly arrived member of the order wrote home in 1699, with excessive optimism:

> The people hold themselves fortunate to live under so accomplished a Prince; but what gives us greater joy is that the Prince favours more and more the Christian religion. He says it is the true law; he was delighted to learn that some great Lords had embraced it, and who knows if the time is not approaching when he will embrace it himself.[13]

These were the golden years of the mission, but within a decade they began to fade.

The Rites controversy

The Jesuit interpretation of Confucianism meant that, despite a few doubters among them, they took a tolerant view of the common Chinese practices of ancestor worship and of the rituals honouring Confucius himself. They interpreted these as civil not religious practices. They argued that ancestor worship was an expression of familial respect to past generations, and that the tablets set up to honour ancestors were simply memorials, not repositories of souls. Further, the rituals honouring Confucius did not make him a figure of divine status and authority; he was honoured by the Chinese as a sage, not a god. The Jesuit emphasis was on the early and basic texts of Confucianism, which they interpreted as having much more spiritual content and awareness than the exegesis of those texts by later Confucian scholarship suggested. Respect to images and memorials of Confucius or ancestors was allowable, while respect to Buddhist and other idols was condemned. It was a fine line that was being drawn.

As well there were other difficulties, such as how best to translate the word God – whether to use an existing term (*shangdi* = emperor on high), thus implying that the concept as understood in the West was present in traditional Chinese thought, or to use a neologism (*tianzhu* = lord of Heaven), thus emphasizing the novelty and challenge of the Christian message. Ricci himself, writing in the early years of the mission, had used both terms, but his successors settled on *shangdi*, the term that was later to be adopted by Protestant missions. Other Catholic missionary orders, such as the Dominicans and the Franciscans, which had entered the China field in the wake of the Jesuits, used *tianzhu* and insisted that Confucianism was basically atheistic and materialistic, that the rites associated with it and ancestor worship were indeed idolatrous. For them it was not possible to practise faithfully both Confucian and Christian ceremonies. Thus developed the complex, protracted Rites Controversy in the Catholic church which was to cast a very deep shadow over the whole Christian mission to China during the eighteenth century.

Appeals for rulings on these questions of rites and terminology were made both to the Chinese emperor, by the Jesuits, and to the Papacy, by their Dominican and Franciscan critics. In a petition to the Kangxi emperor the Jesuits stated 'We have always judged that Confucius is honoured in China as a legislator, and that it is to this end, and solely with this in view, that the ceremonies established in his honour are performed.'[14] The emperor agreed. In a sense he was a logical person to appeal to for an authoritative statement of the Chinese understanding of such things, but it was perhaps not altogether good tactics for the Jesuits to do so while the issue was *sub judice* in Rome. When the first papal legate sent to enquire into and judge the matter, de Tournon, arrived in China in 1705, he was certainly not favourably disposed towards the Jesuits. But appealing to the dragon throne in Beijing before the papal throne in Rome probably made no difference, for the kind of cultural flexibility that would have been necessary to sustain the Jesuit approach was still lacking among the religious leaders of the West. Indeed at this point in time the Chinese appear to have been the more flexible and tolerant, at least in the person of the Kangxi emperor. He reigned more or less contemporaneously with Louis XIV of France, with whom the Jesuit missionaries often compared him. It was the French king who revoked the Edict of Nantes in 1685 and sought to impose, by force and with papal approval, religious uniformity on his subjects, while it was the Chinese emperor who issued an Edict of Toleration in 1692, permitted considerable diversity of faiths in his kingdom, and honoured personally many of the missionaries from the West. Of course, by this time there were many in the West arguing in favour of religious toleration, and Western civilization was moving far more rapidly towards greater liberality of thought and recognition of a right to dissent than was China. Still, the contrast between Louis XIV and the Kangxi emperor is a warning against generalizing too glibly.

By the end of his long reign, however, the emperor had just about had enough of these Christian missionaries, much as he had respected and enjoyed contact with some of them. By the time of his death in 1722, two papal legates had come to China and passed judgment against the Jesuits. A papal pronouncement in 1715 approved the first legate's judgment, and when the Jesuits temporized by arguing that this was not a formal Bull which they were bound to obey, a second legate came in 1721 to repeat and reinforce it. After reading the Chinese text of the papal pronouncement the emperor wrote on the document, in imperial vermilion ink,

> On reading this proclamation I can only conclude that the Westerners are small minded. How can they talk about the great ideas of China? No Westerner understands Chinese books, and when they discuss them our people find many of their remarks ridiculous... I have never seen such nonsense as this. Henceforth no Westerner may propagate his religion in China. It should be prohibited in order to avoid trouble.[15]

Just 30 years after issuing an edict tolerating and promoting Christianity the Kangxi emperor was threatening its suppression.

Suppression began in earnest in 1724 when his successor issued an edict making confession of the Christian faith illegal for Chinese. Missionary work was forced underground, and those Jesuits who continued to reside in the capital had less status and were more and more limited to practical functions. By 1752 one of them wrote sadly, after setting up a mechanical theatre to help celebrate the birthday of the then Empress Dowager,

> It is thus we try, in the interests of our religion, to gain the good will of the Prince and to make our service so useful and necessary to him that in the end he will become more favourably inclined towards Christians and persecute them less than he had done.[16]

A few Jesuits were tolerated still around the court as useful functionaries, but the suppression of the order by the Papacy itself during the late eighteenth and early nineteenth centuries meant that eventually none remained. In 1742 a papal Bull had reaffirmed the 1715 pronouncement and required all missionaries working in China to swear an oath that they would obey the apostolic command regarding the Confucian Rites and ensure that their converts gave up observing them. This Bull remained in force until 1938. Such hostile judgment from Rome, on top of the far less interested and tolerant attitude of those who succeeded the Kangxi emperor, meant that by the later eighteenth century Ricci's door was hardly even ajar.

The Jesuit mission, which centred strongly though not exclusively on the imperial Court, had failed, but a few missionaries remained in the provinces, 'ministering secretly to a cowed remnant of lower class Christians'.[17] By the nineteenth century these were mainly French Lazarists or representatives of the *Missions Étrangères*, and one study of them has claimed that, on the evidence of their letters in the *Annales de la Propagation de la Foi*, 'there were, deep inside China, substantial communities of the faithful', while admitting that an estimate of two hundred thousand is guesswork.[18] Given the size of the task this was not much to show for two hundred years of dedicated effort by several hundreds of missionaries. The missionary influence on China before the door was forced more widely open in the nineteenth century had proved minimal. The Jesuits among them had introduced many Western technical and scientific ideas, but it is not apparent that these had any greater impact than their religious ideas. In his great study *Science and Civilisation in China*, Joseph Needham suggested that, after the coming of the Jesuits, Chinese science 'fused with world science', that these missionaries began 'a work of liaison' that has led China to take its place in the world community of science.[19] But this is far from obvious, and Needham himself had to go on to admit that the process was slow during the eighteenth and nineteenth centuries, 'inhibited by the same factors in Chinese society which had hindered it throughout all earlier history.' Traditional Chinese civilization remained basically unmoved by these Jesuit missionaries, accommodating, intelligent, patient and informed though they were. It was the traders and the diplomats who were to prove to be the main agents bringing China into the wider world of science as a spin-off from their basic objective of bringing China into the wider world of commerce and diplomacy. The main influence exerted by the Jesuit missionaries of the seventeenth and eighteenth centuries was upon Europe rather than China, and I turn now to consider that briefly.

China and the Jesuits Help Enlighten Europe

The two centuries during which the Jesuit mission to China was launched, flourished briefly and then declined sharply, were centuries during which Western perceptions of both Heaven and Earth changed radically. The process had begun earlier with the humanist scholars of the Renaissance expanding the West's intellectual horizons by their close study of Europe's classical past. The voyages of discovery widened geographical horizons, greatly increasing awareness of the variety of cultures on our globe, while Copernicus brought into question the place of that globe itself within the cosmos. In addition there was the Protestant Reformation, which fractured the theoretical religious unity of Christendom and raised acutely the questions of the rights of individual conscience and of the authenticity of many accepted religious beliefs. Our modern globalized, pluralistic and secularized world was emerging during the fifteenth and sixteenth centuries. But it was during the seventeenth and especially the eighteenth century that that world was decisively defined. More and more, critical reason was applied to every aspect of being, to the whole world of nature and of man, including religious faith, while every continent was drawn, to at least some degree, into an expanding global economy. The nineteenth and twentieth added a greatly quickened pace and extended range to this process, but the direction was firmly set in those earlier two centuries. There has always been, and still is, much confusion, resistance, doubt and debate about this process, both within the West itself and beyond it, but it continues and, however rough the ride in places, seems irreversible. For good or ill a globalized, largely Westernized world, is our world of the foreseeable future. The Jesuits, so active and experimental in China and elsewhere, were among its forerunners, contributing significantly, though not altogether intentionally, to its formation.

Jesuit reports, letters, translations and commentaries from China were widely published, especially in the eighteenth century, and provided a mass of information to Western readers about this great culture on the far side of the world, a culture which displayed, in their accounts, many admirable features and seemed, in general terms, at least the equal of the West in civilization. China was by no means the only source of such challenging information to Europeans, but by the eighteenth century it was the chief one. In his great book *La Crise de la Conscience européene*, translated into English as *The European Mind 1680–1715*, Paul Hazard entitled his first chapter 'The Ferment Begins' in which he surveyed 'the spate of travel books, Narratives, Descriptions, Reports, Collections, Series, Miscellanea' from which 'Gentlemen sitting comfortably at home by the fireside learnt all there was to know about the Great American Lakes, the Gardens of Malabar, the Pagodas of China, and a host of things they would never behold at first hand.' At the end of this chapter Hazard commented, 'in this panoramic survey of ideas, China holds the most conspicuous place.'[20] China indeed became something of a model for Europe. Late in the sixteenth century, even before Ricci's arrival in Beijing, the French humanist Montaigne, in the last of his essays (Of Experience), included high praise of China,

> a kingdom whose government and arts, having had no contact with or knowledge of ours, offer examples that surpass ours in many excellent features; from whose history I learn how much wider and diverse the world is than either the ancients or we moderns have been able to conceive....

Many others after Montaigne were to learn the same lessons from the Jesuit writings on China.

Leibniz and Voltaire view China favourably, Dr Johnson does not

The general tone of those writings is apparent in the quotations already given from Ricci's journals, edited versions of which were published in Latin and in French only a few years after his death. Other publications followed, and many of the missionaries in Beijing also engaged in direct correspondence with savants in Europe. One of the greatest of these savants, the German mathematician and philosopher Leibniz, edited a volume of Jesuit letters in 1697, and in his preface wrote in visionary terms about China and the West:

> I consider it a singular plan of the fates that human cultivation and refinement should today be concentrated as it were in the two extremes of our continent, in Europe and China...which adorns the Orient as Europe does the opposite edge of the earth. Perhaps Supreme Providence has ordained such an arrangement so that, as the most cultivated and distant peoples stretch out their arms to each other, those in between may be brought to a better way of life... Now the Chinese empire, which challenges (equals) Europe in cultivated area, vies with us in many other ways in almost equal combat, so that now they win, now we...In the useful arts and in practical experience with natural objects we are, all things considered, about equal to them, and each people has knowledge which it could with profit communicate to the other. In profundity of knowledge and in the theoretical disciplines we are their superiors...But who would have believed that there is on earth a people who, though we are in our view so very advanced in every branch of behaviour, still surpass us in comprehending the precepts of civil life...And so if we are their equals in the industrial arts and ahead of them in the contemplative sciences certainly they surpass us (though it is almost shameful to

confess this) in practical philosophy, that is in the precepts of ethics and politics adapted to the present life and use of mortals. Indeed it is difficult to describe how beautifully all the laws of the Chinese, in contrast to those of other peoples, are directed towards the achievement of public tranquillity and the establishment of social order, so that men shall be disrupted in their relations as little as possible . . . To be sure they are not lacking in avarice, lust or ambition. Hence the Chinese do not attain to full and complete virtue. This is not to be expected except by Heaven's grace and Christian teaching. Yet they temper the bitter fruits of vice, and though they cannot tear out the roots of sin in human nature, they are apparently able to control many of the burgeoning growths of evil.[21]

I have quoted Liebniz, one of the most eminent thinkers of his time, at some length, to demonstrate the strength of the impact of the example of China, as understood through Jesuit reports and letters, at a crucial period in the development of modern European thought. Particularly interesting in this extract is Leibniz's idea that human cultivation was concentrated at the two extremes of the Eurasian continent, prompting his hope that 'the most cultivated and distant peoples' might, by stretching out their arms to each other, help civilize the lands between. The interplay between Europe, China and the main land between that Leibniz hoped they might together help bring to a better way of life, that is to say Russia, has never been very co-operative, but it remains an engaging thought!

Like the Jesuits, Leibniz was not totally uncritical, and did not present the Chinese as beyond compare and criticism. But the overwhelming thrust of his comments was positive and admiring. For him China's was clearly a culture from which there was much to learn. Leibniz even went on to suggest 'that Chinese missionaries should be sent to us to teach us the use and practice of natural religion, just as we send missionaries to them to teach them revealed religion.' And it was not just instruction in 'natural religion' that he hoped for from China. As a great mathematician he was interested in the binary mathematical structure he discerned in the arrangement of the hexagrams of the Chinese Yijing (*I Ching* or Book of Change), and had hopes of somehow drawing China into a global scientific academy. About 1700 Ricci's door was still open, seeming to promise movement of men and ideas both ways.

The movement of ideas was in fact virtually only one way, from China to the West, and it was a movement not at all promoted by the Chinese themselves. It was activated by the experimental vigour and curiosity of Western society as it entered what historians call, reasonably accurately, the Age of Enlightenment. The information coming in a growing flood out of China, as well as out of other parts of the globe, was fastened on by a host of writers and commentators, eager to assess and interpret it by the light of reason. From it were drawn conclusions that challenged many deeply entrenched European beliefs and assumptions. Thus, at about the same time as Leibniz was writing his glowing preface, that prince of sceptics, Pierre Bayle, having read many of the same Jesuit reports and letters, saw the Chinese as atheists, yet agreed that they were indeed bound by moral laws. Bayle concluded that morality was not dependent on religious beliefs, and that teaching the Chinese about Christianity was not likely to bring them any nearer to Leibniz's ideal of full and complete virtue. A little further on into the eighteenth century Voltaire, who had attended a Jesuit school, became one of the strongest admirers of the Chinese, seeing them as deists rather than as atheists, praising them for their tolerance and lack of dogma, and for having a religion 'wise, august, free of all superstition and barbarism, never dishonoured by impostures, never troubled by quarrels of priests, never making absurd innovations.' Clearly Voltaire's was a rose-coloured view, but for him any well-ordered society without a crusading church and priesthood, without *l'infame* that he denounced so strongly in his own society, merited high praise. He gave no support to Leibniz's idea of an exchange of missionaries, since 'this mania for proselytising is a disorder confined exclusively to our climes... The Eastern peoples have never sent missionaries into Europe, and it is only Western nations who have been eager to carry their opinions, like their commerce, to the extremities of the globe.'[22]

In addition to the perceived order and morality of this great society, which seemed to have only a 'natural' and no divinely 'revealed' religious tradition, the great antiquity and extent of its historical record posed a challenge to the validity of the biblical account of man's origins and early development. Chinese history, as conveyed in Jesuit accounts, seemed to stretch back to the days of the Flood and the Tower of Babel, and there was much speculation among scholars as to how it could be fitted into this biblical history, long taken as universal in the West. One seventeenth-century scholar, impressed by the supposedly mono-syllabic and uninflected nature of the Chinese language, saw it as the original pre-Babel world language, arguing thus:

> Scripture teacheth that the whole Earth was of one language till the conspiracy of Babel. History informs us that China was peopled

whilst the earth was so, of one language and before the Conspiracy. Scripture teacheth that the Judgment of the Confusion of Tongues fell upon those only that were at Babel; History informs us that the Chinois, being fully settled before, were not there: And moreover that the same Language and Characters which, long preceding that Confusion, they used are in use with them at this very Day... it was Nature that from God taught them their language.[23]

Here we can see how earnestly scholars were striving to match their received Christian tradition to the new information they were receiving from the other side of the world. It was no easy task, and it is not surprising that many of them became increasingly sceptical about that received tradition – as well, it should be added, as sceptical about some of the claims made for China. Sinomania in Europe was at its height in the late seventeenth and first half of the eighteenth century. But even those less enthusiastic, such as Montesquieu, saw China as representing a very serious, even if not necessarily superior, alternative to Western values and institutions.

Voltaire was one of the least critical, but his firm placing of China within the context of world history was an important insight – one rather lost to view during the nineteenth and early twentieth century, when Westerners tended again to equate their history with world history. In his *Essai sur les moeurs et l'esprit des nations* Voltaire set a new standard for universal history by beginning not with Genesis but with China. 'In introducing you to universal philosophy', he told his readers in his foreword, 'you must cast your gaze first upon the East, cradle of all the arts which has given everything to the West.' He then went on to devote his first chapter to China, depicting it as a long lasting civilization that continued to flourish while Europe was plunged into barbarism after the fall of Rome. Voltaire was among the first, if not indeed the first, to move Christian Europe from the fixed central position in world history that earlier Western writers had assumed for it. The antiquity of China, the richness and length of its historical record, was a major influence in developing a broader view of human history in the West, and Voltaire, who had a bust of Confucius in his study at Ferney, was in the vanguard of that revolution in thought.

Economic and political thought in the West were also to some degree affected by the example of China. The French theorists of the mid-eighteenth century, known as the Physiocrats, saw China as providing a model for increasing the nation's wealth through intensive agricultural development, with land tax as the major source of government revenue. They agreed that the Chinese government was despotic, but saw it as benevolently and wisely so, the kind of enlightened despotism they looked for, unsuccessfully, in their own nation. Some, like Montesquieu, were critical of the excessively despotic nature of the Chinese government, while conceding that the country was well governed. Voltaire dismissed Montesquieu's 'vague imputations' and defended China as being despotic only in a formal, literal sense, insisting, mistakenly, that law was supreme in China. Robinson Crusoe, however, saw China through Montesquieu's eyes rather than Voltaire's, Defoe reporting him as saying

> I must confess it seemed strange to me, when I came home and heard our people say such fine things of the power, glory, magnificence and trade of the Chinese; because as far as I saw they appeared to be a contemptible crowd of ignorant sordid slaves, subjected to a government qualified only to rule such people.

Clearly there was by no means universal agreement in the eighteenth century among European observers about the nature and value of the Chinese model, political, moral or religious, but the predominant view was positive. By the latter half of the century, however, once the critical reports of visitors such as Anson became more widely known, the kind of Sinomania apparent in thinkers as eminent but different in outlook as Leibniz and Voltaire waned considerably. By 1778 Dr Johnson, although once respectful toward China, was dismissing all East Indians (that is Asians) as barbarians.

Boswell: You will except the Chinese, Sir?
Johnson: No, Sir.
Boswell: Have they not arts?
Johnson: They have pottery.
Boswell: What do you say to the written characters of their language?
Johnson: Sir, they have not an alphabet.
           They have not been able to form what all other nations have formed.[24]

We have moved a long way from that earlier English scholar who had sought to prove that Chinese was the original, virtually God-given, language. But there can be no question that the impact of China on

European thinking was substantial, strengthening and quickening the trend, deeply inherent within the European tradition, towards critical, rational assessment of all things, including religion. This was certainly an unintended spin-off from the Jesuit mission, though in a real sense they were themselves an expression of the global rationalism characteristic of modern Western civilization. They had set out to convert China to Christianity using carefully calculated, rational methods, but the main result of their informed, judicious accounts of that great civilization was to strengthen the armoury of the growing band of sceptics within Europe itself. History, like God, moves in mysterious ways.

China's influence on artistic taste, especially gardens

Dr Johnson's grudging concession that the Chinese at least had 'pottery' reminds us that drinking tea from fine china was a refinement to living that Europe, most particularly England, gained from its trade with the far east. Such cultural and aesthetic influences deserve some notice, in addition to the intellectual, in any survey of the debt European civilization owed to China during the Age of Enlightenment. A variety of new influences in addition to those from China worked upon European taste during the eighteenth century, among them Indian and the revival of Gothic. This mixture of models could lead to excesses, such that:

> The traveller with amazement sees
> A temple, Gothic or Chinese,
> With many a bell or tawdry rag on,
> And crested with a sprawling dragon.[25]

In this movement of taste away from orderly, balanced Classicism towards freer Romanticism China was a very important influence. In an essay entitled 'The Chinese Origin of a Romanticism' the great historian of ideas, A.O. Lovejoy, concluded that:

> A turning point in the history of modern taste was reached when the ideals of regularity, simplicity, uniformity and easy logical intelligibility were first openly impugned, when the assumption that true beauty is 'geometrical' ceased to be one which 'all consented, as to a Law of Nature'. And in England, at all events, the rejection of this assumption seems, throughout most of the eighteenth century, to have been commonly recognized as initially due to the influence and the example of Chinese art.[26]

In his essay, after illustrating 'the enormous reputation which Chinese civilization had in Europe from the late sixteenth until the eighteenth century', Lovejoy went on to trace the development of the English ideal of the garden that emerged strongly during the eighteenth century. This style of garden was in sharp contrast to the formal, geometrical layout of great continental gardens, such as at Versailles.

By the later eighteenth century the chief enthusiast and propagandist for Chinese gardens was Sir William Chambers, who had visited China in his youth. In 1757 he published a lavishly illustrated folio of 'Designs of Chinese buildings, furniture, dresses, machines and utensils...To which is annexed a description of their temples, houses, gardens and so on.' The gardening section, Lovejoy notes, was subsequently reprinted. While rather dismissive of Chinese architecture as toylike, worth only an occasional place 'among compositions of a nobler kind', Chambers was insistent that:

> The Chinese excel in the art of laying out gardens. Their taste in that is good, and what we have for some time past been aiming at in England, though not always with success...Nature is their pattern and their aim is to imitate her in all her beautiful irregularities...As the Chinese are not fond of walking, we seldom meet with avenues or spacious walks as in our European plantations: the whole ground is laid out in a variety of scenes and you are led, by winding passages cut in the groves, to the different points of view, each of which is marked by a seat, a building or some other object. The perfection of their gardens consists in the number, beauty and diversity of these scenes.[27]

Stimulated by such writings, and helped immeasurably by the variety of new plants that were brought in from China and other exotic places, the English also came to excel in the art of laying out gardens. But what we think of today as the English garden should, in justice, be thought of as, at least in its origins, 'Anglo-Chinese'.

Garden layout, fine porcelain, glowing silk fabrics, picturesque wallpapers, bright lacquer ware, light furniture, the occasional pavilion or pagoda – all these things, plus tea – that cup 'which cheers but not inebriates' – flowed in strongly from China, enriching European and especially English culture during the eighteenth century. Even though, towards the end of the century, the earlier Sinomania faded, and more and more Europeans came to think of China as quaint rather than admirable, respect for its culture and government remained the norm in European thinking. The nineteenth century was to see a great turn around in the prevailing Western attitude, but until then most Europeans seem to have recognized that they had gained much from this growing relationship – far more, one would have to say, than had China.

Yet China during these centuries was by no means unchanging or stagnant, as it became fashionable for Westerners to see it during the nineteenth century. Consider this recent assessment from a wide ranging study of China in world history:

> In the Enlightenment Europe and the European world progressed . . .
> Yet it would be hard to say China declined except relatively. The
> Ch'ing was an era of creativity . . . Without, the Ch'ing had solved the
> Inner Asian problem which had baffled the Han, the T'ang, the Sung
> and the Ming. Within, they provided some of the best government
> China ever saw and also the peace which allowed Chinese society to
> indulge in an unparalleled increase in population. It was two boom-
> ing worlds which were increasingly involved with each other . . . But
> the two worlds, Chinese and European, inscribed and circumscribed,
> ran on different time scales. They were desynchronized, China con-
> scious of the past, Europe conscious of the future; China living from
> hand to mouth, Europe building for the long term. The pattern of
> exchanges in the Enlightenment was shaped by these differences of
> temporal orientation.[28]

As this scholar, S.A.M. Adshead, emphasizes, both China and Europe were expanding worlds. But China was expanding and consolidating only within its own region and rich tradition, while Europe was expand-ing globally, bursting well beyond the geographical and intellectual bounds of its own equally complex and rich tradition. Between 1500 and 1800, the period I am surveying in this chapter, these two worlds, so long widely separated, began to converge. That they could indefinitely maintain peaceable separate courses, merely drawing from each other such benefits as each wanted (in China's case very little) in a kind of remote partnership of mutual self-interest was, in the nature of things, improbable. By the late eighteenth century the forces driving them beyond convergence towards collision and confrontation were steadily mounting.

The Diplomats

Turning back now to the diplomats who were, in the mid-nineteenth century, to draw up the new rules under which relations between

China and the West would become ordered, during these earlier centuries there were only sporadic diplomatic relations, but what there were generally fitted in to the traditional Chinese view of the world. After the disaster of the Tomé Pires embassy of 1520 there were no more attempts by Western diplomats to reach the court of Beijing until the later seventeenth century. The merchants engaging in trade with China gained what concessions they needed at the local level, as had happened in 1557 at Macao, while the missionaries who entered the country and reached the capital dealt individually with provincial or court officials as they required. The missionaries very clearly fitted into the Chinese order of things. As the famous edict of the Qianlong emperor, quoted at greater length below, observed when rejecting a British request in 1793 to have a diplomatic representative reside in Beijing,

> Hitherto, whenever men from the various Western Ocean countries have desired to come to the Celestial Empire and to enter the Imperial service we have allowed them to come to the capital. But once having come they were obliged to adopt the costume of the Celestial Empire, they were confined within the Halls, and were never allowed to return home. These are the fixed regulations of the Celestial Empire.

One might almost say that the Jesuits became prisoners, though willing ones, of the Chinese system.

Unlike the missionaries, Western merchants were not permitted to enter the country, only to trade at its boundaries. The Chinese court was flexible enough to turn a more or less blind eye to the fact that this trade, carried on in the far south of its Celestial Empire, was not made absolutely conditional on regular tribute bearing, as in strict Confucian theory it was supposed to be. So long as those traders came and went at outposts such as Macao and, when permitted to go for a few months each year up river to Canton, observed the strict, confining rules laid down there, the court in Beijing did not demand regular submission for what, in its eyes, was a relatively remote and expendable trade. On such a matter Confucian bureaucrats could be creatively and benevolently passive, not requiring too much in the way of civilized behaviour from such distant, seafaring barbarians. So, for most of the period under review in this chapter, the Westerners who came to China were accommodated one way or another into the Chinese order without much need of high level diplomatic relations. The great growth of trade at Canton by the late eighteenth century was eventually to put considerable strain on this comfortable, long-lasting give and take way of handling relations.

The Portuguese and Dutch embassies of the seventeenth century

In the later seventeenth century there was a flurry of diplomatic activity from the West, following the change of dynasty from Ming to Qing, and then no more for another century, apart from some Papal representations at the time of the Rites controversy. The new Manchu dynasty was not at first very secure in the south, where European trading interest was confined, with the Dutch and the English just beginning to enter the scene. Both Dutch and Portuguese sent embassies between 1666 and 1670, and again between 1678 and 1687, partly to indicate their loyalty to the new regime but also with an eye, especially the Dutch, to further trading opportunities.[29]

Having provided some naval help to the Qing, the Dutch wanted the right to trade freely at many more ports and also to have a representative in the capital, the kind of concessions eventually forced from the Chinese in the treaties of the nineteenth century. They were, however, directing their efforts mainly to South East Asia and, though they retained some presence in China and Japan, did not press the issue of wider access to China as the British were later to do.

For two years the Portuguese embassy of 1667–70 did not receive permission to proceed to the capital since, among other reasons, its leader was described as a captain of horse – in Portuguese eyes a highly honourable status, but not to Confucians. Cultural contretemps of this kind have often been a feature of Sino-Western diplomatic relations. This Portuguese embassy was concerned mainly to win for Macao exemption from the strict coastal control regulations that the new dynasty had laid down to defend the country against possible incursions from Taiwan, then not yet part of the Chinese empire. Altogether, between 1667 and the end of the next century some eighteen embassies came from the West, including about six from Russia. Two went the other way, but only as far as Russia which, as an emerging new continental Asian power was in a very different category to the Western maritime states which were seeking trade but not territory. In settling border disputes in the far north, in regions well beyond the Great Wall, the Manchu rulers of China were prepared to negotiate with the Russians on a basis of virtual equality and reciprocity, as in the treaty of Nerchinsk of 1689. But with the Western maritime powers, which wanted increased commercial and other contacts with China proper, the diplomatic traffic was decidedly one way, with no acknowledgment of near equal status. Of the embassies from the West, as distinct from Tsarist Russia, four came from the Portuguese, four from the Dutch, the last in 1795, three from the Papacy, between 1705 and 1725, and one, in 1793, from Great Britain.

Records for these embassies vary in completeness, but it appears that most of them, including the Dutch embassy as late as 1795, performed the ritual ceremony known as the kowtow. Thus, in Chinese eyes they fitted into their system of a superior–inferior tributary world order, with the central kingdom at its apex. 'The established order was not challenged by this contact,' J.K. Fairbank concluded in his study of *Trade and Diplomacy on the China Coast*,[30] and it seems clear that, right down to the beginning of the nineteenth century, the Confucian rulers of China had little reason to doubt that the Western barbarians accepted their status as tributaries, not equals, within the international order as understood by the Chinese. Not, it should be added, that the Chinese were particularly anxious to have to fit them into that order. They had not sought the West out, for trade or for any other reason. But Confucian principles of righteousness and benevolence required that, once present, Westerners should be allowed to share, to some controlled degree, in the riches which Heaven had bestowed on the central kingdom. Regular tributary submission, which imposed some costs on the Chinese state, was not to be expected from men coming from so far away, and so long as they did not attempt to rock the diplomatic boat they were welcome enough, at least tolerated. And, despite the fact that during this period the Europeans were developing strongly among themselves their own very different system of nation-based international relations, those Westerners who did come to China for whatever purpose did not try to rock the diplomatic boat while in Chinese waters. When circumstances demanded it, and self-interest indicated the wisdom of it, they kowtowed. 'The Dutch did not mind going through a few tiresome ceremonies, even giving substance to a few heathen illusions, in order to carry on important negotiations with great sovereigns and their officials', writes J.E. Wills, the historian of the late seventeenth century Dutch and Portuguese embassies,[31] and that pragmatic attitude remained strong among Western envoys to China right down to the nineteenth century. One reason for this is that most of the envoys who came were basically merchants who might carry letters of credit from their governments but were not diplomats representing national governments first and foremost. For them it was not worth compromising the advancement of their commercial interests by questioning the custom of kowtowing. So overall, until the 1793 embassy from Britain, this ritual and the relationship it symbolized did not become an issue between China and the West. Both sides were, in their respective ways, flexible about it, and diplomatically speaking things went along smoothly enough, but on China's terms.

The kowtow ritual

Before moving on to review the embassy which began the Western challenge to this comfortable-seeming balance, some brief consideration of the principles behind the kowtow ritual seems desirable. The three kneelings and nine prostrations, accompanied by knocking the head on the ground, ('ke-tou' in Chinese, hence the English kotow or kowtow) was a very clear physical demonstration of the respect required by court protocol to be paid by all when received in audience by the emperor. But not only before the emperor. The kowtow was performed on special occasions between any superior and inferior, beginning within the family, the basic unit of society. It was not primarily a government or political requirement, designed to emphasize Chinese superiority over all other peoples, although at the diplomatic level it inevitably came to carry that kind of connotation. In essence, it was an act which expressed the performer's recognition of his place under Heaven. It expressed a quasi-religious or philosophical view of the world under Heaven in a manner which was much more energetic than, but comparable to, a Christian kneeling or a Moslem prostrating in prayer. A major difference, but one consistent with the very diffused nature of the Chinese religious tradition, was that this act was not directed primarily to spiritual symbols on religious occasions, save perhaps before tablets to Confucius or ancestors, but was performed at many levels throughout the social system – by filial children before parents, by supplicants before government officials, by all before the emperor, and by the emperor himself before Heaven, or before the tomb of Confucius when he visited it. Indeed the emperor might kowtow not only to Heaven but, in private and as a filial son, before a surviving parent. It was, in short, a rule of conduct of universal application. To refuse to kowtow was to deny not just your place under the superior before you, be they parent, elder, high official or the emperor on the dragon throne, but to deny Heaven itself. To perform the ritual was to 'centre' yourself, to align yourself correctly with the ruling forces of the cosmos, to which the emperor was subject like everyone else.[32]

The deep-seated basis of this kowtow ritual needs to be understood if one is to appreciate why the court and the Confucian officials of China, far into the nineteenth century, were so much more concerned over this issue than over such things as extraterritorial rights or the cession of the island of Hong Kong. Their values and priorities were not those of the West, nor were they those of later generations of Chinese nationalists, for whom the kowtow and all it symbolized became irrelevant compared to ending extraterritoriality or to regaining control of the foreign concessions in the treaty ports and, ultimately, Hong Kong. In due course China would adapt itself pretty well to Western patterns of diplomacy, where principles of national sovereignty dictate the rules. But well into the nineteenth century the idea that its emperor should not receive obeisance by kowtow from all, including these Westerners from afar, was, to put it mildly, deeply disturbing to these Confucian-trained bureaucrats. *Fiat kowtow, ruant coeli,* they might have said, and indeed Heaven was to fall in rather heavily on the Confucian-based Chinese state over the next century or so. But until far into the nineteenth century the kowtow was to remain for them a ritual of central symbolic importance. Without it their world collapsed.

The British send an embassy in 1792

It became an issue between China and the West from 1792–3, when a British embassy under Lord Macartney was sent from Britain to attempt to negotiate new terms for trade and diplomacy. There had been no embassy from the West for some years – one from Portugal in 1753 and another from Russia in 1767, but none from the country which had by this time become the chief trader at Canton. The East India Company, which then had a monopoly of English trade to the far east with its profits rising steadily from the escalating trade in tea, was not very keen to challenge the existing system. Its Directors were 'apprehensive lest by eagerly contending for the redress of grievances, or prematurely insisting upon further privileges, the government of China should take alarm and stop entirely the foreign trade.'[33] The initiative therefore came from the British government which, having brought the East India Company under tighter control by the India Act of 1784, obliged it to help mount the embassy. An embassy was attempted in 1788, but had turned back when its leader died en route. It is a measure of the determination of the British government to promote trade with China by this time that a second embassy was sent fairly quickly, even as events in France were moving Europe towards a serious crisis for Western civilization. So in 1792–3 one of the nation states of Europe, Great Britain, a state far smaller in extent and population than the celestial kingdom but far better able to organize and concentrate its resources, and far readier to direct them towards commercial ends, was about to challenge, at this point peacefully and politely, the system of trade and diplomacy that China had evolved over many centuries. It was a moment of great truth in world history, though it would take quite some years for its full impact to work itself out. It is worth spending some time examining this embassy and the behaviour of its leader, my favourite Westerner in China.

Lord Macartney

Lord Macartney, who led this 1793 British embassy to China, was an experienced diplomat, having served in his twenties as ambassador to the court of Catherine the Great in Russia from 1764 to 1767, and subsequently as Chief Secretary for Ireland and governor of such diverse places as Grenada and Madras, where he applied diplomacy rather than force to Indian princely politics, and had not used his position to enrich himself to become a nabob. A highly cultivated product of the Age of Enlightenment, he was elected in 1786, the same year in which he was wounded in a duel, to the Literary Club, of which Dr Johnson had been one of the founders and which included such notables as Edmund Burke, Sir Joseph Banks, Edward Gibbon, David Garrick, and Johnson's biographer, James Boswell. In his biography, Boswell referred to Macartney as 'eminent for his variety of knowledge' and 'remarkable for an elegant pleasantry'. Earlier, Dr Johnson himself thought him 'in some degree a literary man', but noted that 'his genealogy was a good deal less glorious than his career', being a newly created member of the Irish, not the superior English, aristocracy. Ambitious but very capable, he was often lucky during his career, and no doubt counted himself so when he was appointed to the ambassadorship for which he is now best remembered.[34]

He was not so lucky in his efforts to persuade the Chinese government to take a new view of trade and diplomacy, and returned in 1794 to cartoons and journal comments critical of what many saw as an expensive and fruitless enterprise. But some of history's failures deserve attention as much as its triumphs, as we have seen with the Jesuit mission. Macartney had the 25-volume collection of the Jesuit *Lettres édifiantes et curieuses* in his library and, like many an educated gentleman of eighteenth century Europe, learned a great deal about China from them. Like the Jesuits, he tried patiently, intelligently but unsuccessfully to convert the Chinese to Western views, in his case of Earth rather than of Heaven.

Macartney's instructions

Macartney was commissioned by George III in September 1792 to go to China, ostensibly to congratulate the Qianlong emperor on his 83rd birthday but in reality to negotiate better conditions for trade with a country now being seen as not just a source of highly desirable commodities but as potentially the greatest market in the world for British products. The Instructions issued to him, drawn up by the Home Secretary, Henry Dundas, warrant some close examination, since they encapsulate much that was to become at issue later.[35]

Dundas began by emphasizing that the recent great growth in the tea trade made it 'particularly desirable to cultivate a friendship and increase the communication with China which may lead to such a vent [sale] throughout that extensive Empire of the manufactures of the mother country and of our Indian territories.' He then complained, with some exaggeration, that Britain had so far been obliged to pursue trade with China 'under circumstances the most discouraging, hazardous to its Agents employed in conducting it, and precarious to the various interests involved in it.' After speculating on possible reasons for these 'evils', the Instructions then asserted that,

> in seeking to improve our connections with China we have no views but the general interests of humanity, the mutual benefit of both nations, and the protection of our Commerce under the Chinese Government, subject nevertheless to its Laws and regulations and formed upon a permanent principle equally beneficial to the subjects of both countries.

The British government hoped that appointing a person of Macartney's rank and experience 'would be most likely to meet with a favourable reception from a high-minded people, accustomed to think lightly of the commercial character.' Thus, although the basic objective was to increase trade, both the agent and the method of approach were to transcend crass materialism in order to emphasize and promote universal values, 'the general interests of humanity'. It was another fine line for a Western missionary to have to tread, this time a secular missionary seeking to convert China to Western economic rather than religious principles. Once in China, Macartney was insistent that no one in the embassy party engage in private trading. It was to be a strictly diplomatic exercise, whatever its commercial objectives.

The Instructions, after discussing the best route to take to Beijing and recommending that if possible it be by gaining permission to sail to a northern port rather than proceeding overland from Canton, then informed Macartney that 'His Majesty, from his earnest desire to promote the present undertaking, and in order to give the greatest dignity to the Embassy', would provide a large naval vessel to convey it to China, and also a military guard 'composed of chosen men from the Light Dragoons, Infantry and Artillery with proper Officers... This guard will add splendor and procure respect to the Embassy.' In addition to these naval and military embellishments another ship, provided by the East India Company (which was required to bear most of the cost of the whole exercise) was to carry 'a great variety of articles of British goods, not for the purpose of Sale but to be dispersed and distributed by you in the most likely manner to excite a taste for and establish the use of such Articles in China.'

Among the gifts, taken to impress the emperor in particular, were an elaborate planetarium and many astronomical instruments, including a large telescope; two carriages, one for winter and one for summer conditions, decorated and upholstered in the imperial colour, yellow; various armaments, ranging from pieces of artillery to flexible sword blades; samples of pottery and chinaware made in modern British kilns; paintings of the royal family and of scenes of English life, both rural and urban. In short, the embassy carried a large, carefully collected cross-section of British culture, calculated to impress as well as inform. The emperor, however, when he came to inspect the collection, dismissed much of it as 'good enough to amuse children', though he was interested in a scale model of the largest British naval vessel of the time, which carried 110 guns and was named after the commodore who, 50 years earlier, had forced his way upriver at Canton in a ship carrying only half as many guns. Were the British sending a message about possible things to come, and was the old emperor, who would not live to see those things but had been on the throne when Anson came to Canton, receiving it? Much of the collection was destined to gather dust and lie unregarded in back rooms of the palace on the outskirts of Beijing that the Jesuits had helped design, the Yuan Ming Yuan (Gardens of Encompassing Brightness), later to be burned on British orders. Included in the disregarded gifts left there were the yellow carriages. That style of conveyance, in which the emperor would be seated below the level of the servants attending him, did not conform to Chinese ideas of imperial status.[36]

Presuming the Chinese would receive such an embassy, Macartney was then instructed by Dundas to procure an audience as early as possible after arrival, 'conforming to all ceremonials of that Court which may not commit the honor of your Sovereign or lessen your own dignity so as to endanger the success of your negociation.' It is interesting that at this point the Instructions went on immediately to qualify the reservation expressed here about Chinese court ceremonials by adding, 'Whilst I make this reserve I am satisfied you will be too prudent and considerate to let any trifling punctilio stand in the way of important benefits which may be obtained by engaging the favorable disposition of the Emperor and his ministers.' Thus Macartney was not receiving any very clear instruction about what was to become a major issue for him, whether or not to kowtow. Did that ritual 'commit', that is compromise, the honour of his sovereign and his own dignity as ambassador? Was it, or was it not, 'a trifling punctilio', a mere ceremony? To the Chinese, as I have endeavoured to show, it was much more, and a good many Westerners had already gone along with the ceremony as something necessary to win favours. Macartney too was seeking favours and would have a problem in deciding how far performance of this ritual would help him gain them. His Instructions did not help him much in deciding what course to take.

On another issue which was to loom even larger in the future, the growing trade in opium, his Instructions were clearer. I quote the relevant paragraph in full:

> It is necessary you should be on your guard against one stipulation which perhaps will be demanded of you, which is that of the exclusion of the Trade of Opium from the Chinese Dominions as being prohibited by the Laws of the Empire. If this subject should come into discussion it must be handled with the greatest circumspection. It is beyond a doubt that no inconsiderable portion of the Opium raised within our Indian Territories actually finds its way to China, but if it should be made a positive requisition, or an article of any proposed Commercial Treaty that none of that drug should be sent by us to China, you must accede to it rather than risk any essential benefit by contending for a liberty in this respect, in which case the sale of our Opium in Bengal must be left to take its chance in an open market, or find a consumption in the dispersed and circuitous traffic of the Eastern Seas.

In 1792 the amount of opium being traded from India to China was only a fraction of what it was to become. The British government which drew up these Instructions in the name of George III recognized, however, that this trade could become a problem, and indicated that it was prepared to see it end rather than risk general trade. In the event opium did not become an issue for Macartney, as the kowtow did. But looking ahead, as his Instructions were attempting to do, it was not enough for the British government to say 'none of that drug should be sent by us to China' if that was what the Chinese government required, while still allowing the production and sale of the drug in India to continue, leaving the trade 'to take its chance in an open market'. It was under just such circumstances that the opium trade did grow rapidly over the next few decades, even though neither the British government nor the

British East India Company 'sent' it to China. Private merchants and free trade principles ensured that it got there, where there was certainly a market, even if not one exactly 'open'. Until the British were ready to check the production and free sale of the drug in their Indian dominions, which did not happen for over another hundred years, there remained a deep ambivalence and inconsistency, indeed dishonesty, about their policy on this trade, an inconsistency clearly reflected in these Instructions to Macartney.

A number of other issues and possibilities were raised by Dundas – a treaty of friendship and alliance; the exchange of representatives on an occasional or permanent basis; the grant of a small tract of land or detached island as a base for British trade which, should it be conceded, 'you will endeavour to obtain on the most beneficial terms, with the power of regulating the policies and exercising jurisdiction over our own dependants'. This was an anticipation of the cession of Hong Kong and of extraterritorial rights that were to eventuate 50 years later. Finally, looking beyond China, it was suggested Macartney might also visit Japan, which he did not attempt. The Instructions ended with the ambassador being wished 'a prosperous voyage and complete success in the very important objects of it'.

Macartney's reception, rejection and reaction

There are many accounts and studies of the Macartney mission. The first 'authentic' and official one by the second ranking member of it, Sir G.L. Staunton, appeared in 1797 in two large volumes, plus a folio volume of entrancing engravings made by artists in the embassy. A French version of this account was read by the exiled Napoleon on St Helena and prompted the *bon mot* about China attributed to him: 'Let it sleep, for when this dragon wakes the world will tremble.'[37] Other accounts by participants also soon appeared, though not Macartney's own detailed journal. In recent years that has been published, as well as several major studies of the mission. Its bicentenary was marked by an international conference in Rehe (Jehol) in Manchuria, where Macartney was received in audience a year after setting out, by the aged Qianlong emperor, on 14 September 1793. Thus the dedicated reader may readily pursue in a number of texts this coming together at the highest level of two great cultural traditions.[38] Here I will pursue briefly only some of the issues raised in the Instructions given Macartney, Instructions which so clearly reflect the expectations and assumptions the British brought with their gifts, expectations and assumptions so very different from those of the court they were approaching.

Before reaching Rehe, in the original homeland of the dynasty where the court regularly moved to avoid the summer heat of Beijing, Macartney had several interviews with high officials about the ceremonies he was expected to perform. He turned a blind eye to the fact that the banners on the Chinese barges or yachts which carried the embassy upriver from the coast to the capital proclaimed that they were carrying 'the English Ambassador bringing tribute to the Emperor of China', but he was resistant to repeated urgings, with demonstrations, that he prepare himself for the kowtow procedure. These began even before he reached Beijing. As he recorded on 15 August in his journal:

> They then introduced the subject of the court ceremonies with a degree of art, address and insinuation that I could not help admiring. They began by turning the conversation upon the different modes of dress that prevailed among different nations, and, after pretending to examine ours particularly, seemed to prefer their own, on account of its being loose and free from ties, and of its not impeding or obstructing the genuflexions and prostrations which were, they said, customary to be made by all persons whenever the Emperor appeared in public. They therefore apprehended much inconvenience to us from our knee-buckles and garters, and hinted to us that it would be better to disencumber ourselves of them before we should go to Court. I told them they need not be uneasy about that circumstance, as I supposed, whatever ceremonies were usual for the Chinese to perform, the Emperor would prefer my paying him the same obeisance which I did to my own sovereign. They said they supposed the ceremonies in both countries must be nearly alike, that in China the form was to kneel down upon both knees, and make nine prostrations or inclinations of the head to the ground, and that it never had been, and never could be, dispensed with. I told them ours was somewhat different, and that though I had the most earnest desire to do everything that might be agreeable to the Emperor, my first duty must be to do what might be agreeable to my own king; but if they were really in earnest in objecting to my following the etiquette of the English court, I should deliver them my reply as soon as I arrived in Pekin.

There may have been no real meeting of minds occurring, but the confrontation, if one can call it that, was certainly being conducted on both sides with considerable politeness and diplomatic finesse.

In the reply, which Macartney delivered a few days later, he expressed the strongest desire to do whatever

I thought would be most agreeable to the Emperor, but that, being the representative of the first monarch of the Western world, his dignity must be the measure of my conduct; and that, in order to reconcile it to the customs of the Court of China, I was willing to conform to their etiquette, provided a person of equal rank with mine were to perform the same ceremony before my Sovereign's picture that I should perform before the Emperor himself. The Legate shook his head, but Wang and Chou said it was a good expedient, and offered immediately to go through the ceremony themselves on the spot; but as they had no authority for the purpose I civilly declined their proposal.

That was as near as Macartney ever got to performing the kowtow. It would have been an intriguing scene had this urbane, cultivated aristocrat from Britain performed the three kneelings and nine prostrations before the Son of Heaven while a Chinese or Manchu official of equal birth and rank did the same publicly before a portrait of George III. But it was not to be; the compromise offered by Macartney was not taken up by the Chinese. Given what the kowtow really symbolized for them it could not be.

Macartney, however, was not sent packing, as 23 years later another aristocratic British ambassador was to be when he too demurred about kowtowing to the next Son of Heaven occupying the dragon throne.[39] The emperor himself kept quite a close eye on all these preliminaries, and was critical of some of his own officials, as well as of the British who, in contrast to an embassy from Portugal that he had received 40 years earlier, were acting like 'ignorant foreigners'. Nevertheless, as the author of the most searching and detailed analysis of this diplomatic contretemps presents it,[40] the emperor was prepared to adjust the ritual process for Macartney since, although the British Ambassador lacked proper comprehension of the significance of the kowtow, he had shown that his intentions were proper and, like the king he represented, that he was sincere. So on this basis this embassy could be incorporated into the dynasty's overall theory of imperial sovereignty. This British kingdom was seen to be different from, and more troublesome than, others that had come from the Western Ocean. But in 1793, under an intelligent, very experienced and highly honoured emperor, some condescending allowances might be made, because of the sincerity he discerned behind British ignorance and obstinacy. But it would not happen again, as Macartney's successor as ambassador to China, Lord Amherst, was to discover in Beijing in 1816, and a third British negotiator also, Lord Napier, at Canton in 1834.

Although by the time he reached Rehe it was fairly clear that Macartney would not kowtow, he was received in audience in a great circular tent, or yurt, not in the nearby palace. Several other minor tribute bearers from Inner Asia and Pegu were received at the same audience. Macartney, who had dressed in splendour for the occasion, with his court decorations and a plumed hat, did not think these other ambassadors very splendid, but they certainly kowtowed and kept at a respectful distance from the Son of Heaven. Macartney, the last to be received, went down on one knee and, bowing his head, handed directly to the emperor a jewel encrusted box containing a letter from George III. It was in reply to this letter that the Qianlong emperor's famous edict to George III came, though it appears to have been drafted well beforehand.[41]

We by the Grace of Heaven, Emperor, instruct the King of England to take note of our charge. Although your country, O King, lies in the far oceans, yet inclining your heart towards civilization you have specially sent an envoy respectfully to present a state message, and sailing the seas he has come to our Court to kowtow and to present congratulations for the Imperial birthday, and also to present local products, thereby showing your sincerity...As to what you have requested in your message, O King, namely to be allowed to send one of your subjects to reside in the Celestial Empire to look after your country's trade, this does not conform to the Celestial Empire's ceremonial system, and definitely cannot be done...there are a great many Western Ocean countries altogether, and not merely your one country. If, like you, O King, they all beg to send someone to reside at the capital, how could we grant their request in every case...If it is said that your object, O King, is to take care of trade, men from your country have been trading at Macao for some time, and have always been treated favourably. For instance, in the past Portugal and Italy [that is the Papacy] and other countries have several times sent envoys to the Celestial Empire with requests to look after their trade, and the Celestial Empire, bearing in mind their loyalty, treated them with great kindness. Whenever any matter concerning trade has arisen which affected these countries it has always been fully taken care of...Why, then, do foreign countries need to send someone to remain at the capital? This is a request for which there is no precedent and it definitely cannot be granted. Moreover, the distance between Macao, the place where the trade is conducted, and the capital is nearly ten thousand li, and if he were to remain at the capital how could he look after it?

Finally, the most frequently quoted section read:

> The Celestial Empire, ruling all within the four seas, simply concentrates on carrying out the affairs of Government properly, and does not value rare and precious things. Now you, O King, have presented various objects to the throne, and mindful of your loyalty in presenting offerings from afar, we have specially ordered Yamen to receive them. In fact, the virtue and power of the Celestial Dynasty has penetrated afar to the myriad kingdoms, which have come to render homage, and so all kinds of precious things from 'over mountain and sea' have been collected here, things which your chief envoy and others have seen for themselves. Nevertheless we have never valued ingenious articles, nor do we have the slightest need of your country's manufactures. Therefore, O King, as regards your request to send someone to remain at the capital, while it is not in harmony with the regulations of the Celestial Empire we also feel very much that it is of no advantage to your country. Hence we have issued these detailed instructions and have commanded your tribute envoys to return safely home. You, O King, should simply act in conformity with our wishes by strengthening your loyalty and swearing perpetual obedience so as to ensure that your country may share the blessings of peace.

As this document makes very clear, although this Chinese Emperor might charitably have given a little ground on the issue of the kowtow, he gave none at all on the issues that had been the driving impulses behind the Macartney embassy. On these he was so adamant and dismissive that there can be little doubt that even had Macartney kowtowed it would have made no difference.

Bertrand Russell remarked that no one understands China until this edict has ceased to seem absurd.[42] Given what has passed since, its bland and condescending dismissal of everything the West brought and sought, and the supreme confidence it displayed in China's continuing position as the centre of the world and the prototype of civilization, does make it appear to be one of the most unrealistic and hubris-loaded of historical documents. To a degree, so it was. But it should also be recognized that the Qianlong emperor was simply stating what was true of the world China knew down to the end of the eighteenth century. The central kingdom was truly the font of civilization for the extensive East Asian and Central Asian region. Its traditional economy, though beginning to come under severe pressure from rising population numbers, did still provide for the needs of its people without much recourse to foreign goods; its polity, under a joint Manchu-Chinese ruling elite, had greatly extended and stabilized the bounds of empire and was, given its size, remarkably well-ordered and integrated, as European observers, including Macartney, recognized. China under the Qing was on a very even stretch of its dynastic cycle, and seemed well set for a continuing smooth run for a long time to come. Why try to change the existing order of things to humour an importunate, distant kingdom? That might only upset the current harmonious balance between Heaven and Earth, and perhaps precipitate a transfer of the mandate. It was no wonder that the emperor and his top officials waved the British away.

An impasse was building up, though perhaps neither side was fully aware of what was developing. The emperor's edict reflected a calm and not unreasonable confidence in the achievements and universal appeal of the Chinese system, a system which did not need to seek out men from afar but rather drew them benevolently to itself. The West too, with the British as its vanguard was increasingly confident of its achievements and the universal validity of its principles, hence the embassy with its full and (save on the kowtow issue) precise Instructions. But whereas the Chinese principle, derived from its Confucian heritage, was *laihua*, that is come of your own free will and be transformed, come and be fully civilized, the Western principle, derived from its Christian heritage, was to go out actively and preach to all the world, if necessary compelling the reluctant to come in. The kowtow debate, from one perspective a debate over a mere ceremony, encapsulated this contrast in fundamentals. In 1793 a temporary compromise on this was achieved, thanks to a degree of flexibility and sincerity on both sides. But basically nothing had changed. On the issues of central importance to the West the Chinese had given no ground.

This was underlined by a further imperial document handed to Macartney when he was enroute on the long trek overland back to his ship in the south, and in no position to attempt further substantive negotiation. This document rejected six requests Macartney had put to the emperor's chief minister, Heshen, such as access to additional ports as well as to Beijing, and an island base. A seventh request, which Macartney never made and was not mentioned in his Instructions, was also rejected in this late arriving document. This was for permission to preach 'the British religion', which the emperor dismissed with the observation (probably prompted by the Catholic missionaries still at the court) that this was 'not the same as what the Christian religion had earlier been.' Macartney's embassy was not at all concerned to promote missionary enterprise in China, so adding this to the list of rejections was really rubbing in the totality of the dismissal of what it did seek. On this seventh, unprovoked rejection Macartney bravely responded that 'the English had anciently been of the same religion as the Portuguese and the other missionaries, and had adopted another, but one of the principal differences between us and them was our not having the same zeal for making proselytes which they had.'[43] That was certainly true, and the British government was never to be active in promoting missionary work in China. It might have been less surprising to Macartney had the emperor added opium rather than religion to the list of rejections, since that had at least been raised as a possibility in his Instructions. But the growing opium trade seems never to have been raised during the course of the embassy – an opportunity lost?

Receiving these final rejections the disappointed Macartney asked in his journal:

> How are we to reconcile the contradictions that appear in the conduct of the Chinese government towards us? They receive us with the highest distinction, show us every external mark of favour and regard, send the first Minister himself to attend us as cicerone for two days together through their palaces and gardens; entertain us with their choicest amusements and express themselves greatly pleased with so splendid an embassy, commend our conduct and cajole us with compliments. Yet, in less than a couple of months they plainly discover they wish us to be gone, refuse our requests without reserve or complaissance, precipitate our departure and dismiss us dissatisfied . . . [44]

Macartney's confusion over Chinese style reception and negotiation was to be experienced by many later Westerners in China, but from their point of view the Chinese were as bemused by what they saw as the inconsistencies and contradictions, as well as the presumptions, of British behaviour and requests. But for the present they were secure and confident in their world, and it was the British who had to give ground. It was the West's inexorable pursuit of wealth wherever it was to be found around the globe that ensured that before long the debate would resume, next time with less diplomatic finesse and tolerance.

Macartney, cultivated representative of the age of reason as he was, did not dramatize the frustrating outcome of his mission. Certainly he thought the Chinese 'a singular people', but they were also 'men formed of the same materials and governed by the same passions as ourselves', and so were surely open to rational persuasions. The ordinary Chinese, 'the lower orders', were 'all of a trafficking turn', he noted,[45] and were happy to have Western ships in their ports however much their rulers affected to disdain and marginalize trade. Enlightened self-interest would eventually lead China's rulers to welcome participation in a wider world of trade, he argued. Though well aware of the vast superiority of Western arms, he insisted that force, even haste, was not necessary. Towards the end of his journal he wrote:

> Our present interests, our reason and humanity equally forbid the thoughts of any offensive measures with regard to the Chinese whilst a ray of hope remains for succeeding by gentle ones. Nothing could be urged in favour of a hostile conduct but an irresistible conviction of failure by forbearance. By my embassy the Chinese have had what they never had before, an opportunity of knowing us, and acting towards us in the future.[46]

Clearly Macartney was putting the best construction possible on his mission, but his measured optimism was misplaced. The Chinese displayed less flexibility and the West less forbearance than he hoped for. Meanwhile Europe had to cope with revolution in France and its Napoleonic aftermath, while the Chinese, only a year or so after Macartney's departure, received another Western Ocean embassy, this time from the Dutch. That embassy kowtowed readily and frequently,[47] so for China's rulers at the turn of the century there seemed every reason to suppose that, despite the difficulties experienced with the British, relations with these Western Ocean men could remain much as they long had been. The diplomats, like the missionaries, appeared to have made no real progress.

After Macartney – no turning back

Yet the challenge that the Macartney embassy posed could not be much longer turned aside, as the Qianlong emperor and his bureaucrats had so confidently done. China, the most self-contained of the world's great cultures, still felt very secure and satisfied within its traditional boundaries, both geopolitical and intellectual, and was justifiably proud of its achievements within those boundaries. But once technology in the world beyond had advanced to a point where China could be reached relatively easily, the challenge to let in more of that world, and conversely for China to go out into that world, was inescapable.

The Macartney embassy is the defining moment when that challenge was clearly and fully posed, and it is for that reason that I have given it more space than any other episode in this broad survey of the West's relations with China, once the semi-mythical kingdom of Cathay.

For good or ill, the world was moving, and China could not avoid being moved with it. By the later eighteenth century the West, with Britain in the vanguard but by no means alone, had the technical power as well as the intellectual conviction to reshape the world. It recognized that China was a major part of that world. The irony was that, as outlined in the previous chapter, traditional China had itself earlier displayed a technical capacity suggesting that it might have anticipated the West in exploring, opening up and changing the world. But whether or not it had the potential to do so it chose not to try, whereas the West, once it developed the necessary skills, did not hesitate to apply them widely, consistently, relentlessly.

'Relentless' is a pejorative-sounding word, and the historian may well wish that the West had pursued the process somewhat less insistently, somewhat more sensitively. But the history of the expansion of the power and influence of the West is a very complex one, not to be understood simply in terms of aggression, greed and exploitation, all too common in the process though those qualities were. Macartney certainly adopted an approach that was, while very clear in its objectives, quite moderate, patient and reasonable – reasonable not only in a narrowly modern Western sense but also, I believe, in the wider human context. Its basis was, as summed up in the title of Adam Smith's great text, which was part of the intellectual baggage Macartney took with him to China, that the wealth of nations, all nations, increases as the flow of trade, the exchange of products, techniques, ideas, and ultimately people, between them is encouraged and made freer. If increasing material wealth and productivity is to be regarded as a desirable development – and, whatever doubts contemporary consumerism and commercialism may prompt, most societies through human history have acted as if it were – then the basic Western message being conveyed to China through Macartney was a positive one for China, as it was for the West itself and for the world at large. Its actual implementation was, of course, to be marred everywhere by misunderstandings, confrontations, great inequities and, in the case of China, the particular evil of the opium trade. Maybe without the opium problem, of which the British were already uncomfortably aware, China might have been slowly nudged towards the position Macartney hoped for and which it has now come to accept, even embrace. But it would certainly have taken a long time, and was probably beyond the bounds of patience and possibility so long as Confucian orthodoxy directed Chinese government decisions on trade and diplomacy. Macartney observed that the Chinese populace was by no means averse to trading, or 'trafficking' as he called it, and it seems reasonable to assume that his message on trade was far more acceptable to them than to their rulers. Whatever the Qianlong emperor stated in his famous letter to George III, it is too simple to conclude from it that 'China' was not at all willing to trade more extensively. Given the opportunity its people have displayed as much interest in and talent for it as Westerners.

It is not easy to tease out the possible rights and wrongs involved in this confrontation, undoubtedly imposed upon China by an expanding and all too readily aggressive West. Both China and the West were, I suggest, behaving in ways determined by their own long traditions, and the leaders of both were being consistent to the rationale of their particular world view and value system. In an ideal world they might, once technology had made their closer contact inevitable, have adjusted gradually, co-operatively and peaceably to a mutual accommodation of interests. But opium among other things ensured that the post-Macartney world was far from ideal, that the closer contact of these two great cultures would generate much friction, and be especially painful and difficult for China. The history that was to come would certainly not show the West in China in a very kindly light. But that history should be seen in the longer perspective I have endeavoured to sketch in these first two chapters, and also with a recognition that there were broad issues of principle, going beyond just greed and force, at stake.[48] As well as sheer greed and search for profit it was a conviction that reason, the laws of nature itself and the longer term benefit of all, justified the drive of the West by the later eighteenth century to challenge China to break with its past attitudes and restrictions on trade with men from afar. Opium blurred the issue, but did not create the basic problem. So great a part of the world as China had somehow to be drawn into the full circle of the globe.

But about 1800, after nearly three centuries of sustained and increasing contact between China and the West, contact which had impacted far more strongly on the West than on China, the central kingdom seemed still well in control of the terms and the extent of the process. At the beginning of this chapter I questioned the validity of any 'dominance of maritime power over the land masses of Asia' model for this period of Sino-Western relations, and suggested that a better model might be of a curve of European influence rising slowly at first, more rapidly in the eighteenth and steeply in the nineteenth century. It is time to question that model too, for it is in the nature of things that such overarching constructs are at best only approximations to reality. The detail I have set out about these pre-nineteenth century traders, missionaries and diplomats serves to make plain that the curve varied a good deal between the three main agents of Western influence. The traders had a generally consistent, if not always smooth, ascending rise, but for the missionaries it was decidedly wobbly, going down rather than up by the later eighteenth century. The major Western diplomatic initiative of these centuries simply ran into a brick wall, and cannot be counted as having, at the time, any influence upon the Chinese beyond confirming them in their intention to contain and control the contact in accordance with their traditional values and institutions. What was rising over this period was not so much 'European influence' as European presence. This was certainly becoming more and more substantial, at least in the south of China. Ultimately presence is likely to result in influence and power. That became very plain in the course of the next century, to which we should now turn.

3
Closer Encounters, on the West's Terms (1800–1900)

The nineteenth century is the period in the history of the West's relations with China when the domination model appears clearly to fit the facts. During this century the West succeeded in forcing from the Chinese all and more of the concessions that Macartney had sought, obliging them to accept, after several wars, treaties which imposed conditions on China that greatly extended contact between the two cultures. Western traders, diplomats and missionaries all gained far wider and more regular access to the central kingdom, thereby forcing upon it a radical reassessment of many of its traditional values, institutions and assumptions about its place in the world. The massive Chinese revolution of modern times has deep roots within China's own tradition, and is not to be explained simply in terms of the mounting impact of Western ideas and techniques. But that impact was certainly very great, helping to determine the form and direction of many of the ongoing changes that have made contemporary China so crucial a force in the modern world. To a very significant degree modern China is a creation of the West. In waking Napoleon's sleeping dragon we have also helped substantially to transform it.

In textbook terminology, during the nineteenth century China, that once secure, proudly self-contained central kingdom, was forced open by the West and then kept under control, most obviously by the 'gunboats' which for a century ranged freely, not only around its coast but also up the Yangzi river to cities far inland, such as Nanjing and Wuhan. Those gunboats were potent symbols of the superior force the West was able to bring to bear at will upon China, as it not infrequently did until the mid-twentieth century. Indeed, at the turn of that century China seemed to many not just opened by but prostrate before the West, ripe for carving up among the powers as Africa had been not long before.

That did not happen, and the speed and extent to which China was in fact opened up to Western influence and made subject to Western controls are often exaggerated. Nevertheless the nineteenth century can reasonably be seen as a period of Western domination and of increasing Chinese humiliation, save only that history does not fall so neatly into century-long segments set by the Western calendar. There were certainly a hundred years or so of considerable Western power and privilege in China, amounting to something like domination, but those years began about 1840, when the first of the Western wars with China was fought, and the first of the treaties was drawn up. They ended in the 1940s, when the treaties embodying Western, and by then also Japanese, power and privilege were finally abrogated, when China was recognized alongside the United States, Great Britain, France and Russia as one of the five veto-wielding powers in the newly created United Nations, and when the last of the gunboats sailing on Chinese rivers was forced to run for safety from the guns of Chinese nationalists, who happened also to be Communists. It was their nationalism as much as their communism that prompted Mao Zedong's forces to fire on the H.M.S. *Amethyst*, as it was nationalism that prompted his famous claim in 1949 that China had at last 'stood up'. By then a good many Chinese, including Mao's rivals for power, had helped get China to its feet, but his claim did reflect the new reality that the Indian historian, K.M. Pannikar, exulting in comparable events for his own country, celebrated in his book as the end of 'the da Gama epoch' for Asia.

But although the actual century of domination began in 1840 rather than 1800, in this chapter I will confine myself still to the calendar century, which I suggest has a logic beyond mere numerical convenience. Stretching it a little ('long' and 'short' centuries are an accepted part of modern historical discourse) that century may be said to have begun with the 1793 reply of the Qianlong emperor to George III, already quoted at length, a reply demonstrating that China and not the West still determined the terms upon which the two cultures were meeting. For some decades into the nineteenth century China continued setting the terms, rejecting further British diplomatic efforts in 1816 and 1834 to win equal status and wider access, though the bases of power, economic as well as military, had by then shifted decisively to the West. It was the free ranging activity of merchants engaged in the opium trade, a trade extending by the 1830s well beyond the hub of officially sanctioned trade in the Canton estuary, that was undermining the Chinese control system and was to bring on the crisis that led to war and the forcing from China of the concessions that radically altered the character of its relationship with the West. The process of putting more and more pressure on China, though it stopped short of actual partition and direct Western rule, continued into the early twentieth century, until after the debacle of the Boxer uprising in 1899–1900.

1898: An emperor attempts to lead China to adapt to the West

However, in the year before that disaster, that is barely a century after the Qianlong emperor's edict, another imperial statement, much less well known but hardly less significant in defining China's position, was issued. This was the edict promulgated by the young Guangxu emperor on 11 June 1898 and, like the Qianlong edict, is worth quoting at some length.[1]

> Some of our aged ministers, who have grown grey in the service of the State and whose fidelity is unquestioned, in their anxiety for the Empire, have argued that we ought to stick to the very letter of our ancient institutions and cast away from us the suggestions in favour of a new régime. In fact, all sorts of suggestions have been made by any number of memorialists most of which are empty and vain and impracticable. Let us ask what other country except our own is there that is labouring under such difficulties because of being behind the times? . . . The methods of government inaugurated by the Sung and Ming dynasties, upon investigation, reveal nothing that is of any practical use or that may be of advantage to us. . . . Changes must be made to accord with the necessities of the times. It is apparent that we must issue a plain and unvarnished decree on the subject so that all may understand our wishes. Let this therefore be made known to one and all in the four corners of this Empire, from Prince to Duke, from highest to lowest among the officials of the capital and the provinces, from Court Minister to the most humble of our subjects – let them know that it is our earnest and sincere desire that one and all bend energetically to the duty of striving for higher things, to show all that they are men ambitious to succeed and to advance their country; let us, keeping in mind the morals of our sages and wise men, make them the basis on which to build on newer and more advantageous foundations. We must also select such subjects of Western knowledge as will keep us in touch with the times and diligently study them and practise them in order to place our country abreast with other countries. Let us cast off from us the empty, unpractical, and deceiving things which obstruct our forward progress, and strive with one-heartedness and energy to improve upon all things that we have learned; let us eliminate the crust of

neglect that has accumulated on our system, and cast away the shackles which bind us. In a word, let us evolve useful things out of those which hitherto have been useless, and let us seek by able instructors to fashion the materials in our possession. With these objects in view let us strive toward advancement and progress.

The change of tone and direction is very evident. Instead of confidently and complacently dismissing the West and all its ingenious works as the Qianlong emperor had done, by the end of the nineteenth century the reigning emperor was stating in an imperial edict – that is in the ultimate expression of his administrative status and authority – that China had to change radically, that it had to assess critically the value of its own tradition while seeking out Western knowledge in order to maintain a strong place in the world. In addition to the defeats suffered at the hands of the Western powers in the middle and later decades of the nineteenth century, China's humiliating defeat in 1895 at the hands of its far smaller but rapidly reorganizing neighbour Japan helped prompt this great change of emphasis from the dragon throne. By the end of the century the pressure on China to modernize was coming from within its own traditional sphere of influence and not just from an alien, distant West.

After issuing this edict, one of the most revolutionary documents in the Chinese historical record, the young Guangxu emperor sought to begin a process of radical change for China by issuing a stream of edicts authorising many innovations, thus provoking much alarm among the still numerous and powerful conservatives around him, including the empress dowager, Cixi. The reaction was swift and ruthless. After only one hundred days of attempted reform the armed forces backed the conservatives, and the emperor was put into isolation, to die mysteriously about ten years later, just before the empress dowager. Six of his young advisers were executed, while others, including the leading thinkers of the reform group, Kang Youwei and Liang Qichao, fled into exile, some with the help of foreign legations. Practically all the reforming edicts were rescinded. One which was not was that founding a university in Beijing, the institution which was to be at the centre of many future demands for change. But as yet it was too soon for the new University, now known as 'Beida', to play such a role. Following soon after the crushing of this emperor-led reform movement came the Boxer uprising, the siege of the foreign legations in Beijing, the occupation of the city by an international relief force, and the imposition of a settlement which placed yet more burdens on a once great and powerful empire, now apparently prostrate before its predators.

If one looked only at the court and the capital about 1900 China would seem still fixed in the Qianlong time frame, hopelessly and unrealistically so. But Beijing was not China, though a crucial part of it. In the provinces and the by then numerous treaty ports there were many Chinese, including high officials, merchants, and especially a younger generation of scholars, still Confucian trained but also avid for other learning and ideas, who were well aware that China had somehow to adapt itself to a radically changed world order. Just what this process of reassessment and adaptation would involve was still very unclear, and for the peasant masses, as well as for the Boxer zealots and the court conservatives, it still seemed it should not even be attempted. But it was inescapable and, by the end of the century, there was a growing awareness, especially among many provincial officials and the educated youth, that this was so. The young Guangxu emperor was clearly and bravely, if naively, reflecting that awareness. Although his shaft of light was quickly dimmed it could not be extinguished. Despite setbacks from within and increasing pressure from without, by the 1890s the recognition that the world Qianlong knew was irrevocably past had become clear to many Chinese. It is in that decade that the Chinese revolution can be said to have truly begun. For half a century more that revolution had to struggle to make headway, not only against conservative forces within China but also in the face of a still strong Western presence. The West's response to that revolution was to be decidedly mixed, but that is an issue for the next chapter. In this chapter, having begun with a rapid sweep over the whole of the nineteenth century, I turn now to survey three major aspects of the Western presence in nineteenth century China – the opium trade, the treaty system and the missionary attempt to convert China to Christianity, concluding the chapter with some examination of the changes in prevailing Western ideas about China.

The Opium Trade

The moral dimension

In the long history of Western relations with China nothing is more widely known than that opium is a major part of that history. A very shameful part, most would add, since it is generally believed that the West, the British in particular, forced the drug on the Chinese who, when their government attempted to take strong action against its illegal import, were defeated in wars begun by the British and known appropriately as the Opium Wars. Defeat meant that the Chinese were obliged to make concessions in unequal treaties which, among other enormities, legalized the trade in opium so that its consumption in China became ever larger, creating a long term social evil for the country, an evil for which the West must bear a large part of the responsibility. This is, broadly, the standard view, shared by Westerners and Chinese alike. J.K. Fairbank, the leading Western authority on the history of Western trade and diplomacy in nineteenth-century China, when reviewing a book on the first of the opium wars, judged that 'the opium trade from India to China was the most long-continued systematic international crime of modern times', a judgment sure to resonate strongly with many, especially Chinese.[2]

However, given some of the other ongoing international crimes of modern times not everyone, including the author of the book then under review as well as the author of this book, is altogether comfortable with so comprehensive a condemnation of the trade in opium to China. Fairbank himself has also emphasized that responsibility for this crime was widespread, many Chinese being as deeply involved in marketing the drug as were Westerners, and that the rapid growth of the trade was largely unexpected. Justified though severe moral judgments on the opium trade and the wars it precipitated certainly are, such qualified condemnation from a leading authority may serve to warn us that the straightforward text book view may be a little too straightforward. If a balanced understanding of the past, insofar as we can approximate to such understanding, is our objective then we need to place the opium trade in a nineteenth-century British as well as a Chinese context. The comments on it which follow are directed to such an understanding, while not denying that this is a subject where the Actonian injunction, 'to suffer no man and no cause to escape the undying penalty which history has the power to inflict on wrong', may appropriately apply.

The moral dimension was emphasized by the Imperial Commissioner sent to Canton in 1839 to suppress the trade in opium, Lin Zexu. He addressed a lengthy communication to the rulers of Great Britain, part of which read:

> Let us ask, where is your conscience? I have heard that the smoking of opium is very strictly forbidden by your country, that is because the harm caused by opium is clearly understood. Since it is not permitted to do harm to your own country then even less should you let it be passed on to the harm of other countries – how much less to China! Of all that China exports to foreign countries there is not a single

thing which is not beneficial to people . . . Take tea and rhubarb for example; the foreign countries cannot get along for a single day without them. If China cuts off these benefits with no sympathy for those who are to suffer, then what can the barbarians rely on to keep themselves alive? . . . How can you bear to go further, selling products injurious to others in order to fill your insatiable desire? Suppose there were people from another country who carried opium for sale to England and seduced your people into buying and smoking it; certainly your honourable ruler would deeply hate it and be bitterly aroused. We have heard heretofore that your honourable ruler is kind and benevolent. Naturally you would not wish to give unto others what you yourself do not want . . . May you, O King, check your wicked and sift your vicious people before they come to China, in order to guarantee the peace of your nation, to show further the sincerity of your politeness and submissiveness, and to let the two countries enjoy together the blessings of peace.[3]

The fate of this communication is obscure. If it was ever received by anyone in power in Britain they would certainly have been bemused by some of the assumptions behind it. Whatever the degree of their dependence on rhubarb as well as on tea, the British were also quite dependent on opium. Certainly they did not smoke it, as the Chinese did, but it was widely and legally consumed by them in other ways. The usual method in Britain was to drink it dissolved in alcohol as laudanum, or in concoctions with names such as Godfrey's Cordial, Venice Treacle or, for children, Mother Bailey's Quietening Syrup. It was also available in pill or lozenge form. Before the development of modern synthetic medications opium in some form or other was the main painkiller, and it was also used to help cure conditions such as diarrhoea. Until the passing of the first Poisons and Pharmaceutical Act in 1868 its dispensing was unregulated, so that 'the corner shop and not the doctor's surgery was the centre of popular opium use . . . Customers often dictated the type of remedy they wanted. Families had their own private remedies which the shopkeeper or chemist would make up.'[4] This comment comes from a study on opium use in nineteenth century England which provides tables of the quite substantial imports of the drug, mostly from Turkey, as well as estimates of home consumption, and of death rates attributed to narcotics, figures which indicate that opium had a not insignificant place in nineteenth-century British life.

As one would expect, in such circumstances a good many people in nineteenth-century Britain became seriously addicted, most famously the poet and savant Coleridge. The biology of addiction was not well understood, and treatment for it was haphazard, as Coleridge's experience demonstrates. For most of the nineteenth century the consumption and sale of opium in Britain was not criminalized, as Lin assumed it was, but was freely available. As the century advanced the problems associated with it were more clearly recognized, and regulation of it began. But the British engaged in the trade mostly saw themselves as supplying the Chinese with a commodity used quite extensively in their own society and regarded as having many useful, even if also some dangerous, features. William Jardine, one of the leading early suppliers seemed to have no qualms about the trade and advised a friend that it was 'the safest and most gentleman like speculation I am aware of', but others, including some of the Matheson family who were also early suppliers, were less comfortable with it.[5]

The growth of the trade

Opium was a commodity known to the Chinese at least as far back as the seventh century, when Arab traders brought it in, and was used for both medicinal and recreational purposes. During the seventeenth century the characteristic Chinese method of absorbing the drug became to smoke it, at first mixed liberally with tobacco, but by the later eighteenth century generally in pure form. Smoking seems to be a relatively efficient way of absorbing the drug, more so than chewing or drinking it in mixtures. This method of use possibly helps explain why addiction became a more serious problem in nineteenth-century China than in the many other societies where opium was also freely available. The first Chinese imperial edicts against smoking it were issued in 1729–31, but were not strongly enforced. Edicts against the import of the drug began in 1796, by which time many in the military forces as well as the bureaucracy had acquired the smoking habit, which had spread from the south as far north as the capital and into court circles. For whatever reasons – boredom among garrison troops; corruption among officials; social pressures arising from over-population; a coastline which facilitated smuggling – the market in China continued to grow strongly. A French observer commented in the late eighteenth century that the Chinese were developing a passion for the narcotic which passed all belief, and it has been estimated that by the time of the outbreak of the first Opium War in 1839 about one per cent of the population, that is up to four million people, were consumers, mostly in the coastal provinces.[6] By then British vessels, having carried the drug from India where it was grown and sold in bulk, were ranging extensively up the coast, supplying Chinese middlemen who carried it ashore, under the usually averted eyes of well-bribed officials. Although there were occasional campaigns of enforcement, notably at Canton in 1821 when the opium supply ships were forced out of the port and had to take up anchorages off the coast, the imperial edicts against both the smoking and import of the drug were observed more in the breach than in the performance. The trade became 'no hole in the corner petty smuggling trade but probably the largest commerce of the time in any single commodity.'[7]

The British began to enter the trade in the late eighteenth century when the East India Company first sent shipments, not always successfully, to Canton. But the market there strengthened, so that imports from India increased from around 200 chests in 1729, coming then from Portuguese not British India, to 1000 by 1770 and 4000 by 1790. A chest contained about 140 lb of raw opium, enough to supply the needs of a hundred or more consumers, depending on the degree of use. East India Company ships ceased to carry the drug after the issue of edicts prohibiting its import, but the Company maintained production and sale in India, licensing private traders to carry it wherever they chose, mostly to China. It perfected a neat system of growing and selling opium in India but disowning it in China.

The East India Company, and behind it the British government, had strong economic reasons for turning a blind eye to what had become, on Chinese paper at least, an illicit trade. A staple commodity to balance the rapidly growing purchases of tea from China had long been sought. Opium, high in value relative to its bulk and with an assured, expandable source of supply in India, met the need admirably. Given the long standing imperial edicts against the smoking of the drug there was at first a degree of official British tentativeness about the trade and, as we have seen, Macartney's Instructions did not direct him to defend it at all costs. Had the Chinese been ready to negotiate seriously with Macartney that was perhaps, though only perhaps, a point in time when the trade in this commodity might have been contained. But a combination of factors – economic imperatives driving the British to try to balance their trade with China; the existence of a large and readily exploitable market in China; a Chinese administration ill-equipped to enforce its own rules; a lack of scruple among British merchants about smuggling a commodity they regarded as normal enough – suggests that there was a degree of inevitability about the growth of the opium trade to China in the early nineteenth century.

It grew very rapidly indeed by the 1820s. The traders forced out of Canton began trying other ports up the coast, thus effectively undermining one of the basic principles of the established official Chinese system for allowing trade with the West, that is confinement to just one port. In addition, new and cheaper sources of supply were being developed in India. Imports rocketed to the 30–40 000 chests a year range by the 1830s, by which time about one-sixth of the revenue of the East India Company was coming from its opium sales, while about one-tenth of the revenue of the British government came from duties levied on the tea trade, the financing of which had become heavily dependent on the trade in opium. Large public revenues, as well as private profits, were involved in the business of opium.[8] The balance of trade moved against China, causing a drainage of silver out of instead of into the country, disrupting the currency and helping cause some inflation. By the mid-1830s China had strong economic as well as social reasons for reviewing its policy towards opium. It faced a choice between attempting to enforce fully its long standing edicts against both the smoking and the import of the drug or of moving towards legalization and regulation rather than prohibition. It was a policy choice with which many contemporary governments are familiar.

Free trade – including opium?

By the time the Chinese had reached this point the British also were reassessing their position in China and the overall conditions facing them there. Although other Westerners, including the newly independent Americans, were present in not insignificant numbers at Macao and Canton, the British were far and away the predominant group, the most inclined to mount a strong Western thrust into the supposedly immense China market. By the early decades of the nineteenth century the free trade principles defined so clearly by Adam Smith and others in the later eighteenth century were becoming the new orthodoxy, especially for the British. A sign of this was the abolition in 1833 of the formal monopoly over British trade with China long held by the East India Company, a monopoly already much modified by the practice of granting licences to private traders to engage in the opium trade. The private traders who now took over the whole range of British trade at Canton were far less disposed than the Company had been to accept the conditions imposed by the Chinese. As already quoted, the Directors of the Company had been prepared to state as late as 1817 that nations had a right to regulate their commerce as they saw fit. Contrast the view put in 1821 by John Bowring, the man who was later to precipitate the second Opium War, that 'governments are but too much the victims of self deception when they imagine that their

Decrees of prohibition do really produce the effects they contemplate.' Rather, Bowring suggested, such decrees were as absurd and ineffective as trying to direct the winds by Order in Council, or to manage the tides by Act of Parliament. Equally pointed, and specifically directed at China, was the forceful statement in the merchant journal *The Canton Register* in 1833: 'In all parts of the world trade will find its level and a people's wants be satisfied maugre [despite] the opposition of a government far stronger than the inefficient weakness by which this empire is ruled.'[9] In short, the market rules and governments cannot effectively control it. Basically Macartney had represented the same philosophy, but it was now being put to China by men not cast in his urbane, diplomatically patient mould.

The traditional Chinese approach to trade and diplomacy with the West prevailed for the last time in 1834–5 at Canton. Lord Napier had been sent there by the British government to take over the task of supervising British trade from the East India Company. His Instructions were not as precise or as realistic as they might have been, the Foreign Secretary Lord Palmerston – another definitely not in the Macartney mould – adding almost casually at the end of them 'Your Lordship will announce your arrival at Canton by letter to the Viceroy.' When Napier did so and tried to elevate his role from that of Chief Superintendent of Trade, his actual title, to that of an accredited ambassador, comparable to Macartney and Amherst, the Chinese Viceroy at Canton refused to see him. To the Viceroy Napier was merely a commercial agent, a Headman, 'the barbarian eye', who might petition through the Co-hong but certainly not negotiate directly with China's ruling mandarins. Napier's attempts to do so provoked suspension for a time of all British trade as well as a contretemps, reminiscent of the kowtow controversy, over seating precedence at the one meeting with lesser officials which was set up. Eventually, frustrated and ill, Napier had to withdraw to Macao, where he died. His attempt to assert diplomatic equality as a prelude to negotiations over the general terms of trade ended, as Macartney's had done, in total failure.[10] But British patience was running out and its position had moved. A kind of stalemate developed, and Palmerston instructed Captain Elliott, a former Company official who succeeded Napier as Superintendent of Trade, not to use the Co-hong merchants as channels of communication, nor to present any form of petition. Thus, even before the Chinese decided to get really tough with the opium traders, the situation was drifting towards some kind of a confrontation because the West was increasingly reluctant to continue under the long-standing Chinese rules for trade and diplomacy which, 40 years after Macartney, still frustrated Napier and irritated the private traders. At this time 'the West' meant essentially the British, but others, such as the Americans and French, though sometimes critical of British methods, were quick to follow their lead – what has been aptly called hitch-hiking diplomacy.

War consolidates the trade

Yet it was the conservative Chinese rather than the aggressively innovative British who, within a few years, brought on the actual confrontation. 'The Ch'ing [Qing] government and *not* the British took the really active role in forcing a military and diplomatic showdown over the drug question in 1840; it did so under the influence primarily of internal political pressures and not foreign economic or military threat.' This is the conclusion of a recent closely argued study, based on the detailed Chinese record, which its author entitled *The Inner Opium War*.[11] From about 1836 a major debate developed within the upper levels of Chinese government over whether to legalize, subject to certain conditions, the trade in opium, or whether to take more vigorous steps against both consumers and suppliers. Like a good many contemporary governments, the Chinese in 1839 decided on zero tolerance, on a war against the then favoured drug of choice of their subjects, opium. In doing so they certainly did not intend to precipitate actual war with the West, and were understandably shocked that this became the outcome, as many, including many Westerners, have been ever since.

How things deteriorated to that point is a complicated story, well told by others whom I will not attempt to summarize. Chinese decisions and actions certainly contributed, as of course did British. The author of one of the most comprehensive and sympathetic studies of Commissioner Lin Zexu suggests that his main error was in putting pressure directly on the foreign suppliers, specifically by holding some hostage for a time until bonds were signed and chests of opium, not all yet actually in the possession of those held hostage or even within Chinese territory, were handed over for public destruction.[12] Had he been content just to tighten the screws on domestic suppliers and consumers, as was being done fairly successfully, the trade might have withered, at least for a time. In the mid-twentieth century Lin's communist heirs carried through successfully the kind of zero-tolerance domestic policy which was one prong of his programme, but they did not have to do so in the face of powerful and persistent foreign suppliers. Lin's task was more difficult, much more difficult than he realized. The British did not deny the right of the Chinese government to ban the import of opium, but they did complain that, as Palmerston put it, it was unjust that such a law 'should for a great length of time be allowed to sleep as a dead letter, and that both Natives and Foreigners should be taught to consider it as of no effect and that then, suddenly and without sufficient warning, it should be put into force with the utmost rigour and severity.'[13] It was true that imperial edicts against the import of opium had been very imperfectly observed by the Chinese themselves, but to make this somehow grounds for justifying resistance to Lin's actions seems a bit rich. The illegality was clearly on the British side.

Effectively the British government was unwilling to help suppress this trade as they were willing, over this same period, to help suppress the slave trade. The parallel, or contrast, is not perfect, since slavery was illegal in the United Kingdom whereas the consumption of opium was not, but some contemporaries drew attention to it. 'I am fully convinced that for this country to engage in this nefarious traffic is bad, perhaps worse than encouraging the slave trade,' said the social reformer Lord Shaftesbury in 1843. But as the hard headed Palmerston pointed out, the cost of providing a large number of revenue cruisers to be employed patrolling the China coast from Canton to the Yellow Sea 'for the purpose of preserving the morals of the Chinese people, who were disposed to buy what other people were disposed to sell them', would be very great, and possibly was logistically unsustainable, even for the powerful British navy.[14] What the British could have done would have been to cut back on the Indian sources of supply, at some considerable cost to their revenues, and declare opium an impermissible cargo for all ships of British registry. But that prompted the objection that other sources of supply, such as Turkey, and other carriers, such as the Americans, would soon be in the market. Lin certainly exaggerated the power of governments to control developments, but British self-interest, legalism and evasions ensured that his well-meaning attempt to check the consumption of opium by the Chinese was soon frustrated.

The first Opium War, fought 1840–2, did not result in the formal legalization of the trade, though the British negotiators of the treaty that settled the war sought to persuade the Chinese to this course. For some time yet 'the inner opium war' continued to be waged in Chinese government circles, but eventually the lack of British co-operation toward suppressing the trade, the continuing pressure from the Chinese market for the supply of the drug, and the evident revenue advantages in taxing it, led to reluctant Chinese acceptance of a form of legalization. This came after a second war fought between 1858 and 1860, precipitated by the actions of the aforementioned Bowring, by then

Governor of Hong Kong and Chief Superintendent of British Trade with China. This was a war condemned by many in England who were, like Shaftesbury, critical of the trade. But though forced to an election because of it Palmerston, now Prime Minister, retained power and fought the war to a rather messy conclusion, of which more later. Thereafter, for nearly sixty years, the import of opium ceased to be a smuggling matter, but it remained the largest item in Western trade with China for many years, the Chinese domestic market proving, despite the opening of more and more treaty ports, a difficult one for foreign manufactures to penetrate. Kerosene, oil for the lamps of China, was one of the few articles of foreign origin apart from opium to find a large market there during the later nineteenth century. By that stage more and more of the opium consumed in China was grown within the country. Imports of opium from British India, now subject to import duties and consequently providing an important source of government revenue for China, peaked at over 80000 chests a year during the 1880s. Such a volume, added to a growing amount of native opium, meant that addiction to the drug became very widespread. Hudson Taylor, founder of the China Inland Mission, who worked and travelled in many parts of China, reflected in 1893 that 'When I first reached China (in 1854) the opium habit was comparatively rare, but it has spread very rapidly during the last twenty years... it is frightfully prevalent now.' In his comprehensive history of opium Martin Booth estimates that by the 1930s there were 40 million consumers of the drug in China, that is almost ten per cent of the population. In an interesting short discussion of the use of opium in China, in which he emphasizes the importance of medical considerations, S.A.M. Adshead states that 'Opium was never epidemic in China: 12 million regular users would be a reasonable estimate.'[15]

The British eventually withdraw from the trade

By the late nineteenth century pressure to end the trade was mounting within Britain as well as in China, though there were still many who defended it and dismissed evidence that opium was a seriously addictive or dangerous drug. It was not until the first decades of the twentieth century that measures to control the trade from India began to be taken, such that by 1917 the trade ceased, although that did not mean that opium consumption ceased to be a serious problem within China itself. At the cost of extending the time span of this chapter a little it seems convenient to summarize at this point the ending of British involvement in the opium trade to China. It provides an example of cautious co-operation, in contrast to the evasion, obstruction and pressure that characterized earlier British policy and attitudes.

There were always many Western critics of the trade, the missionaries prominent among them. In 1874, the Anglo-Chinese Society for the Suppression of the Opium Trade was founded, with the aged Lord Shaftesbury as its president and with much Quaker support. The Society petitioned and published actively for some years, but without making much headway. Defenders of the trade made claims such as that opium smoking was 'a strictly harmless indulgence, like any other smoking, the essence of pleasure being not in the opium itself so much as in the smoking of it.'[16] The Victorian age did not lack spin doctors and corporate apologists! Governments in Britain were resistant to the idea of any substantial change in policy. Even the liberal Gladstone, who had once denounced this 'most infamous and atrocious trade', stalled in his last year in power by appointing a severely nobbled Royal Commission. This reported in 1895 'that the habit is generally practised in moderation, and that when so practised the injurious effects are not apparent...We may fairly compare the effects of opium smoking among the Chinese population to those of alcoholic liquors in the United Kingdom.' The Chinese were perfectly free agents with regard to opium, the majority report claimed, and there was 'no evidence from China of any popular desire that the import of Indian opium should be stopped.' The British government's response was simply to state that unspecified controls would be introduced at some time in the future.[17]

That time arrived ten years later, with the election in 1906 of a Liberal government after a campaign in which many candidates stood on an anti-opium ticket and some had been returned. A resolution condemning the trade from India as morally indefensible and requesting the government to bring about its speedy close was passed, and the new Secretary of State for India, John Morley, soon indicated that he was ready to work with the Chinese to restrict the trade. The Qing dynasty, by then actually on its last legs but in reform mode after the Boxer disaster, quickly responded. There may have been, as the Royal Commission report had claimed, no strong popular demand to end the trade, but the ruling dynasty was still committed to doing so. An agreement was negotiated by which the British were to reduce their export of opium to China from India by ten per cent a year, on condition that the Chinese reduced their very substantial native production at a comparable rate. Over a trial period of several years British officials toured Chinese provinces to check that this was happening and, satisfied that the exercise was not simply resulting in the protection of native growers, the original agreement was confirmed in May 1911, just five months before the Qing dynasty was overthrown. Within a few years China was to disintegrate politically into rule by warlords, under whom opium production and consumption continued on a large scale, but for a few years after the 1911 revolution a sufficient degree of political integration was sustained, despite the collapse of the dynasty that had negotiated the agreement, for both sides to continue to honour it. By 1917 imports of opium from British India ceased.

In addition to this Sino-British campaign against the opium trade an International Opium Commission was set up and conferences held, at Shanghai in 1909 and The Hague in 1911–12, at which programmes for international co-operation on drugs began, a process stemming from the experience of China, the first, but not the last, state to attempt to grapple with a widespread drug habit among its citizens. The opium trade, the source of so much bitterness in the history of Sino-Western relations became, at the beginning of the twentieth century, the catalyst for one of the more fruitful and honourable episodes in that history. The anti-opium campaign of 1907–17 'may have been the largest and most vigorous effort in world history to stamp out an established social evil', wrote Mary Wright in a seminal collection of essays on early twentieth-century China.[18] Whatever the truth of that claim one can only be glad that it was at last begun jointly, while wishing it had started earlier, back with Macartney or Lin Zexu.

The Treaty System

The opium trade had precipitated two wars between Great Britain and China, the first fought between 1839 and 1842, the second between 1856 and 1860. Out of these wars came the treaties which were the foundation documents governing relations between China and the West for a century, and to some degree even longer, until China resumed full control of the last outposts of Western empire on the China coast, Hong Kong and Macao, in the last years of the twentieth century.

Distance and other complicating factors protracted both wars, but eventually the naval and military strength Britain was able to deploy across the world resulted in the total defeat of China, the French assisting substantially in the second campaign. The first war ended at Nanjing, with the British preparing to storm that second city of the empire, while also blockading the Grand Canal and in occupation of the large island of Chusan at the mouth of the Yangzi, as well as of several ports to the south. The first phase of the second war ended much farther north at Tianjin, close to the capital, in June 1858, but British accusations of bad faith against the Chinese government over ratification of the treaty led to a renewal of conflict in 1860. This second phase of the second Opium War culminated in an Anglo-French occupation of Beijing and the burning of the Summer Palace. That unfortunate act was meant to be a limited, exemplary punishment directed against an allegedly untrustworthy court, sparing the people at large, but it is remembered today by the Chinese people as an outstanding example of Western aggression, indeed barbarism, against their culture.

With two wars within two decades these were indeed crisis years in the history of Sino-Western relations, leaving deep suspicions and bitter memories. They were not, however, years of anything like total warfare, of the kind later generations became familiar with. Normal trading relations often went on between British and Chinese in one place while somewhere else they fought one another, and the great mass of the Chinese people knew nothing of what was happening on their coast or in some of their major cities. But, total or not, they were years of great disaster and humiliation for China, especially for a court forced to flee from its capital in 1860 – those successors to that emperor who, barely a lifetime earlier, had so disdainfully dismissed Macartney and his king. Though for many years much remained still unchanged in the greater part of that vast empire, the middle years of the nineteenth century mark the point in time when the Chinese world began to be turned upside down.

The first of the treaties ending these wars was signed at Nanjing in August 1842, and was followed by a supplementary British treaty in 1843 as well as by separate treaties negotiated by the French and Americans in 1843 and 1844. These early treaties contained many, though not all, of the basic provisions of what came to be an extensive system of agreements binding China into what was for it a still unfamiliar system of international law. The first treaties worked to no one's real satisfaction, however. The Chinese, especially the court and its officials at Canton, did their best to minimize their impact and to maintain the old arms-length pattern of relations. The British, soon disappointed in their hoped for great commercial and diplomatic gains, argued for their revision and extension, but to no avail. Out of these frustrations came, predictably enough at one level but actually rather inadvertently, the second war and the events outlined above. A much more detailed treaty was imposed by the British at Tianjin in 1858 and, after the Summer Palace episode, a further Convention was added at Beijing in October

1860. The French and Americans also extended their treaties, as did the Russians. The latter took the chance, even before the Anglo-French campaign of 1858 was concluded, to revise the treaties they had made with Jesuit assistance back in the late seventeenth and early eighteenth centuries. They gained far more territory, in what is now eastern Siberia, than did the British to whom the small island of Hong Kong had been ceded by the Treaty of Nanjing in 1842.

Acquisition of territory was not what these treaties were essentially about, except for the Russians. None of the Western powers involved sought more than greater trading, diplomatic and, for the French, religious access to China. Insofar as China's territorial integrity was ever at stake it was Russia and Japan that were to be the main threats. Though peripheral regions were later to be loosened from Chinese influence – Tibet and Burma by the British; Indo-China or modern Vietnam by the French; Mongolia and other parts of Central Asia by the Russians; Manchuria by Japan – there was never any serious intent by Western powers to take over as colonies any part of China proper. 'No more Indias' was a common refrain in British official documents of the period, especially after the traumatic 'Mutiny' of 1858 there, which had helped delay the British campaign in China. The small peninsula of Kowloon was added to the island of Hong Kong as British territory by the 1860 Convention of Beijing, but that toe-hold on the mainland of China was never seen as a potential gateway to larger acquisitions. Even the so-called Battle of Concessions, which developed between various treaty powers at the end of the century and prompted some contemporary observers to anticipate the carving up of China among Western imperialist powers, was about exclusive trading and investment rights rather than territorial take-overs. Opening the country securely to traders, investors, diplomats, missionaries, not to colonial administrators, was the objective of the treaty system as far as the West was concerned. These nineteenth-century treaties were clearly 'imperialist' in character, but they were not 'colonialist'. China, unlike India, Africa and the Americas, was never colonized by the West, and the treaty system did not work, and was not intended to work, in that way by its originators.

Nevertheless, the treaties made after 1842 certainly increased Western power and influence in China considerably, though less quickly and comprehensively than is often presented. They are known collectively as the unequal treaties, and this description is fair enough insofar as nearly all of the clauses in them required concessions and changes only from the Chinese. But treaties made at the end of wars in which one side is decisively defeated are usually very one-sided and unequal, and from that standpoint the treaties imposed on China are not so exceptional. They certainly required the Chinese to begin to act more in line with Western ideas about how trade and diplomacy between the two cultures should be conducted, and also required the Chinese to tolerate and protect, to a degree only briefly achieved by the Jesuit missionaries, Christian enterprise in their country. For many years much of the deep interior of the country was little affected by these treaties, at least directly. Missionaries penetrated to some degree, but the traders and diplomats mostly stayed in the cities and ports opened to them, of which only a few became major centres for Western enterprise. China was by no means at once flung wide open to the West, even by the treaties of 1858–60, though over time the treaty system provided the means whereby Western influences, cultural and intellectual as much as economic and political, did penetrate China deeply. Assessing how these treaties really operated, judging how oppressive and exploitative as well as stimulating they were, is a challenge for the historian. A first step towards attempting such an assessment is to summarize their main provisions.[19]

The terms of the treaties

Beginning with the provisions concerned with trade and commerce, many more ports were opened to Western residents, at first a few only and all on the south coast, but after 1860 more widely, including some in the interior, up the readily navigable reaches of the Yangzi river. The old monopolistic and restrictive Co-hong was abolished, so that trade could now be conducted with any willing Chinese, who could also be employed in any lawful capacity by Western firms, most of which came to rely heavily on their Chinese agents or compradores. As already noted, the trade in opium was at last legalized, not formally but indirectly, under the detailed tariff provisions of the treaty of Tianjin in 1858. What the first treaty called 'a fair and regular tariff' was to be drawn up by mutual agreement and publicly notified, later treaties providing that at ten year intervals 'either of High Contracting Parties... may demand a further revision of the Tariff'. China thereby lost autonomous control of its tariff revenues, and the treaty powers of course generally interpreted 'fair' as meaning 'low'. This naturally became a major source of grievance for the Chinese, though at first it worked as much in their favour as against. The setting up in the 1860s of an efficient customs service, administered by Westerners in the employ of the Chinese government, meant that, although kept at relatively low rates (opium was higher) tariffs became a much larger and more reliable source of revenue for the Chinese government than had ever been the case under the old order of things. 'The new rates, while hurting the private coffers of local customs officers actually worked in favour of the imperial treasury', Immanuel Hsu comments in his study *China's Entry into the Family of Nations*.[20] Also, it should be recognized that Britain, at this time by far the biggest Western trading nation, was itself a low tariff country and an advocate of world-wide freer trade. Whether low tariffs seriously inhibited the development of a more modern industrial economy in late nineteenth – early twentieth-century China is arguable. Many factors contributed to the slower pace of economic modernization in China in contrast to Japan, another East Asian country then being forced by the West to open up under restrictive treaty terms comparable to those imposed on China. The issue of customs control and administration demonstrates the mixed nature of the treaty system in its actual operation in late nineteenth-century China. It brought gains as well as losses, but the restoration of tariff autonomy understandably became a major demand of later Chinese nationalists.

Secondly, at the diplomatic, government to government level a main provision of the treaties was that high level foreign representatives could reside permanently at the capital, a clause only insisted upon by the British after the crisis over the ratification of the 1858 Treaty of Tianjin. Of all the treaty provisions this was the most objectionable to the court at Beijing. For some years that court, dominated by the Empress Dowager, continued to resist receiving these non-kowtowing, non-tribute-bearing Western representatives in formal imperial audience. A separate foreign legation quarter developed near the imperial palace, and a new bureau known as the Zongli Yamen, not quite a Foreign Office, was set up to handle dealings with the treaty powers, but appointment to it was for many years regarded as a disgrace by most within the governing bureaucracy. There was still considerable resistance, especially in the capital, to China entering fully into what the West called the family of nations. In the treaty ports consuls were appointed, active merchants often doubling in this diplomatic role, though not the consuls appointed by the major trading power, Great Britain. The consuls administered the foreign settlement or 'concession' areas that were created at the major treaty ports, such as the large International Settlement at Shanghai, and were empowered by various clauses in the treaties to deal directly with local Chinese officials as equals, using terms such as 'communication', 'statement' or 'declaration', but never 'petition'. Early on some consuls, especially John Bowring at Canton, had great difficulty in getting recognition on such terms, and even after the harsh lessons of 1858–60 old-style local officials could be decidedly haughty towards any Western 'barbarian eye' in their region. But in many ports, most importantly at Shanghai, the treaty-based pattern of relations between government representatives was more readily accepted than in Beijing. By the late nineteenth century the treaties had swept away the old restrictive Canton system and entrenched Western traders, diplomats and consuls at many points around the coast, up the main inland waterway, and in the capital itself. Macartney, while regretting the method, would have approved the outcome.

Thirdly, on the religious front, the missionaries also benefited handsomely from the treaties, from those of 1858–60 in particular. Article VIII of the British treaty of Tianjin read:

> The Christian religion as professed by Protestants or Roman Catholics, inculcates the practice of virtue, and teaches man to do as he would be done by. Persons teaching or professing it, therefore, shall alike be entitled to the protection of the Chinese authorities, nor shall any such, peaceably pursuing their calling and not offending against the laws, be persecuted or interfered with.

Thus the Chinese government was made responsible for the security of Western missionaries and their converts, a treaty requirement which was to become perhaps the most troublesome to all parties, as the next section of this chapter will outline. The British government was never very committed to promoting the missionary enterprise in China, though often reluctantly obliged to insist on the treaty terms protecting it. The French were more proactive on the missionaries' behalf, and their treaty of 1860, or more accurately a clause apparently slipped by a missionary interpreter into the Chinese version of the treaty, promised to restore all properties seized from earlier missions, and gave permission for Catholic missionaries in the future to purchase and build on land anywhere within the country. This right to carry on missionary work and acquire property, not just in the treaty ports but far beyond them, was taken full advantage of by Protestants as well as Catholics. In the judgment of P.A. Cohen, the leading historian of the Christian missions in nineteenth-century China, 'The missionaries of both faiths guarded their treaty privileges as treasured possessions and often applied pressure on their governments to enforce them. None, at the time, seemed concerned over the manner in which these privileges had been won.'[21] In fairness to the missionary this judgment could be said to apply with equal force to the traders. Some of the diplomats, as I will endeavour to illustrate in a moment, were somewhat more sensitive and ambivalent about these treaties and their enforcement.

To complete this summary of the treaties, two other general provisions benefiting all Westerners need to be added to those outlined so far. One was the most favoured nation principle, common to many treaty arrangements before and since these Chinese treaties but of particular force in their case. This is the principle that a power granted most favoured nation status is automatically entitled to any new concession made to any other treaty power. The British included it in their 1843 treaty supplementing the terms of the treaty of Nanjing and reaffirmed it in Article LIV of the 1858 Treaty of Tianjin. This stated that 'the British Government and its subjects will be allowed free and equal participation in all privileges, immunities and advantages that may have been, or may be hereafter, granted by His Majesty the Emperor of China to the Government or subjects of any other nation.' The Americans and French, when making their own first treaties with China in 1843–4, wrote most favoured clauses into them, and subsequently this provision became general among the wide group of other powers which made treaties with China after 1860 (for example Prussia 1861, Denmark 1862, Belgium 1865, Italy 1866, Austria-Hungary 1869, Spain 1877, Portugal 1887).

The Chinese at first had no great objection to this principle, since in Confucian theory all who came to the central kingdom should be treated with equal benevolence. Thus an Imperial Edict stated in November 1843: 'Now that the English barbarians have been allowed to trade, whatever other countries there are, the US and others, should naturally be permitted to trade without discrimination, in order to show our tranquillizing purpose.'[22] Old habits and attitudes changed slowly. But soon enough it became clear, as shown by the missionary clause in the Chinese version of the French treaty, that this provision created something of a free-for-all situation, and encouraged the powers to urge one another on to greater gains for all. J.K. Fairbank summed up the process as 'a one way street... China could never reverse the tide and, by abolishing the privileges of one power eliminate those of others. Treaty privileges steadily accumulated against her interest.'[23] As with the tariffs, what in origin was a reasonably acceptable principle to the Chinese came increasingly to be seen as onerous and unjust.

Finally, what came to be seen as the greatest imposition of all in the treaty system was extraterritoriality, that is the provision that Westerners residing in China be subject not to Chinese law but to their own national jurisdictions, as administered through consular courts. Articles XV and XVI of the Treaty of Tianjin stated that

'All questions in regard to rights, whether of property or of person, arising between British subjects shall be subject to the jurisdiction of the British authorities...British subjects who may commit any crime in China shall be tried and punished by the Consul, or other public functionary authorized thereto, according to the laws of Great Britain.' By the end of the century over a dozen treaty powers enjoyed such extraterritorial rights in China.

As with the most favoured nation provision, extraterritoriality was not a totally new principle, created by Western negotiators especially for China, nor was it a practice entirely unknown or unacceptable to the Chinese. There was a long tradition in both cultures of some degree of self-regulation being permitted to resident foreigners, at least in the settlement of disputes among themselves. The Chinese had permitted this to Arab traders back in Tang times, and the treaties made with the Russians in the seventeenth and eighteenth centuries included some such concessions. Even in the modern world, one historian of extra-territoriality states, 'An alien within the territory of a State never fully loses the right to protection by his own State, unless the latter voluntarily renounces the right.'[24] Given the contrasting philosophies and practices of law, and the sometimes alarming experiences Westerners had of the Chinese system of law under the old Canton trading regulations (and may still have today), it was not surprising that the Western powers took the opportunity provided by victory in war of making their legal status in China clearer and more secure. They certainly did so very comprehensively, as the clauses from the Treaty of Tianjin just quoted demonstrate. Later developments, such as the growth of foreign conces-sion into areas much larger and more populous than was at first anti-cipated, and within which many Chinese came to reside beyond the easy reach of Chinese authority, meant that extraterritoriality became, like tariff autonomy and the most favoured nation principle, an increasingly serious invasion of Chinese sovereignty. The development of a mixed court system for cases involving Chinese and Westerners, and the readi-ness of many missionaries in the interior to assert their extraterritorial status even on behalf of their converts, heightened Chinese objections to the principle, and by the early twentieth century it became, with the tariff autonomy issue, a major ground of hostility towards the West and its treaties.

'Unequal' but limited?

Overall, however, it is easy to exaggerate the degree to which China was oppressed and exploited by these treaties. They were not intended, even the more detailed and exacting treaties of 1858–60, to 'squeeze China until the pips squeaked', as could be said with some justice of the terms imposed on China after the Boxer crisis. As ever in pursuit of historical accuracy it is important to distinguish outcomes from origins, to be aware that how things develop is no reliable guide to the intentions and expectations of those who set them in motion. In the case of the unequal treaty system to which China was subjected between 1842 and 1943 it seems to me reasonable to argue that it became more oppressive than its original architects anticipated or intended.

It is worth noting at this point that the 1842 treaty of Nanjing, which initiated Western treaty relations with China, was not the first treaty in Chinese history containing such provisions as extraterritorial rights, tariff concessions and most favoured nation treatment. Only a few years before the first of the opium wars China had, after a protracted struggle, negotiated with the powerful Kokand Khanate in Xinjiang what Joseph Fletcher, in the authoritative *Cambridge History of China*, described as China's first unequal treaty settlement.[25] Fletcher judged that 'the Ch'ing concessions to the coastal trading powers in 1842–4 paralleled the concessions to Kokand in 1831–35.' Coping with the barbarians from the West was by no means the only major external relations issue facing the Chinese in the early nineteenth century, and they brought to their dealings with these seaborne trouble makers tactics and attitudes shaped by their long-standing experience of Central Asia. In 1842 they were ready to buy off the British and their Western followers with treaties containing provisions similar to those they had recently conceded to the trade-hungry Kokandis in Xinjiang, hoping it would be a purely temporary necessity. The difference was that the Western-imposed treaty system applied not to relatively remote frontier regions, well beyond the walls of China proper, but to major centres of population within the central kingdom itself. Also, although the first Western treaties were relatively limited and fairly readily agreed to by the Chinese negotiators, circumstances soon led to their becoming more extended in scope and application, with other non-Western powers, such as Russia and Japan, joining in the process.

But at the beginning little of this was anticipated by either side, certainly not by the Chinese. When the terms of the Treaty of Nanjing were settled on 29 August 1842 the chief negotiator on the Chinese side, actually a Manchu official, was reported as saying 'Is that all?'. The historian could benefit from a video of that moment, to help judge by the tone of voice and body language with which the question was asked whether it meant simply 'Is there anything else on the agenda?', or (more likely) 'Is that really all you want?'. The modern Chinese historian who recounted this story, though not altogether certain of its authenticity, was certain that it demonstrated 'the incompetence and shortsightedness of the Chinese authorities in the treaty negotiations.'[26] This is very much the judgment of a modern Chinese nationalist, understandably viewing this moment across one hundred years of treaty operation. Yet in the circumstances of the time, and remembering – as that Manchu official surely did – that only a few years earlier an agreement including extraterritorial, tariff and most favoured nation provisions had been made with other troublesome border traders, the Qing negotiators at Nanjing may well have been surprised and relieved that more was not being exacted from them. After all, in mid-1842 British guns were threatening Nanjing, the second city of the empire, their navy was blockading the Grand Canal, and their military forces were occupying the large island of Chusan off the mouth of the Yangzi, as well as the island of Hong Kong and the ports of Canton, Amoy (modern Xiamen) and Ningbo. They had not breached the Great Wall nor occupied Beijing itself, as the Manchus themselves had done two centuries earlier, but their capacity to do so and penetrate to the very heart of the empire was becoming clear. It is no wonder that the Chinese negotiators at Nanjing were anxious to settle as quickly as possible, nor that they were relieved, given the evident strength of the British naval and military position by mid-1842, that so little seemed to be being demanded of them by these first Western treaty makers.[27]

Nevertheless, these British treaty makers, then the cutting edge of Western penetration into China, were certainly making significant demands, backed by substantial force. Yet something of the moderate Macartney approach was still present, even as they imposed a treaty system containing both novel and familiar elements on a reluctant but somewhat relieved Chinese government. The chief British negotiator of the treaty of Nanjing and of the Supplementary Treaty that followed it, Sir Henry Pottinger, wrote in 1843: 'Now that peace is made I consider myself to stand as it were in the light of an umpire between the two Empires... I am resolved that all commercial arrangements shall be as reciprocal as far as it is possible to make them.'[28] Making reciprocity work proved not to be easy, but was certainly Pottinger's intent. Thus, although convinced of 'the utter impossibility of suppressing the trade so long as the Chinese *will* have and *will* use opium', he accepted the continuing unwillingness of the Chinese negotiators to legalize the trade. Instead of demanding that such a clause be included in the treaty he sought to work out some indirect means of regulating the trade, in co-operation rather than in confrontation with them. This in-between approach to what remained a very open but technically still illegal smuggling trade broke down within a decade or so, as the volume of imports continued to grow rapidly, and as officials who proved far less ready to compromise came into office both at Canton and Hong Kong. But in the person of Pottinger the treaty system began with some British recognition of official Chinese sensibilities over the issue that had precipitated war between them.

Pottinger also took an in-between line on the issue of tariffs. In Article II of the first treaty he made clear the legal responsibility placed on consuls 'to see that the just duties and other dues of the Chinese government, as hereafter provided for, are duly discharged by Her Britannic Majesty's subjects.' In the subsequent negotiations about those 'just duties and other dues', he resisted pressure from British merchants to keep them so low as to deny the Chinese government any chance of raising much revenue from them. Opium was not yet included in the list of legal trade items subject to tariff, but informally at various ports a sort of de facto legalization and collection of dues had developed, to the benefit of local officials rather than of the Imperial government.

Thus, despite its undoubtedly unequal character, the treaty system did not begin as a totally one-sided system. The American historian, J.K. Fairbank, in his detailed and authoritative study of trade and diplomacy on the China coast during these Opium War years, sums up these early treaties as 'not British-made blue prints, but Anglo-Chinese compromises. They took account of Chinese values and institutions almost as much as Western.' This is certainly not the standard Chinese nationalist view, which is that 'the British wrote the Articles; the Chinese were only permitted to polish the translation and re-word some small items.'[29] That was the judgment of a Chinese historian writing in the 1920s, some years before Fairbank's searching analysis, but it remains fairly representative of the orthodox, still current, Chinese interpretation of the treaty system. Like beauty, historical truth lies in the eye of the beholder!

Lord Elgin attempts to balance toughness with moderation

Pottinger's successor as the chief British negotiator of the next series of unequal treaties, drawn up at Tianjin and Beijing, was Lord Elgin, son of the man who removed the marbles from Greece and who was himself to order the burning of the Summer Palace in Beijing in 1860, another act of apparent cultural vandalism. He was certainly tougher and more demanding than Pottinger had been, but not very comfortably so. 'I made up my mind, disgusting as the part is to me, to play the role of the "uncontrollably fierce barbarian"', he wrote in his journal in mid-1858 while at Tianjin. 'These stupid people, though they cannot resist and hardly even make an attempt to do so, never yield anything except under the influence of fear; and it is necessary therefore to make them feel that one is in earnest, and that they have nothing for it but to give way.'[30] These were not exactly kindly thoughts, but Elgin was not without sympathy and respect for Chinese culture. On his way up to Tianjin he had admonished the British merchants of Shanghai, who were intent on opening up the country as fully and quickly as possible, that 'When the barriers which prevent freer access to the interior of the country shall have been removed the Christian civilization of the West will find itself face to face not with barbarism but with an ancient civilization in many respects effete and imperfect, but in others not without claims to our sympathy and respect.' Like Pottinger he did not try to force legalization of the opium trade, writing that he could 'not reconcile it to my sense of right to urge the Imperial government to abandon its traditional policy in this respect.'[31] But by 1858 the inner opium war was over, and many Chinese officials had come to the conclusion that, since prohibition was not working, it would be best to recognize the existence of the trade and raise revenue from it. Thus it was agreed that opium be included in the tariff scales drawn up under the terms of the treaty concluded at Tianjin, although it was not formally recognized within the treaty itself. It was a compromise of sorts which worked until, as outlined on pp. 85–7, 50 years later the British were ready to end their part in the trade.

Elgin adopted a much tougher approach on the diplomatic front, insisting that the right to appoint an 'Ambassador, Minister or other diplomatic agent' who would 'not be called upon to perform any ceremony derogatory to him as representing the Sovereign of an independent nation on a footing of equality with China', should be firmly written into the treaty. This was a most sensitive issue, where the two cultures were still eyeball to eyeball, the reigning Xianfeng emperor resenting this aspect of the settlement more strongly than any other of the treaty provisions. But on the principle of a Western right to residence in the capital as diplomatic equals, Elgin was insistent, though he was prepared to yield a little on its actual implementation. The relevant clause in the treaty was phrased to read that the British representative might reside permanently at the capital, 'or may visit it occasionally at the option of the British Government.' After the treaty was signed, but before it was ratified, Elgin made a further less formal agreement to the effect that the soon-to-be-appointed first British Minister to China would in fact reside at Shanghai, visiting the capital only for such formalities as presenting his credentials and exchanging ratifications. In return the Chinese agreed to the opening of the Yangzi river to British trade earlier than was strictly required by the treaty. After exploring the river as far as modern Wuhan, Elgin then left China, satisfied that his disagreeable duty was done. Before returning to England to become (briefly) Post Master General in Palmerston's government, he also went to Japan, making a treaty there, as the Americans had done some years earlier.

Events quickly overtook him and the treaty he had made. The first British minister appointed under the terms of the new treaty was Elgin's younger brother, Frederick Bruce, who was to reside at Shanghai but to present his credentials to the court at Beijing and exchange ratifications of the treaty there. The Chinese endeavoured to persuade him, as well as the new French and American ministers, to do this at Shanghai, but all insisted on proceeding to the capital. They travelled as far north as possible by ship, accompanied by a substantial British naval and military force. The British were determined that there would be no repetition of their Macartney-Amherst-Napier diplomatic put-offs. However, on 25 June 1859, the progress of their rather provocative entourage was resisted successfully, though unwisely, by the Chinese at the Dagu forts at the mouth of the river leading to Beijing. The British forces, when they tried to force the opening of the river, were repulsed with four gunboats sunk and over 400 men lost, a notable early victory of Chinese forces over Western. The Russians, not long before the enemy in the Crimean war, were suspected of aiding the Chinese who, in British eyes, were showing themselves reluctant to ratify the just concluded treaty of Tianjin in a manner which made plain their acceptance of Western diplomatic practice. Elgin was therefore sent back to repeat and reinforce the lesson, and the second Opium War was reignited.

Elgin had been criticized in parliament by the free trader John Bright and others for having insisted too strongly on the principle of the right of residence at the capital, an unnecessary humiliation of the Chinese, Bright claimed. Elgin defended himself by insisting that 'if we intend to maintain permanent pacific relations with some 400 million of the human race scattered over a country some 1500 miles long by so many broad . . . we must establish direct diplomatic relations with the Imperial Government of Pekin.' It was, he added, 'the greatest kindness you could possibly confer upon the Chinese Emperor.'[32] In short, one had to be cruel to be kind.

The Emperor and his officials certainly did not see it that way, and Elgin's hoped for 'permanent pacific relations' between China and the leading Western power seemed a very long way off in 1859–60. Mistrust and misunderstanding on both sides marked a sorry sequence of events, including the seizure by the Chinese of truce negotiators, who were maltreated, some dying, while in captivity. This event particularly outraged the high-minded Elgin, who became determined to punish what he viewed as a perfidious and untrustworthy government. The Chinese court fled west to Xian in September 1860 while a joint Anglo-French force advanced to occupy Beijing early in October, the French not so willing this time, being heavily involved in north Italy and resentful of British criticism of their role there. After looting – the 'allies' blamed each other for that – and burning the Summer Palace (Elgin's misguided way of trying to punish only the rulers, not the populace), the Convention of Beijing was added to the 1858 treaty, now finally ratified. This Convention was signed late in October 1860 by a terrified remnant of the Imperial government which had returned to face these manifestly 'uncontrollably fierce barbarians'. The Convention reasserted the principle of residence and effectively cancelled the concession Elgin had made in 1858. It also doubled the war indemnity payment to about £3 million, facilitated the emigration of Chinese overseas, and added the peninsula of Kowloon to the British possession of Hong Kong. By the end of 1860 the basic structure of the treaty system was firmly in place.

The system was, I have been suggesting while at the same time describing it, more even handed in origin and intent than it is commonly presented. Its main architects, acting fairly flexibly within the general guidelines of their instructions from the British government, sought to balance firmness, sometimes certainly amounting to downright toughness, with at least some sensitivity to what the changes meant for China. Further evidence for this argument that the intent, even if not the methods, of the British government in forcing the system on China was not totally crude and one-sided (as concentration on the opium aspect of the confrontation, or events such as the burning of the Summer Palace, encourages one to believe) is to be found in the proclamation with which Elgin prefaced the publication of the Convention of Beijing in November 1860. In this he urged moderation upon all his compatriots in China in tones similar to those he had used in his admonition to the merchants at Shanghai in 1858. The proclamation read in part:

> The Earl of Elgin trusts that by a considerate treatment of the natives with whom they may come into contact, and a faithful observance of

their obligations towards the Chinese Government, Her Majesty's subjects in China will do what in them lies to reconcile the people and authorities of China to the changes in their relations with foreigners, which are about to be introduced under the international compacts herewith promulgated – changes which, if they be carried into effect in such manner as to afford greater scope to the commercial activity of the Chinese people, without doing unnecessary violence to their habits and traditions, will, it may be hoped, prove beneficial to them, and to all who have dealings with them.

Due notice will be given whenever the arrangements for carrying into execution the provisions of this Convention and Treaty, at the Ports thereby opened to British Trade, shall be completed.

GOD SAVE THE QUEEN.[33]

This proclamation, probably about his last public statement before finally leaving China, reflected Elgin's genuine concern, shared with his predecessor Pottinger, that the treaty system should operate to the benefit of both sides, and that it should be applied in such a way as to do as little violence as possible to Chinese habits and traditions.

Needless to say, the actual working of the system over the remaining decades of the nineteenth century, which is the time frame of this chapter, was a good deal less smooth and mutually beneficial than Elgin hoped for. During the 1860s his immediate successors as chief British diplomatic representatives in Beijing, along with others such as the American minister Anson Burlinghame, did do their best to apply the treaties as moderately as possible.[34] But given, on the one hand, the conservatism and understandable apprehension and suspicion of the Chinese government as to how far the Western invasion of China might go – perhaps as far as the Manchus themselves had gone two centuries earlier – and on the other hand the determination of merchants and missionaries to exploit as fully and quickly as possible their new rights in China, the treaty system in practice became more oppressive than its original architects intended. For them the system was the necessary means of educating, of leading China into the ways of the modern Western-defined world of trade and diplomacy. 'Our office is that of the schoolmaster who educates, not of the tyrant who imposes', Frederick Bruce wrote home to his sister Augusta in 1864, after several years of residence in Beijing.[35] But his Chinese pupils, though not stupid, as his brother had once impatiently described them, were certainly fearful and reluctant, and therefore slow to learn the lessons Bruce and his colleagues wished to impart. Although after

1860 some steps towards the insistent, powerful world beyond its borders began to be taken by some of China's leaders, more in the provinces than in the capital, movement was slow, and Western impatience mounted, especially among traders convinced they were still being denied ready access to what they saw as the biggest potential market in the world. The British Foreign Office, less convinced about the potential of the China market, was under constant criticism for what merchants complained was a too accommodating stand towards the Chinese.[36] Most merchants, as well as many missionaries, showed little inclination 'to reconcile the people and authorities of China to their relations with foreigners', as Elgin had hoped for in his well-meaning proclamation.

It was soon evident that the capacity of the diplomats to control and soften the working of the system they had helped create was decidedly limited. Official relations with China remained strained throughout the later decades of the century, and Western impatience with what came to be seen as an incorrigibly conservative society mounted. Insistence on treaty rights became entrenched. In the minds of many Westerners, especially those resident in treaty ports, the whole system and all the privileges associated with it came to be seen as fixed and permanent to an extent, I suggest, that was not intended by diplomats such as Pottinger, Elgin and Bruce. Just how permanent a system they thought it would be is unclear, but here the parallel with Japan should be borne in mind. That country, admittedly far smaller and more integrated than the great sprawling mass of China, was also subjected to the same kind of pressure from the West, but by the beginning of the twentieth century had shaken off the unequal treaties it had been obliged to accept after the visit of Perry's black ships in 1853–4 and Elgin in 1858. This was achieved, not without some reluctance on the part of Japan's treaty powers but ultimately with their full acceptance. Japan very rapidly transformed itself into a modern state, politically, economically, and also, as its success in wars against China in 1895 and Russia in 1904 demonstrated, militarily. The treaty system there clearly operated more as a stimulus than as a drag upon its emergence out of isolation and feudalism into the modern world. China found that process of change and transformation far more difficult. In consequence the treaty system there became longer lasting and more burdensome.

There is more that should be said about the working of the treaty system, including the possibility that at the end of the century the Powers, Russia and Japan as well as the West, might have attempted to go beyond it by partitioning the country and attempting to rule it directly. But I leave that for the next chapter, and turn now to look at another aspect of the nineteenth-century Western impact on China.

The Missionary Confrontation

'Take away your opium and your missionaries and you will be welcome' said Prince Gong, head of the section of the Chinese government set up to handle relations with Western powers under the treaty system, to a departing British minister in 1869.[37] It is a nice question which he thought the greater problem. My guess is that it was the missionary, for by 1869 the Chinese government was at least beginning to raise some revenue from the opium trade, but the missionary seemed to bring only costs, troubles and disturbances, even rebellion against the dynasty itself. It was only a few years since the final suppression of the great Taiping uprising, which had been led by a religious mystic who had been greatly influenced by his reading of Christian tracts and by contact with an American missionary in Canton. That had required 15 years of often savage struggle in southern and central China. The Taiping preached a recognizable, if very unorthodox, Christian creed, fiercely anti-Confucian and anti-Manchu, and had come close to establishing a new regime, one socially as well as religiously radical, before its Heavenly Kingdom of Great Peace was finally overthrown in 1864. Four years later there had been a serious attack on British missionaries of the recently founded China Inland Mission at Yangzhou, not a treaty port but a sizeable city of which Marco Polo claimed to have been once the governor. In 1870 there was to be a still more serious attack on French missionaries at Tianjin, resulting in many deaths and a crisis that might have led to war had the French not been then also having trouble with the Prussians. It was little wonder that Prince Gong and the government he represented wished heartily to be rid of the missionary.

By the later nineteenth century the missionary posed a far greater problem for relations between China and the West than had ever been the case earlier. The Jesuit missionaries of the seventeenth and eighteenth centuries had, as we have seen, adopted a highly accommodating stance towards Confucian culture. When that approach had been abandoned, after adverse rulings by the Papacy in the early eighteenth century, the Chinese state had had no difficulty in reversing the policy of toleration the Kangxi emperor had adopted towards the Christian enterprise in China, and no Western power could alter that reversal. By the early nineteenth century Christian missions in China were struggling to survive. Although Protestant missionaries had also begun to enter the field, the number of missionaries working there, never very large, had shrunk to a Jesuit remnant in Beijing and a handful of others operating in secret in a few provinces beyond the Macao-Canton region. By 1800 the always tiny ratio of converts to the large and steadily growing population of China had probably halved from what it had once been. The judgment of K.S. Latourette, in his comprehensive 1929 history of the missionary movement in China, was that 'in the first quarter of the nineteenth century the future of the Church was very dark. . . . Had missionaries after 1835 gradually ceased coming to China instead of increasing in numbers, the Church would probably have passed out of existence within a few generations, leaving behind it no permanent mark.'[38] To a degree this is a surprisingly pessimistic judgment from a historian of Latourette's faith. Given the deep seated strength of the Western impulse to preach and convert, plus the magnitude of the China challenge, I, a historian of much less faith, am inclined to the view that, even had China not been opened up soon after 1835 to the missionary as well as to the trader and the diplomat, Christian missions would somehow have battled on, and the Church in China would not have been totally lost. But certainly on the eve of the first opium war the prospect for the Christian faith in China did not look bright.

A Chinese alternative to Western Christianity

That, though, is to state the case very much from a Western standpoint, to assume that without missionaries in large numbers to lead the way the faith could not be established and flourish in this very challenging, stony Chinese field. Before surveying the later nineteenth-century missionary approach to the sowing and harvesting of that field it seems appropriate to say something more about the Taiping effort to convert China from within. Might China have become Christian through them, with only limited, marginal missionary involvement? Would the missionary, and the West generally, have been wise to respond more positively than they did to this remarkable, quasi-Christian movement?

The origins of the Taiping uprising lie in a complex mix of personal, social, economic and political factors, but crucial to its appeal and power was the ideology that its messianic leader, Hong Xiuquan, shaped from his reading of various Christian texts, plus his two month stay in Canton in 1846 receiving instruction preparatory to a baptism (which he did not take) from the eccentric but earnest American Baptist missionary, Issacher Roberts. Hong's version of Christianity, which was to inspire his early followers to many victories as they swept rapidly northward from their original base in Kwangxi, capturing Nanjing in

1853 and threatening Beijing itself by 1854, was far from orthodox in Western eyes, Catholic or Protestant. As with Marxist communism, then just being defined and later to inspire other Chinese revolutionaries, this Western-derived Christian ideology was interpreted by its Taiping protagonists in such a way as to contain many Chinese characteristics.

After experiencing visions or hallucinations in 1837, which his later reading of Christian tracts seemed to explain, Hong presented himself as the younger brother of Jesus Christ, sent by Jehovah to be the bearer of a new revelation updating the Christian message. In another time and place Mahomet had done something similar with considerable success, so there were certainly great possibilities in Hong's claim. According to Hong's teaching, as summarized by Jonathan Spence in his biography of *God's Chinese Son*, Jesus himself came back to Earth several times in 1848, sang them 'songs newly composed by God' and told them of all the events in Heaven since Hong left 11 years before.

> They talk of Hong's young son, conceived and born in Heaven, but still unnamed, who lives in Heaven with his grandmother, the wife of God. They talk of the boy's mother, the First Chief Moon, of how she lives with her divine in-laws, or with Jesus and his wife, and of how she yearns for her husband to come back to her... She talks of the kindness shown to her and her son by Jesus' wife, and of Jesus' five children, three boys, two girls... [39]

Clearly this was an extended, very Chinese style Holy Family.

Gathering many followers among the poor peasantry of south west China, by 1851 Hong proclaimed a new kind of dynasty, bearing not just the mandate of Heaven but itself of heavenly origin and authority. Nanjing when captured was renamed Tianjing, meaning the heavenly capital. One of Hong's close associates defined himself as the Holy Ghost, so that his pronouncements might theoretically override even those of the younger son of God, a claim that was to lead to some savage internal struggles which for a time seriously weakened the movement. Hong survived, though the would-be Holy Ghost did not, and by 1860 the movement had regenerated itself to capture many major cities of central China and to advance on Shanghai. There, however, it was repulsed by some of the Anglo-French forces sent to China to punish the Manchu court in Beijing for its failure to ratify the Treaty of Tianjin in a manner acceptable to the British. Thus, the West was attacking the Chinese government in one place, its capital, while in another helping it resist a rebellion claiming to be Christian and more accepting of the

Western presence than the ruling dynasty. It was a complex, one might say farcical situation, politically, militarily and theologically.

The Protestant missionaries were uncertain and divided as to how to respond to the Taiping, though the Catholics were always definite in their rejection of what they saw as a distorted outcome of their rivals' methods and influence. Scattering the seed broadcast seemed to have produced a jungle rather than a harvest. The hope of some of the more evangelical Protestants was that if they could establish sustained contact with the rebels – a distinct possibility by 1860, as Taiping forces neared Shanghai – their leaders might be led on to more orthodox paths. Several missionaries, as well as other Westerners, paid visits to Nanjing during 1860–1, and Roberts, the only one to be actually received in audience by the now very remote and mystical Hong, stayed for over a year. But all left disillusioned, Roberts pronouncing Hong 'a crazy man, unfit to rule' and despairing of missionary success among them or of any good coming out of the movement. Some left more in sorrow than in anger, but all moved on to establish new mission stations in the now much more accessible China. Within a year or two of the Protestant missionaries' withdrawal from the Taiping the movement was finally suppressed, Westerners giving most of the credit for that outcome to the force of mercenaries called the Ever Victorious Army led by then Major, later General, Gordon, though in reality it was the steady encirclement of Nanjing by Chinese provincial armies that was decisive.[40]

The Taiping were thoroughly exterminated, and left no continuing heritage of native Christianity, only one of rebellion against the Manchu rulers of China. But for a mid-nineteenth-century ruler of China such as Prince Gong their manifestly Christian message was central to the movement, their religion and their rebellion were inseparable. The twentieth-century Chinese memory of them has focussed on their political and social rather than their religious radicalism, though its religious ideology was undoubtedly central to the movement. The Taiping became a hostile memory for that late convert to Christianity, Chiang Kai-shek, but a sympathetic one for the definitely non-Christian rebel he faced, Mao Zedong. The Western missionaries of the time seem simply to have turned aside, ready to forget this Chinese Christian movement while hopeful that, with the treaties now firmly in place, they would achieve great things by their own efforts.

But was a great opportunity lost? Could the Taiping, if more strongly supported and tolerated by Western missionaries, have established a strong and lasting native tradition of Christianity and possibly brought on, more rapidly than the Western missionary could ever achieve, the conversion of the whole country to a new version of Christianity? 'Did ever Christians have so golden an opportunity of winning a great heathen nation for Christ?' asked Eugene Stock, the historian of the Church Missionary Society writing at the end of the nineteenth century, and in his 1935 popular history of China C.P. Fitzgerald also seemed to get close to suggesting that a real opportunity was lost when he commented, rather tartly, 'the missionaries, having rejected the millions of Hong's followers have had to be content with the few thousand of their own converts, and are unlikely to find a second opportunity.'[41]

But to suggest that the Protestant missionaries might have changed either the fate or the character of the Taiping movement is to exaggerate greatly their capacity to influence policy making and the course of events. It is also to expect from them a degree of cultural flexibility and sensitivity towards Chinese institutions and values well beyond what any other Westerners then displayed. At the political level, by 1862 British policy was decidedly hostile to the Taiping, who had come to be seen as incapable of creating in China the kind of order needed if the laboriously created treaties were to be worth anything at all to the West. Although still very uncertain of the Qing dynasty's acceptance of the treaties, some British aid was soon forthcoming to help it suppress these rebels, and missionary visits to Taiping-held areas were deplored. Many Protestant missionaries opposed British intervention against the Taiping, but none argued for decisive action to support them. It is difficult to see that the missionaries, even had they been more accepting of Taiping Christianity, could have done anything effective to preserve the movement, or to change British policy towards it. Roman Catholic missionaries were consistently hostile to the Taiping, and the French assisted in suppressing the revolt. The Americans were then too busy fighting their own civil war to be interested in intervening in China's, though in the mid-twentieth century they were ready to become more actively involved in China's internal struggles.

At the religious level, it is also not surprising that the missionary, even those most concerned to make meaningful contact, in the end rejected Taiping Christianity and gave up trying to influence or defend the movement. It would have required a high degree of tolerance for the missionary to have adjusted to the essentials of the Taiping faith. The modern missionary, better trained to adapt to local conditions and traditions, may have such flexibility, but Taiping Christianity was well beyond any nineteenth-century Western standard of acceptability. Even the culturally sensitive Jesuits who followed Ricci and were ready to foster a Confucianized Christianity for China, would surely have found it impossible to accommodate to the Taiping. I conclude there-fore that the missionary cannot seriously be said to have lost a great opportunity in not supporting the Taiping more energetically. It would have required a great leap of faith and understanding for him to have attempted to do so and, even if he had, he lacked the political resources and capability to influence the power wielders decisively. Perhaps the Taiping movement represents the point in history when China came as close as it ever has to being converted on a large scale to some kind of Christianity. 'Hong's adaptations may strike us today as undoubtedly the best chance Christianity ever had of actually becoming part of the old Chinese culture. What foreign faith could conquer China without a Chinese prophet?' asked J.K. Fairbank in the last of his many studies of Chinese history.[42] But it would have been a form of Christianity radically altered from its Western origins – just as that other Western faith, Marxism, to which many Chinese were to be converted in the next century, was to be altered by Mao. Chinese values, Chinese character-istics were never to be overwhelmed by any orthodoxy from the West, Christian, Communist or capitalist.

The Western missionary confronts China

The nineteenth-century missionary, however, buoyed by the military and diplomatic triumphs of the Opium War years, and confident that he was doing God's work, did not doubt the possibility of converting China thoroughly to a Western faith. Even before the uncertainties of the Taiping uprising were behind them the missionaries dedicated them-selves energetically to the vast task ahead. Their numbers grew steadily. By the end of the century there were some 800 Catholic priests and nuns of foreign origin, mainly French, plus about 500 native priests, who between them served, according to official propaganda figures, a total of 552 448 converts in 1897. In 1889 there were about 1500 Protestant missionaries, mostly British and American, and including many 'missionary ladies', serving about 100 000 converts. Though there was clearly much work yet to be done, many souls yet to be saved, by the end of the century the Christian presence in China was a great deal more substantial, and far more widely spread, than it had been before the treaty system began.[43]

Despite the many good works they performed in addition to their basic commitment to preaching the Christian gospel throughout China – establishing schools, hospitals, orphanages and campaigning against such social evils as opium smoking and footbinding – and despite the readiness of most of them to dedicate their lives (in the case of many Protestant missionaries, the lives of their wives and children also) to the task, of all the Westerners who came to China the missionaries aroused the greatest hostility, the strongest and most lasting resistance from the mass of the Chinese people. Paul Cohen begins his comprehensive chapter surveying the Christian missions and their impact on China down to 1900 in Vol X of the *Cambridge History of China* by asking why this should be so. 'Traders came to China in the nineteenth century to extract profits', he writes. 'Diplomats and soldiers came to extract privileges and concessions. Alone among the foreigners, Christian missionaries came not to take but to give, not to further their own interests but, at least ostensibly, to serve the interests of the Chinese. Why, then, of all those who ventured to China in the last century was it the missionary who inspired the greatest fear and hatred?'[44]

Any attempt at an adequate answer must take into account many factors. Cohen himself puts most weight on the commitment of the missionary to the proposition that the true interests of the Chinese people could be served only by means of a fundamental reordering of Chinese culture. However conservative they might be individually in their personal and religious outlook, they were collectively iconoclastic, he emphasizes. Even those few among them who were appreciative of certain facets of Chinese culture insisted on the need for a compre-hensive overhauling of Chinese ways. Thus, he writes, 'for the vast majority of Chinese who remained closely identified with the status quo, Christianity not only lacked appeal, it appeared as a definite menace. And among all the social classes resistance – both passive and active – was rampant.'[45]

Cohen goes on to give considerable weight also to a xenophobic, anti-Christian tradition in China, going back to Ming times, and argues that, 'even if it is true, as I am certain it is, that missionaries in the late Qing were a major irritant, the fact that they encountered a population many of whose members were *predisposed* to be irritated cannot be so lightly dismissed.' On the other hand, the French scholar Jacques Gernet, after a detailed examination of seventeenth-century Chinese writings which challenged Ricci and his successors, concluded that

If the doctrine of the Master of Heaven (that is Christianity as pre-sented by the Jesuits) was regarded by many Chinese as a threat to the most venerable traditions of China, to society, morality and the State, this cannot simply have been a xenophobic reaction as has so often been suggested.[46]

Cohen is certainly not suggesting that the nineteenth-century anti-Christian movement in China was simply, nor even primarily, xenophobic in character, but it seems clear that irrational fear of the foreign, and a readiness to take violent action against it, was a major element in the later Chinese response to the Western missionary. Earlier anti-Christian writing and sentiments certainly fed into that response and helped sharpen it. The mix of forces and feelings at work was very volatile. The contrast in basic religious tradition and ideas, plus the increasingly aggressive nature of the Western presence in China, of which the missionary was a very vigorous as well as the most exposed part, make the generally hostile reaction of the Chinese during the later nineteenth century understandable, with or without any xenophobic predispositions.

At this point it seems worth listing some of the missionary actions which, however well meaning, aroused resentment at all levels within Chinese society, with populace and ruling elite alike. These included:

● the building of Western style churches, some quite large, often on sites which ignored Chinese geomantic principles (*feng shui*), so disturbing sensibilities about the harmony of Heaven and Earth and arousing fears of possible dire consequences;
● the bringing together of men and women for public worship, contrary to traditional standards of propriety;
● the rescuing of abandoned children for baptism, many soon dying within the orphanage, giving rise to rumours of dark deeds by the missionaries and the nuns, who were very active in this work;
● the assumption, central to the missionary's main objective, of the role of teacher and instructor on behaviour, belief and moral principles, thus challenging the authority and status of the traditional leaders in Chinese society, and moreover inculcating heterodox, un-Confucian ideas;
● the readiness of some missionaries to intervene on behalf of their converts in cases of dispute brought before a magistrate;
● the close association of the missionary with the treaty system, so that however troublesome he might be in the eyes of many Western diplomats and merchants, in Chinese eyes he was as much a representative and agent of imperialism as they.

One could extend the list, but these may serve to illustrate the many points of friction involved. The inflammatory anti-Christian propaganda resulting – broadsheets, pamphlets, cartoons, rumours – was commonly scurrilous, one of its relatively milder thrusts being to pun on the term *tianzhu*, meaning ruler of Heaven and used by many missionaries for 'God', by changing the second ideograph in the Chinese compound to another, pronounced identically but meaning 'pig', so that Christianity and its agents could be represented in a crude and disparaging way.

The missionary and the responses he provoked remained an acute and ongoing issue in Sino-Western relations throughout the second half of the nineteenth century, to the frequent dismay of the diplomats. In response to Prince Gong's 1869 complaint, the British diplomats, long before they took away their opium, would have been glad to take away their missionaries, or at least confine them to the treaty ports, had they been able. But when troubles arose they felt they had perforce to protect the missionary, not infrequently by sending a gunboat, lest the Chinese get the idea that other aspects of the treaties could also be challenged. The dilemma persisted into the twentieth century. Some other diplomats, particularly the French, were more supportive of the missionary enterprise, and the American minister Anson Burlinghame, who died while leading a delegation to the West and Russia in 1867 to urge moderation in the interpretation and application of the treaties, talked of planting the shining cross on every hill and in every valley there, an American-style sentiment not readily found in the British diplomatic records of the time. The missionary himself, whether Catholic or Protestant, English, French or American, was determined to carry on with his God-given task, whatever governments, Western or Chinese, said. 'We are here not to develop the resources of the country, not for the advancement of commerce, not for the mere promotion of civilization, but to do battle with the powers of darkness, to save men from sin, and conquer China for Christ', the Rev. Griffith John of the London Missionary Society declaimed at a conference in 1877.[47] Although a few other missionaries, such as the Baptist Timothy Richards, who had some contact with and influence on the Chinese reformers of 1898, were less single minded and confrontationist in their approach, Johns' statement summed up the prevailing attitude of the nineteenth-century missionary to his task in China.

The readiness of the nineteenth-century missionary to set about transforming not only Chinese religious belief but its whole culture was apparent in a speech given by one of the directors of the London Missionary Society at a public meeting called by the Society in January 1843, after the signing of the Treaty of Nanjing. Though that treaty had made no mention of religion, the directors were confident that it would prove 'highly favourable to the efforts of Christian benevolence', and so began an appeal 'to meet solemn claims of Providence on behalf of

China' by sending out more missionaries. In launching the appeal the
Rev. Dr Leifchild confidently proclaimed:

> When Christianity once gets into China, and the inhabitants of that
> empire are able to compare the statutes of Confucius and Buddha,
> and all the puerilities mixed with them, with the Christian scriptures
> universally diffused in their own language, and eagerly pursued by
> that inquisitive and reading people, think you not that the objects of
> their idolatrous worship will soon begin to totter, and tumble, and
> fall, and be entombed in the very soil out of which they arose. When
> they see the superiority of our own knowledge and civilization, to see
> how we have carried their arts and inventions to a pitch of refine-
> ment as far above that in which they have suffered them to remain as
> their first discovery was beyond the ignorance of former ages; when
> they shall receive benefits of this kind from our countrymen residing
> among them, can you doubt that their puerile conceits will crumble
> and vanish. When our women – the glory of our land and the charm
> of every circle – whose superiority is acknowledged in every country
> under heaven – when our women who have hitherto been so rigor-
> ously excluded from their outposts, shall mingle with them in the
> person of the wives of Missionaries or the consorts of noble and
> illustrious visitors to the palaces how will the female portion of the
> Chinese population rise in everything graceful and dignified by such
> an association. The Chinese ladies, in a very few years, will be copy-
> ing the manners of English women . . . How wondrous are the ways of
> Providence, how mysterious to our apprehension, that this little
> nation – this handful of people – should be the means of saving, by
> her civil, moral, intellectual and spiritual condition, the teeming and
> swarming population of the globe![48]

This speech, brimming with the over-weening confidence, amounting
to arrogance, of early Victorian England, demonstrates that nothing less
than the overturning of 'the puerile conceits' of Chinese civilization, the
transforming of its civil, moral, intellectual and spiritual condition, was
the goal set for the missionaries sent out in increasing numbers to China
by this and many other similar societies in Europe and America. More
fully even than the traders or the diplomats, the missionary seemed
to embody and articulate the implications of the nineteenth-century
Western thrust into China. That once so securely self-contained world
was indeed to be turned upside down, as the reverend Dr Leifchild
predicted.

But although they could help precipitate this process of radical change, and were confident of achieving their own special goals within that process, in the end the missionary was no more able to control and direct it than was any other Westerner. Eventually the Chinese would come to accept the essence of the changes which the traders and diplomats sought, would open up their country to freer trade and to international relations on the basis of equal sovereignty. But for all save a handful of converts, many of those unreliable 'rice Christians' prompted more by material than by spiritual considerations, the missionary's religious message was unacceptable, especially once it came to be seen as having little to do with the West's material wealth and power. Optimistic Western anticipations as to the changes that would come about by the opening of China under the treaty system were generally misplaced, but by none more than the Christian missionary.

To put a little flesh on the bare bones of such a judgment, consider the report of a member of the China Inland Mission on the progress being made by 1872 at various stations established inland from the treaty port of Ningbo. The main success story, recounted in some detail, is of a woman of 82, 'alone in the world with scarcely a friend or relation left' who had been 'a devoted and sincere worshipper of idols all her life.' Despite her great age and impaired sight and hearing, 'gradually the truths of the gospel were unfolded to her, and what she did comprehend she retained with considerable tenacity' the report affirmed. 'Eventually she became a candidate for baptism. On examination we were convinced of her sincerity, but suggested that it might be well to defer for a time her reception, that she might first gain a more intelligent apprehension of some of the truths of our faith.' The old lady, naturally enough, was anxious to be received at once into Church fellowship, for, as she said mournfully, 'my day is nearly spent, the sun is going down, there is no time for deferring in my case', words which, the missionary reported 'I shall never forget, but by the Lord's grace keep in mind, and work while it is day'. It is almost needless to add that her request was acceded to, and she was received. After this quite extended account of the admission to the faithful of one old lady the report on this station, based in a district city, concluded more briskly 'One of the members, previously suspended, has been restored. But a case of discipline was pending when I left, which may result in the suspension of two others. The total number of natives in communion was twenty three.' Thus, in a centre of some size we hear of one conversion, not bringing in an adherent likely to add much strength to the mission, and evidence of backsliding among the small group of 'natives' in communion, that is receiving instruction but not necessarily baptised.

At the next station visited, in a village about twenty miles away, the report continued

> Here there has been little visible progress for a considerable time. There are now only fifteen members and one candidate for baptism. Owing to the sickness of Wong...the preaching at Dzao-ts'eng has not been so regularly kept up, but when he has been able to go there the attendance has been considerable; but there is at present no visible result from the services. The people of the villages in this district are divided into clans, which makes it very difficult for one of their number to declare himself a Christian. There are often hundreds, or even thousands of people in one village or town, all of one surname; and they are so intimately connected with each other, that any step taken by a member of the clan which is considered by the rest to be a departure from the religion of their ancestors will entail upon him considerable persecution and loss of property, almost in some cases to his becoming virtually an outlaw.

Here it is apparent that acceptance of the missionary's message could have major social consequences, and required considerable courage, as well as conviction, from any potential convert. Very few of those were to be found among the more educated groups within Chinese society, the literati indeed often being promoters of anti-Christian propaganda. In such circumstances it is not surprising that, as the American missionary Justus Doolittle observed in his book *Social Life of the Chinese*, published a few years before the reports just quoted, 'Christianity makes but slow progress in China. The heavyness of superstition and idolatry there does not give way rapidly or readily to elevating and purifying beliefs. Facts show this most conclusively, and were it not for the promise of the Bible, most discouragingly.'[49]

The promise of the Bible kept the missionaries in the field and, as the statistics quoted above show, some small progress was made. But this was at the cost of many serious incidents, resulting often in the loss of lives, Western and Chinese alike. At Tianjin in 1870 some twenty Westerners, including ten nuns, two priests and the French consul (whose provocative actions helped worsen the incident), plus about forty Chinese were massacred. There were serious anti-Christian riots in a number of cities in the Yangzi Valley during 1890–1, though without great loss of life, but at Kutian in Fujian province in 1895

11 Protestant women and children were suddenly slaughtered by a local secret society. The climax came with the Boxer uprising in north China at the end of the century, which resulted in the deaths of nearly two hundred missionaries and many thousands of Chinese converts. The Boxers were intent on expelling all Westerners and, with the connivance of the Imperial court, were able to besiege the foreign legations in Beijing for two months until they were themselves savagely suppressed by an international force. This major uprising was much more than an anti-missionary movement, but the missionaries and their converts were among its main victims. Without the missionary presence the crisis in Sino-Western relations precipitated at the turn of the nineteenth and twentieth centuries would have been far less acute.

There seems to be something profoundly quixotic, as well as pro-vocative, about the nineteenth-century missionary effort to convert the Chinese to Christianity. Converting a long established high culture to a new faith can happen, witness the history of Islam, though total military conquest and occupation may be the necessary starting point. In the case of China, Buddhism from India did penetrate deeply without military invasion, but the process took many centuries and was never total, so that it is as accurate to speak of the Chinese conquest of Buddhism as it is to call it (the title of a major book on the subject) the Buddhist conquest of China.[50] The early Jesuit missionaries thought long term and, had the Papacy and their co-religionists been equally patient and flexible, perhaps a Confucianized Christianity might grad-ually have become as widely established in China as a Sinicized Buddhism did. But the aggressively confrontationist nineteenth-century mission-ary thrust, especially as represented by its most evangelical elements, raised far more resistance than acceptance among the people at all social levels, and in all parts of the country. While seeking to convince and convert it was as if it was designed to provoke. Great skill and devotion, as well as genuinely good intentions went into much of the work and, quite apart from the Christian message, the missionary brought many positives to China. Advances in medicine, education, the status of women, the campaign against opium, all owed much to the missionary. But overall it seems impossible not to conclude that for the Chinese the nineteenth-century missionary was more of an irritant, a complicator of an already difficult and troubled relationship, than he was the bearer of good tidings to a people whose world was beginning to be turned upside down. He was, however, an inescapable part of the confrontation between the West and China. Although he presented some of the better elements of the Western message to China, it was the trader and the diplomat rather than the missionary that in the end China was readier to accept.

The West Changes its Image of China

During the nineteenth century the prevailing Western image of China was transformed from what it had been over the first three centuries of sustained contact with the great empire of the far east. From being generally admired as a stable, well-ordered society, providing in many ways a model for Europe itself, China came to be seen by most observers, even by those having some sympathy for it, as an empire in decay, as a stagnant and backward society having nothing of value to offer a dynamic and progressive West beyond some trade and perhaps some souls to be saved. This was, in its way, as distorted an image of China as that which had been shaped by enthusiasts such as Leibniz and Voltaire from the reports of the Jesuit missionaries, or was to be shaped by Western Maoist devotees, as well as by the extreme critics of China in the twentieth century. Getting so large and complex a phenomenon as China into some reasonably accurate perspective has never been easy, even for informed and open-minded observers. China as a model, as stagnating, as heroic, as exotic and quaint, as a threat, brainwashed and regimented, in chaos and turmoil – the West has seen all those Chinas, and may see yet more.

The end of Le Rêve Chinois

The shift away from the respectful, admiring view taken by most (though never quite all) of those who read the Jesuit reports and the writings derived from them, began back in the mid-eighteenth century. It was the British, by then far and away the most involved in trade and diplomacy with China, who led the way in dispelling the visionary view of China. Anson's account of his dealings with Canton officials and merchants had a particularly strong impact, though even before that appeared Defoe had been dismissive of many of the claims being made in praise of China. By the time of the Macartney mission at the end of the century a decidedly cooler approach to China is clearly evident. In his journal Macartney, while praising such features as the smooth operation of the Chinese administrative system as he experienced it, and admiring of such practical achievements as the Grand Canal, also noted that corruption was as prevalent as elsewhere:

> I remember Chou telling me one day that an inundation had swept away a village in the province of Shantung so suddenly that the

inhabitants could save nothing but their lives. The Emperor (who, from having formerly hunted there, was well acquainted with the place) immediately ordered 100 000 taels for their relief, out of which the first (official) took 20 000, the second 10 000, the third 5000, and so on till there remained no more than 20 000 for the poor sufferers. So we find that the boasted moral institutes of China are not much better observed than those of some other countries, and that the disciples of Confucius are composed of the same fragile materials as the children of Mammon in the western world.

More generally, Macartney described the Chinese empire as

an old, crazy, First rate man of war, which a fortunate succession of able and vigilant officers has contrived to keep afloat for these 150 years past, and to overawe their neighbours merely by her bulk and appearance, but whenever an insufficient man happens to have the command upon deck, adieu to the discipline and safety of the ship. She may perhaps not sink outright; she may drift some time as a wreck and will then be dashed to pieces on the shore; but she can never be rebuilt on the old bottom.

There was a certain prophetic quality to these comments, to which Macartney added the confident rider that Great Britain, 'from the weight of her riches and the genius and spirit of her people...would prove the greatest gainer by such a revolution as I have alluded to, and rise superior over every competitor.'[51] China was being seen primarily as a field for Western, especially British, enterprise and gain, less and less as an equal in civilization, no longer a model to emulate and learn from.

Although Macartney's journal was not published at the time, the views he recorded in it reveal the shift in the tide of Western opinion about China. In 1806 his private secretary, John Barrow, did publish an account of the embassy and his travels in China which echoed many of Macartney's judgments, of which Barrow must have been well aware. Barrow's account, like Macartney's, reveals a mixture of respect and rejection, his conclusions being:

that the Chinese have been among the first nations, now existing in the world, to arrive at a certain pitch of perfection where, from the policy of the government, or some other cause, they have remained stationary; that they were civilized, fully to the same extent they now are, more than two thousand years ago, at a period when all Europe might be considered, comparatively, as barbarous; but that they have since made little progress in any thing, and been retrograde in many things: that, at this moment, compared with Europe, they can only be said to be great in trifles, whilst they are really trifling in every thing that is great.[52]

Once the first among nations; now stationary if not retrograde; great only in trifles. These were severe judgments, far removed from those of Leibniz or Voltaire, but a fair summary of what became the common nineteenth-century Western view of China.

In the year before the publication of Barrow's book, Francis Jeffreys, editor of the influential *Edinburgh Review*, had even attacked the Chinese language, which some earlier writers had speculated might be the God-given, pre-Babel tongue of mankind, thus:

There is no instance, we believe, on the face of the earth of a language so extremely imperfect and artificial; it is difficult to conceive how any race of people could be so stupid, so destitute of invention, as to leave it in such a state of poverty... They have gone on for many thousands of years *pittering* to each other in a jargon which resembles the chuckling of poultry more than the language of men, and have never yet had the sense to put their monosyllables together into articulate words.[53]

One final example of early nineteenth-century Anglo-Saxon dismissal of China may be provided by the American essayist Ralph Waldo Emerson, who wrote in his journal in 1824:

The closer contemplation we condescend to bestow, the more disgustful is that booby nation. The Chinese Empire enjoys precisely a Mummy's reputation, that of having preserved to a hair for 3 or 4000 years the ugliest features of the world... Even miserable Africa can say I have hewn the wood and drawn the water to promote the civilization of other lands. But China, reverend dullness! hoary idiot! all she can say at the convocation of nations must be – 'I made the tea.'[54]

We are embarrassingly far from the high praise once bestowed by Leibniz and others on Chinese civilization, or even the respect accorded it by Macartney, though in fairness to Emerson it should be added that in later years he supported the Burlinghame mission and spoke in praise of Confucius and the Chinese respect for education. A range of views can always be found, sometimes in the same person. Nevertheless, the young Emerson's dismissal of China as 'a booby nation' did express a growing trend of thought, especially among Anglo-Saxon observers. The kind of extravagant Western praise of China to be found earlier, and to reappear among 'kowtow-to-Mao' enthusiasts later, virtually disappears during the nineteenth century, though some still saw China through romantic eyes. The French poet Gautier wrote several poems about China, one of which may be prosaically translated as saying 'She whom I love is in China, living with her aged parents in a tower of fine porcelain, beside the Yellow River, among the cormorants. She has retroussé eyes and a foot small enough to hold in the hand.'[55] This kind of exotic willow-pattern China long held an appeal for many Westerners.

A stagnant China takes shape in the West

The perceived stability of Chinese civilization, despotic though its system of government might be, had been counted in its favour by many, such as Oliver Goldsmith in letter XLII of his *Citizen of the World* series, but by the late eighteenth century such stability was coming to be seen as evidence of stagnation, of resistance to the idea of progress that more and more prevailed in European thought. German scholars in particular presented China as the outstanding example of a nation of 'the eternal standstill' which now stood virtually outside the course of world history. Although, like Voltaire in his *Essai sur les moeurs*, the philosopher Hegel began his influential text on world history *The Philosophy of History* with the case of China, he took a very different view of its place in the progress of human society:

> With the Empire of China History has to begin, for it is the oldest, as far as history gives us any information; and its *principle* has such substantiality that for the empire in question it is at once the oldest and the newest. Early do we see China advancing to the condition in which it is found at this day; for as the contrast between objective existence and subjective freedom of movement in it is still wanting, every change is excluded, and the fixedness of a character which recurs perpetually, takes the place of what we should call the truly historical. China and India lie, as it were still outside the World's History, as the mere presupposition of elements whose combination must be waited for to constitute their vital progress.

This is not only a great deal heavier and more opaque than what Voltaire wrote on China (or on anything else), it is also far more dismissive.

For Hegel China may have a long history but it is one that lacks movement, is fixed in character and provides no worthy stimulus or example. Hegel goes on to say of Confucius, whom Voltaire so respected, that though he presented some correct moral sayings 'there is a circumlocution, a reflex character and circuitousness in the thought which prevents it rising above mediocrity.' One would like to have Voltaire's comment on that judgment, as well as on Hegel's own style of writing! Warming to his task, the great German philosopher went on to add:

> The Chinese are far behind in Mathematics, Physics and Astronomy, notwithstanding their quondam reputation in regard to them. They knew many things at a time when Europeans had not discovered them, but they have not understood how to apply their knowledge... The Chinese have, as a general characteristic, a remarkable skill in imitation, which is exercised not merely in daily life but also in art. They have not succeeded in representing the beautiful, as beautiful; for in their painting perspective and shadow are wanting... the Exalted, the Ideal and Beautiful is not the domain of his art and skill. The Chinese are, on the other hand, too proud to learn anything from Europeans, although they must often recognize their superiority.

For Hegel, and the many influenced by him, China clearly was far behind the West in every particular – science, art, philosophy, life itself.[56]

Following Hegel, Marx also saw China as 'vegetating to the teeth of time'. But, observing and commenting on events such as the Opium Wars and the Taiping uprising, which Hegel had not lived to witness, for Marx China was being drawn into the stream of world history which flowed inexorably towards a communist future for all mankind. Writing in 1850, that is eight years after the first of the Western treaties had been imposed on China and two years after the suppression of a number of liberal nationalist revolutions in Europe itself, Marx told his newspaper readers:

> It is an amusing fact that the oldest and most unshattered Empire on this earth has been pushed, in eight years, by the cotton ball of the English bourgeois towards the brink of a social upheaval that must have profound consequences for civilization. When our European reactionaries, on their next flight through Asia, will have finally reached the Chinese Wall, the gates that lead to the seat of primeval

reaction and conservatism – who knows, perhaps they will read the
following inscription on the Wall:

Republique Chinoise
Liberté, Egalité, Fraternité

In short, there was to be no escape from the coming world revolution,
and even conservative China would necessarily be part of it.[57]

China was now being seen by most in the West, including radicals like
Marx, as a backward and recalcitrant society which needed to learn,
through force if necessary, some new lessons. 'That huge, strange looking, amphibious hulk of antiquity' was how *The Times* in 1853 described
China. Hopes that the then active Taiping uprising might establish a
new regime which would be ready to welcome the Christian West and
all its offerings, were soon dashed, and the impatient, dismissive views
which, by the early decades of the nineteenth century had displaced the
earlier Western view of China, emerged very strongly. When a Chinese
speaking English consul, T.T. Meadows, who had made some contact
with the Taiping rebels, published a book in 1856 defending them and,
furthermore, suggesting that there were features of Chinese civilization
that were worth emulation by the West, such as recruiting civil servants
through competitive examinations, his reviewer in *The Times* was
amused rather than impressed. 'According to our loose barbarian
notions the Chinese Empire is an overgrown anomaly' he wrote. 'But
now let the barbarians, meaning the British, henceforth perform the
kotow with their faces in the direction of Pekin, for their interpreter has
come to the Flowery Land and has been enlightened as to the inferiority
of his countrymen.' Meadow's book, the reviewer suggested, was itself
quite Chinese in character, 'quaintly luminous, like a Chinese lantern;
as destitute of proportion as a Chinese picture; and quite as involved as a
Chinese puzzle.' The idea that China had any lessons to impart to the
West was for him a nonsense. 'The geological transformation of the
Earth's surface affords a fair parallel to Chinese advancement. Coal is
made quicker than Chinese ethics, and continents grow while their
philosophers sleep.'[58]

The readers of another widely read English journal were presented
with something rather nastier than the light-hearted condescension
of *The Times* review, when, a year or so later, the second Opium War
began. *Punch* then published 'A Chanson for Canton', its verses
illustrated by a cartoon showing a mandarin flaunting a long pig-tail,
advancing sword in hand, against a willow-pattern background.
The 'Chanson' ran:

JOHN CHINAMAN a rogue is born,
The laws of truth he holds in scorn;
About as great a brute as can
Encumber the Earth is JOHN CHINAMAN.
Sing YEH, my cruel JOHN CHINAMAN,
Sing Yeo, my stubborn JOHN CHINAMAN;
Not COBDEN himself can take off the ban
By humanity laid on JOHN CHINAMAN.

With their little pig-eyes and their large pig-tails,
And their diet of rats, dogs, slugs, and snails,
All seems to be game in the frying-pan
Of that nasty feeder, JOHN CHINAMAN.
Sing lie-tea, my sly JOHN CHINAMAN,
No fightee, my coward JOHN CHINAMAN:
JOHN BULL has a chance – let him, if he can,
Somewhat open the eyes of JOHN CHINAMAN.

Two years later *Punch* had a cartoon entitled 'What We Ought to Do in China', showing a St George-like figure mounted on a noble looking horse and wielding a heavy ball and chain weapon against a nasty looking, forked-tongued and many-clawed dragon. This was published not long after the burning of the Summer Palace, which had indeed shown what the West was capable of doing in China.[59]

It would be misleading to suggest that the mid-nineteenth century British view of China was only such as that displayed by *The Times* and *Punch*. There were many gentler, more tolerant voices, including Cobden's in parliament critical of Palmerston's aggressive foreign policy and mindful of the achievements of Chinese civilization, hence the inclusion of his name in the *Punch* verses. The Positivist writer J.H. Bridges, in an essay on England and China published in a substantial 1866 collection of essays on foreign relations entitled *International Policy*, argued passionately that:

The theory of the intrinsic superiority of the Anglo-Saxon race and of Anglo-Saxon civilization to all other civilizations and races must be uprooted and abandoned... For feelings of dislike, contempt and cruelty must be substituted not merely benevolence and pity, but also a large measure of admiration and respect. The Oriental represents types of civilization in which we ourselves were moulded centuries ago. He is, as it were, the visible incarnation of the Past of Europe, from which the Present has sprung in unbroken filiation…

Bridges and his fellow essayists argued in strongly moralistic terms that societies such as China's – essays on India and Japan were included in the collection – should be valued and respected for their contribution to civilization, even though their current condition was very different from that of Western, particularly Anglo-Saxon, societies. 'We cannot act rightly towards nations whose phase of civilization differs from our own unless we are prepared to understand that phase, and to yield it the due measure of sympathy and respect. To effect this result is one of the highest purposes of the Positivist theory of the history of man', Bridges concluded, following French rather than German theories about the course of history.[60] The British populace, however, never much disposed to embrace large theories, Marxist or Positivist, continued to see China mainly through the eyes of such publications as *The Times* and *Punch*.

Missionary publications, which were many and widely read in Britain at this time, also tended to reinforce a critical view of China and the Chinese. For example, in November 1850, when celebrating the appointment of the first Anglican Bishop to Hong Kong, the journal of the Church Missionary Society published a review of the China mission. After outlining the many difficulties it faced – difficulties which included the nature of the language (invented by the devil to hinder the spread of the gospel, some wit later suggested) and the nature of the Chinese people, addicted to opium, infanticide, idolatry and gambling, the review concluded,

> Alas! there is nothing but moral decay in China. From the sole of the foot to the head there is no soundness, and whatever of actual vice and corruption can originate is to be found there. What need of the Gospel in China! Despised and scorned it will be, but who can doubt the issue?[61]

Such comprehensive condemnation was certainly extreme, but not altogether exceptional. Beyond as well as within missionary circles the moral regeneration of the Chinese people was seen as a necessary part of the salvation of the country. Where earlier Western observers of China had, for the most part, recognized a strong moral base to Chinese society, the nineteenth-century emphasis was upon its perceived vices (vices not unknown in the West) rather than upon the Confucian inculcated virtues. Out of this emphasis was to develop a popular stereotype of the Chinese as not only inscrutable but as devious, cruel and untrustworthy. This was a stereotype I absorbed as a small boy watching Fu Manchu films at Saturday matinees and looking apprehensively at Chinese market gardeners as they clip-clopped past in their horse drawn vans, dressed all in black and concealing, I was sure, long knives in their loose fitting jackets. I stood well back until they were safely past.

By the later nineteenth century China was penetrating the Western popular consciousness much more strongly than had been the case in previous centuries, when interest in the distant empire of the east was confined mostly to the educated elite. Wars, the growth of trade, the opium question, missionary activity and promotion – all these developments heightened awareness of China in Europe. In parts of the expanded Western world that awareness stemmed also from the presence of Chinese immigrants, who came to seek gold or to do the heavy work building railways. Many Chinese, mainly from the south of the country, travelled and settled overseas after the Opium Wars (Article V of the 1860 Convention of Beijing required the Chinese government to permit emigration, and set the conditions for the expansion of the coolie trade). The cultural confrontation created by this emigration to such outposts of Western culture as California and the Australian colonies was often acute. Racist sentiment and Yellow Peril phobias became widespread in these frontier Western societies, and were expressed in restrictive legislation designed to keep out the unwelcome immigrant, as well as in propaganda, pictorial and other, which often matched in awfulness some of the anti-Christian propaganda circulating in China. 'Our people don't want the country filled up with semi-barbarous Pagans who have absolutely no moral principles, and who bring no women but harlots of the lowest grade. The Chinese are simply "hands" imported for temporary use; they are not and cannot become permanent habitants and citizens', wrote Horace Greeley, editor of the *New York Tribune*, while another American writer, the storyteller Bret Harte, published in 1870 some very popular verses, 'The Heathen Chinee' about a card sharper named Ah Sin, part of which ran:

> My language is plain
> For ways that are dark
> And tricks that are vain,
> That heathen Chinee is peculiar,
> Which the same I am free to maintain.[62]

In frontier Western societies popular prejudices against the Chinese ran deep and wide, and often took violent forms.

Over time the Western communities most affected by this Chinese emigration came to value rather than resent the relatively small Chinese presence that survived in them, their Chinatowns adding an element of exoticism to otherwise often drably Anglo-Saxon cities. But during the nineteenth century tensions were often high, and prejudice was widespread within the populace at large. The diaspora of southern Chinese, though welcomed by some Western interests as a source of cheap labour, added a complicating strand to the basic pattern of Sino-Western relations that was being woven in China itself by traders, diplomats and missionaries.

The increased contact forced upon China by the West during the nineteenth century naturally meant that the volume of Western literature about the country – its language and literature, its history and geography, politics and social characteristics – also increased substantially. Missionaries were of course still very numerous among the writers of this literature, but there were now many other reporters and commentators – diplomats and consuls, naval and military men, and travellers such as the botanist Robert Fortune. After learning the language and wandering extensively through the interior of the country collecting plants, including tea seedlings which he took to India in 1851, Fortune wrote several books on his travels within China, and must be added to the short list of those in mid-Victorian England who were still ready to praise China. He wrote in 1847:

> It is hoped that those who have been inclined to form their estimate of the Chinese character from what has been written about the low rabble of Canton will, after perusal of these pages, look with a more favourable eye upon the inhabitants of China when seen from other points of view. China is far more ancient as a nation, and as industrious if not as civilized as ourselves.[63]

But many others, few as knowledgeable about China as Fortune, wrote less favourably.

Chinese studies also began to find a place in European universities, at first more strongly in France and Germany than in the country that had most dealings with China. In fact it seems fair to say that the scholarly study of China was more advanced on the continent of Europe, in Holland and Sweden as well as France and Germany, than in Great Britain until well into the twentieth century, though one major contribution that came from a British source was the full translation, with detailed commentary and in several large volumes, of the basic Confucian classics – the Analects, the Great Learning, the Doctrine of the Mean, and the works of Mencius. This was done by the Scottish missionary James Legge, who received financial assistance from the opium trading firm of Jardine Matheson and linguistic assistance from the Chinese scholar, Wang Tao. In 1876 Legge became the first Professor of Chinese at Oxford, though there had been earlier chairs set up in London and much earlier ones in France and Germany. Legge's assessment of Confucius was very different from that of his Jesuit missionary predecessors however:

> I hope I have not done him an injustice, but after long study of his character and opinions I am unable to regard him as a great man. He was not before his age, though he was above the mass of the officers and scholars of his time. He threw no new light on any of the questions which have world wide interest. He gave no impulse to religion. He had no sympathy with progress. His influence has been wonderful but it will henceforth wane.[64]

This judgment, by a Protestant missionary who was, like the Jesuits, a considerable scholar, is indicative of the tone of much of the literature, at least in English, that appeared during the nineteenth century. Much earlier Western writing on China had been open to stimulation and inspiration from that civilization but, especially by the late nineteenth century, the Western approach to the study of things Chinese emphasized their deficiencies rather than their achievements and possible value to the West. Books and articles with titles such as *The Problem of China* and *China in Decay: the Story of a Disappearing Empire* were published in increasing numbers, and many anticipated that China would soon be carved up among the Powers.

The limits of Western dominance

The partitioning and the absorption of China into other empires did not happen, though various regions of the country came to be seen as spheres of special interest and control for one or other of the main Powers. Great Britain, no longer so pre-eminent in setting the Western agenda in China as it had been, was dominant in the lower Yangzi valley and in the region around Hong Kong and Canton; Germany established its priority on the Shandong peninsula; Russia and Japan competed for control in Manchuria and north China; France, having fought a war with China in 1883–4 over control of Annam, pushed on into the province of the south-west. The United States claimed no special sphere of interest and was the most vocal in support of the principle that foreign enterprise in China should, as far as possible, face an open door – open, of course, to much more than Ricci had hoped for three centuries earlier. With varying degrees of commitment the Powers reluctantly accepted this principle, so that the growing scramble between them for control of trading and investment opportunities in China was contained short of actual conflict. Carving up 'the melon' that China appeared to have become was recognized as likely to be a risky business. The so-called scramble for China might have precipitated war between Western powers earlier than actually happened, and it is worth noting that a British collection of documents on the origins of the First World War begins with a selection on China.[65] That war, when it came, had vast repercussions throughout the world, not least in China, by then no longer the distant, self-contained great empire it had been but a country and people struggling to reshape itself as a great nation state in a world of such states. The West's response to that very different China is the focus for the next chapter.

But to conclude this chapter, let us look briefly again at the two descriptive models outlined at the beginning of Chapter 2, that is the 'da Gama epoch' domination model of K.M. Pannikar and the unevenly rising curve model of Kling and Pearson. Both seem to fit the nineteenth-century record of the West's relations with China fairly well. There can be no question that, between the opium wars and the Boxer uprising, China was subject to very strong Western pressures, amounting at times to what may reasonably be called domination. At the end of the century China's capital was occupied by Western-led forces for a second time, and resident Western diplomats were imposing yet more treaty terms upon a weak and defeated government. Further, European influence on China, cultural as well as political, military and economic, was increasing during the last decades of the century, with Western concepts such as science and democracy beginning to make their way into the discourse and thought processes of younger Chinese intellectuals even though, like the concept of God earlier, new words had to be added to the language to express them. By the turn of the century what was once defined as the 'Westernization' of China, though later the culturally neutral term 'modernization' came to be preferred, seemed to be proceeding apace.

Yet there were always significant limits to the degree of Western control and the extent of Western influence within China, so that both our models need to be applied with some caution and reservation,

as for example when reading Pannikar's judgment that, at the beginning
of the twentieth century,

> China was totally helpless before any kind of foreign aggression. She
> was in a worse state than any country of reasonable size, resources
> and civilization had ever been.[66]

China by 1900 was indeed very weak among the powers of the world,
but not really totally helpless. Its great size, with many regions quite
untouched by the West; its strong sense of a distinctive cultural identity
and of a tradition of imperial political unity; its people's readiness
to resist the Western presence where it was most strongly felt, as shown
in the frequent anti-missionary outbursts and in the Boxer uprising;
an emerging sense of nationalism – all these and other factors served
to check any foreign ambitions to take over and literally dominate the
country. Pannikar's overall model fits his own country, India, far more
neatly than it does China. Asia is not a bloc, and its experience of the
West, the real degree of domination endured, varied considerably.
In this regard East Asia needs to be distinguished from South and
South East Asia, and China's experience of Western imperialism recognized as being in important respects nearer to Japan's than to India's or
Indonesia's. It took China much longer than Japan to work out its
response to the power of the West, but like that country, it never
surrendered its sovereignty, even if at the turn of the century it seemed
it might be forced to do so. And as the study of the Western experience
in India and China by Rhoads Murphey entitled *The Outsiders* demonstrates, the treaty ports of China, even Shanghai, never penetrated the
vast domestic economy of China, or became bases for Western political
control and administration, in the way that cities such as Bombay,
Calcutta, and Batavia-Jakarta did in India and Indonesia.[67] In short,
even when China seemed most prostrate before the West its traditional
strengths remained considerable. Not far into the twentieth century
China began in earnest the long process of pushing the West back. It is
that process of reassertion and redefinition that is explored in the next
chapter.

4
Hither and Thither, in Search of Comfortable Common Ground (1900–2001)

The twentieth century was to see as great a shift in the position of the West in its relationship with China as the nineteenth had seen. It was a shift not back towards the position Macartney had found himself boxed into but towards one on a more equal footing than had ever previously been the case. Both kowtow and the unequal treaty system disappeared into the mists of time. As one would expect, progress towards this new standpoint was uneven, marked sometimes by co-operation and mutual support, as in the opium trade agreement early in the century and in mid-century resistance to Japan during World War II, but at other times by hostility and mistrust on both sides. This hostility and mistrust was at its peak during the conflicts in Korea and Vietnam during the third quarter of the century and, though tempered considerably during recent decades, has never entirely dissipated. But overall a very different pattern of relationship from that which prevailed during the nineteenth century took shape during the twentieth century. China's renewed strength and status was fittingly underlined at its very end by the return to it of the two last outposts of direct Western rule within its boundaries, Hong Kong and Macao.

Over the course of this century 'the West' came to mean preeminently the USA. Although Britain continued to set the tone for much of the diplomacy and for the social life of Westerners in China down to World War II, by mid-century America was taking the lead in setting the direction and parameters of Western policy toward and relations with China as strongly as Britain had done a century earlier. Other Western powers, weakened by the loss of their empires after the two World Wars, did at times follow a different line of policy towards the regenerating central kingdom, Britain for example extending diplomatic recogniton to its new Communist government long before the US could bring itself to do so. But after the Second World War 'the West and China' came to mean mainly the US and China. Well before then, though, China's relations with the world beyond its borders had become far more multi-layered than during the preceding century. However one defines 'the West', its influence on China's development, though remaining significant, was matched by other, non-Western powers, specifically Japan and Russia. Whereas during the nineteenth century the West, with Britain very much in the van, had been able to set the terms on which China was obliged to face the world beyond its traditional tributary limits, by the early twentieth century the balance of external forces and influences at work within China was more complex. Japan became a major player, sharing in, exploiting and ultimately challenging the Western structure of power in China while, after the 1917 revolution in Russia, Marxism, a Western creed in origin but disowned by all the Western treaty powers, was Sinicized by Mao into a modern revolutionary ideology for China. For a time, after the apparent triumph of that ideology in 1949, it appeared that China would reshape itself on a Russian derived Marxist–Leninist model, rejecting Western liberal economic and political models entirely.

Thus, with powerful new influences and forces operating within the Chinese scene – with the Chinese themselves beginning to reorder and integrate anew their state and society after overthrowing their old imperial order in 1911, and with the West itself torn apart by a Great War – the first decades of the twentieth century saw a major shift in the foundations upon which the treaty system had been constructed. The century began with the West apparently absolutely dominant over China – its treaty system firmly and widely in place; its armies in occupation of Beijing; its diplomats once again imposing new obligations on China; its missionaries entering the country in ever larger numbers; its entrepreneurs seeing China as a field for profitable financial investment as much as trade. Yet the relationship shaped and forced upon China by the West during the nineteenth century was in fact far from stable. Although the Old China Hands who were still enjoying their privileged status in the treaty ports might have found it hard to credit (though some did), China was beginning to reorganize itself, to reintegrate as a modern power, ready to relate more freely and openly with the outer world but determined to do so in its own way. This reintegration of China once more into a strong state, internally and externally, is the central fact of twentieth-century Chinese history. The West, like the rest of the world, has had to adjust to this reality. In this chapter I survey some of the main stages in that up and down process of adjustment but, in contrast to the preceding two chapters, focus less on the main Western agents – traders, diplomats, missionaries – and more upon what the Chinese themselves were doing. Quite soon into the twentieth century they began again to set the terms upon which the West had to approach their culture, deeply influenced though that culture had been by its nineteenth-century experience of the West. The history of the West's relations with China during the twentieth century is one of gradual, uncertain and sometimes fearful adjustment to an awakening giant. This chapter is as much about that awakening as it is about the West's role in and response to a greatly changed China.

China Begins to Scramble to its Feet, and the Treaty System to Unscramble (1900–28)

At the very beginning of the century China seemed to be a quite feeble giant, more than ever at the mercy of the treaty powers. During the last months of 1900 much of north China, including Beijing, was occupied by an international force of over 40 000, and the partitioning of the country was a real possibility. The Boxer uprising had indeed proved to be a catastrophe, the word used in the title of one of the most valuable of the many books about it.[1] But it proved also to be something of a catharsis. After it the question became not whether but in what form, how quickly and successfully China would reshape itself as a modernized nation state. This uprising and its aftermath marked a low point, maybe the very lowest point, in the history of Sino-Western relations, though Russia and Japan were deeply involved this time as well as the West. But it marked also a turning point – 'the major turning point of modern Chinese history', according to Mary Wright in her introductory essay to the 1968 collection entitled *China in Revolution: the First Phase, 1900–1913*. 'Rarely in history has a single year marked as dramatic a watershed as did 1900 in China,' she began her essay. 'The weakness laid bare by the Allied pillage of Peking in the wake of the Boxer Rebellion finally forced on China a polar choice: national extinction or wholesale transformation not only of a state but of a civilization. Almost overnight Chinese – imperial government, reformers and revolutionaries – accepted the challenge.'[2]

'Polar' change begins in China, after the Boxer uprising

If we need to nominate a particular 'major turning point' in China's movement away from its traditional past towards its modernizing future then the year 1900 has at least as good a claim as any other that might be nominated – such as 1842 or 1860, marking the imposition of the treaty system and the beginning of the 'opening' of China; or 1911, marking the end of Manchu rule and the replacement of the imperial dynastic system by republican governments claiming their mandate from the people rather than Heaven; or 1949, when the Communist party took control of an already greatly changed China and claimed it had at last enabled it to stand up. After 1900 it does seem true to say that what Wright called 'polar' change was recognized as inescapable by even the most conservative Chinese, including many who had supported the Boxers. Evidence for this is to be found in the Imperial Edict of 23 January 1901, issued technically in the name of the Guangxu emperor but actually by the Empress Dowager, Cixi, who had two years earlier made that would-be reforming emperor a virtual prisoner within the palace. This edict began:

> Now that peace negotiations have commenced the whole system of government must be radically reformed, in the hope that strength and prosperity may gradually be attained. The Empress Dowager has enjoined on Us the necessity of appropriating the good qualities of foreign nations, so that by aid thereof the shortcomings of China may be supplemented, and that the experiences of the past may serve as a lesson for the future.[3]

The Guangxu emperor, in his own independently issued edict of June 1898, which was quoted in the last chapter, had also emphasized the necessity of appropriating the good qualities of other nations, a message now being promulgated by an Empress Dowager who, only a few months earlier, had been encouraging the Boxers to 'exterminate the foreign'. Her 1901 edict went on to reject 'the Kang factor', that is those who had advised the emperor in 1898, thus indicating that there would still be deep disagreement as to how far radical change should go. But that it had to be set in train was, after 1900, no longer an issue. The Boxer phenomenon, catastrophic as it was from one perspective, did serve to help clear the way for such change, promoted now by the dynasty itself as well as by many others hostile to the dynasty. Political as well as cultural revolution was clearly on the way.

Probably the one fact about China's pre-Communist history generally known in the West, apart from the importance of opium in that history, is that there was a Boxer 'rebellion' which resulted in the deaths of many Westerners, especially missionaries. The complex details of the origin, nature and course of that uprising are beyond the scope of this book, but a few comments about it should be made here.[4] It was a movement directed against all evidences of the foreign presence, not just the missionaries and their converts but against railways, telegraphs, diplomats, traders and all Chinese associated with them. The deep undercurrent of anti-foreign feeling in Chinese society that it expressed was brought violently to the surface in north China during 1899–1900 by various factors, most important being the impact of widespread drought and consequent famine. The foreign presence was blamed for this, as in this poster set up in the provincial city of Taiyuan:

> The Catholic church of Jesus deceives our gods, destroys our beliefs in the saints and disobeys the precepts of Buddha, consequently we are now having a famine and other disasters...Rain does not and will not fall, and very soon there will be fighting and killing. If you do not pass on this message from Buddha you will not be able to escape unnatural death. If on the other hand you copy it and give it to another your family will be safe...If you use kerosene you will be punished by the gods.

Another placard posted in Beijing in April 1900 proclaimed that

> The will of Heaven is that the telegraph wires be first cut, then the railways torn up, and then shall the foreign devils be decapitated. In that day shall the hour of their calamities come. The time for rain to fall is yet far off, and all on account of the devils.

The attacks roused by such propaganda included many on missionary outposts well away from the capital, but the heaviest fighting and the greatest number of casualties occurred in the sieges of the foreign concession area of the major treaty port of Tianjin and of the legation quarter in Beijing, as well as of a Roman Catholic cathedral there. In this fighting at Tianjin and Beijing, and along the railway line between the two cities, government troops took a large part, the court issuing a general declaration of war against the treaty powers in June 1900. Many high officials opposed such a policy of support for the Boxers, and took steps to ensure that in the central and southern provinces, where the foreign presence was greatest, Boxer-like disturbances did not occur. The precise number of foreigners killed in the uprising is uncertain, but over two hundred of them were missionaries and their families, while many Russians and Japanese were also victims. By far the greatest number killed were the 'secondary hairy ones', that is Chinese who had converted to Christianity or who served (or were just suspected of serving) foreigners in some way. Some 30000 of these were victims of the Boxers.

The movement has been seen by many as an early expression of Chinese nationalist and anti-imperialist feeling, and this interpretation is understandable, even though the Boxers certainly did not think or express themselves in such modern political terms. With their 'spirit soldier' concepts and their magic rituals, which they claimed conferred invulnerability, they were expressing traditional superstitions derived from popular religious beliefs and from traditional stories and operas, rather than any ideas that can be accurately expressed in modern political terminology. Their objective was to preserve the old, not to bring on the new. But their actions, disastrous though they were, did in fact help bring on the new, so they are rightfully accorded a place in the pantheon of modern Chinese nationalism even if, from a Western standpoint, they seemed merely destructive, reactionary, satanic.

Only north China was infected, if that is the right word, by the Boxer virus, but the whole country was to suffer from it. The international force sent to suppress the uprising, and to punish the towns and officials who supported it, may be seen as a kind of early United Nations exercise, though one far from neutral, in the enforcement of international law as defined and understood by the West. There was no formal treaty power declaration of war against China, but for a second time in less than half a century China's capital was occupied and looted by Western forces. When setting out for Beijing late in July, arriving too late to help raise the siege of the legations but not too late for punitive action, the German contingent of this international force was instructed by its emperor thus:

> No quarter will be given, no prisoners taken. Let all who fall into your hands be at your mercy. Just as the Huns a thousand years ago, under the leadership of Etzel [Attila], gained a reputation by virtue of which they still live in historical tradition, so may the name of Germany become known in such a manner in China that no Chinese ever dare again look askance at a German.[5]

The English use of the epithet Hun applied to Germans during World War I apparently derives from this exhortation, but in 1900 such sentiments, and the actions they prompted, were widely shared in the West. There could be no doubt that China would be severely punished for the temerity of some of its citizens and officials in attempting, so desperately and violently, to overturn the treaty structure the West had imposed on it.

The Protocols to settle the Boxer score with China, laboriously thrashed out between treaty powers deeply suspicious of one another, predictably increased the obligations imposed on China, and mark the high, or low, point of the treaty system. It took nearly a year for these Protocols to be agreed upon. Russia, which had seized the opportunity to occupy much of Manchuria, remained entrenched there until forced to withdraw after defeat in the war with Japan in 1904–5. That such occupation and partitioning of China did not go further in 1900–1 was due in part to the fear that if that was attempted the kind of conflict that soon escalated between Japan and Russia would become general, and no one seemed quite ready for that. The caution and moderation displayed by Chinese officials in central and southern China reassured powers such as Great Britain and the US that the treaty system was still basically secure, and support for 'open door' principles was reiterated, though reluctantly by some of the powers. So China was preserved as a still separate but even more tightly treaty-bound sovereign state, and its ruling dynasty, complicit though it had been in the Boxer troubles, was still recognized as the legitimate government, there being no clear alternative in sight. Things would soon change, but for the present it seemed sufficient just to tighten the screws on the dynasty that had been forced, half a century earlier, to make treaties with the West.

The terms of settlement finally agreed upon between the powers in September 1901 and submitted to on behalf of China by Li Hongzhang, a leading reform-minded official not associated with the Boxers, contained 12 articles, of which the most important provided for:

- An indemnity totalling £67 million, equal to about five times the then annual revenue of the central government, payment to be spread over 39 years at 4 per cent interest and to be secured as a primary charge on the collection of the foreign administered customs. Of this indemnity which, given the course of future world history, was never fully paid out, (unlike the much smaller indemnities imposed after the Opium Wars) approximately 29 per cent was to go to Russia, 20 per cent to Germany, 15 per cent to France, 11 per cent to Britain and $7^1/_2$ per cent each to the US and Japan. Japan had also imposed a sizeable indemnity after its defeat of China in 1895, so that in the early twentieth century all Chinese governments faced a large burden of debt prescribed by formal treaties.

- Punishment by demotion, exile or, in a few cases, death of a number of the high officials judged to have most encouraged the Boxers.
- Suspension of the traditional examination system in 45 cities where foreigners had been killed, which led to the abandonment in 1905 of the whole system and the end of a basic Confucian institution of great antiquity, requiring replacement by a more modern education system.
- The destruction of many forts, and the permanent garrisoning by foreign troops of an enlarged legation area in Beijing, as well as of the line of railway communication between the capital and the treaty port of Tianjin.
- The prohibition, under pain of death, of membership in an anti-foreign society.
- The reorganization of the Zongli Yamen, long spurned by conservative officials, into a full ministry of foreign affairs with high status, as was normal in Western governments.

Other provisions included a requirement for the Chinese government to send envoys to Germany and Japan to make formal apology for the killing of diplomatic representatives of those two countries during the uprising. In addition the German minister was to be commemorated by the erection of a monument on the spot of his death, a monument joyfully demolished by the Chinese after Germany's defeat in World War I. There was more, but that is sufficient to convey the punitive nature of the Boxer settlement. The historian W.L. Langer in his great work *The Diplomacy of Imperialism* (1935) concluded that:

> European diplomats as a whole had no ground for priding themselves on the handling of the Boxer movement and its aftermath. Europe's treatment of China in the whole period from 1895 to 1900 had been devoid of all consideration and of all understanding. The Celestial Empire to them was simply a great market to be exploited to the full, a rich territory to be carved up like a sirloin steak... It is well known that the Chinese government tried to prevent an assault on the foreigners and that it spared the legations, which could easily have been taken. Against this you have to place the merciless looting of Peking by the associated forces after the relief of the legations. It was a chapter of European activity which the Oriental cannot be expected to forget for a long time to come.[6]

A severe judgment, but surely justified. The Boxer settlement displayed the ugly face of Western imperialism in China far more crudely than did the treaties imposed after the Opium Wars.

Some tentative moves towards treaty revision

Yet even at this low point in Sino-Western relations the historical record is mixed and complex. During the Boxer crisis the Western powers reacted with varying degrees of sternness. Though presenting a broadly united front, and certainly determined to preserve the treaty system, 'the West' was not then, nor has it ever been, an absolute monolith in its approach to China. Germany, like the Russians and with some support from the British, had insisted on severe terms and its troops were most active in exacting reprisal. The US was the most moderate, and showed a measure of sympathy for China in its predicament in various ways. It took the lead in advocacy of 'open door' principles, though that was certainly a policy concerned to protect American interests as much as Chinese. Also, a few years after the signing of the final settlement, it returned a large portion of its share of the indemnity payments on condition that the funds received be used to fund scholarships for study in the US. This ideal of helping educate and reform China – of course along Western lines – was, as I argued in the previous chapter, present to some degree in the minds of mid-nineteenth-century British diplomats who were the chief architects of the treaty system. But it was certainly a stronger and more consistent characteristic of US policy towards China throughout the century between the Opium Wars and World War II than it was of any other Western power. This long-standing idealistic and educative element in the US approach to China is important to recognize, since it helps explain the extremes of US reaction to the so-called 'loss' of China to the Communists in 1949, felt by many Americans as betrayal by a people they had, as they saw it, so long sought to help and protect. US policy and actions during and after the Boxer crisis, significantly more moderate and idealistic than those of any other power, helped shape the form that relations between China and the leading Western power of the twentieth century were to take. It is worth adding here that after the Boxer trauma an even greater number of US missionaries went to China, so that personal and emotional involvement with the country became far stronger in the US, both within government and the people generally, than anywhere else in the West. By 1925 over half the approximately 8000 Protestant missionaries in China were American.

Great Britain too was edging towards some softening of its policies towards China, despite having supported the German hard line in the Boxer negotiations. In 1902 a commercial treaty was negotiated which provided for a substantial increase in the tariff rates China might impose on British imports, subject to the abolition of internal tariffs known as *lijin*, a tax which merchants had long held to be a major reason for the failure of their goods to penetrate the China market more effectively.[7] But this concession was subject to other treaty powers with most favoured nation rights agreeing to accept the change, which only the US and Japan were prepared to consider. In addition, the internal tariffs were too valuable to provincial governments for them to accept any move by the central government, with which the treaty had been negotiated, toward abolition. The treaty fell far short of restoring tariff autonomy to China, but was a faltering step in that direction.

This 1902 British commercial treaty also included the following clause:

> China having expressed a strong desire to reform her judicial system, and to bring it into accord with that of Western nations, Great Britain agrees to give every assistance to such reform, and she will also be prepared to relinquish her extra-territorial rights when she is satisfied that the state of Chinese laws, the arrangement for their administration, and other conditions warrant her in so doing.

Thus the principle, if not quite the desirability, of ending extraterritoriality in China, as was currently being done in Japan, was also acknowledged within a year or two of the Boxer trauma by the diplomatic representatives of Great Britain, the power chiefly responsible for the creation of the system. These commercial and legal concessions, limited and not immediately applied though they were, suggest that the treaty system was not being regarded by the British and the American governments as absolutely set in concrete. It must be added though, that most of the beneficiaries of that system, especially the traders and business men in the treaty ports, displayed little inclination to make any concessions to growing Chinese demands for full sovereignty and rights recovery. It was to take a few years yet for real changes in the system to eventuate, and then more by Chinese than Western action.

Change in China gathers pace

Whatever faint stirrings by the West towards some readjustment in its formal relationship with China which may be discerned early in the twentieth century, these were far outmatched by the stirrings within China itself. The three decades between the crushing of the Boxer uprising and the coming to power of the Guomindang saw the rise of a torrent of new political and intellectual forces that was, within another couple of decades, to sweep away the whole Western-devised structure of special status for treaty powers. By mid-century, China was once again defining the terms upon which, and the extent to which, it would deal with the world beyond its borders, including the Western world. The West's own internal divisions, manifested in two great wars within the space of a generation, greatly weakened its capacity to direct China in the manner that it had so strongly asserted during the second half of the nineteenth and into the early twentieth century. But ultimately the treaty system was unsustainable once China, whatever its internal divisions, began consistently and purposefully to set about modernizing itself – as Japan had done from the arrival of Perry's black ships there in 1853. China's size and the basic strengths of its culture were too great for any external power to be able indefinitely to dictate the direction of its development, or the terms upon which it had to relate with others.

At this point it seems appropriate to summarize the main political developments occurring in China between 1901 and 1928. Briefly these were:

- The revolution of 1911 which brought about the end of Manchu rule, despite the efforts of the dynasty in its last years to initiate extensive reforms in government, law, education, the economy, transport and the armed forces.
- The failure, between 1912 and 1916, of the strong man who emerged from that revolution, Yuan Shikai, to set up a new dynasty, with some constitutional trappings, and the concomitant failure of the Guomindang, the republican party founded in 1912 out of the various anti-Manchu revolutionary secret societies centred around Sun Yat-sen, to establish itself as either an effective parliamentary or military opposition to Yuan.
- The slide into warlordism after Yuan's death in 1916, and the virtual collapse for a decade of any effective central power, while the main warlords competed for dominance in the north and the lower Yangzi valley and while the Guomindang gained a small, tenuous base in the south, in temporary alliance with the minor, moderate warlord who held Canton.
- China's rather reluctant entry into the World War in 1917 on the side of the Allies, providing manpower for labour behind the lines in France and the Middle East; but finding that its hopes of gaining some significant benefit from this co-operation were to be disappointed by the Versailles settlement of 1919. This made no reference

to treaty revision and, despite Chinese protests, handed over former German concessions in Shandong to Japan.

- The subsequent outburst of national protest known as the May Fourth Movement, which saw the rapid and widespread growth of a radicalized, strongly anti-imperialist nationalism, demanding full rights recovery, including the ending of extraterritoriality, the restoration of tariff autonomy, and the return to Chinese control of the Western administered concession areas at major treaty ports.

- The emergence of organized political parties, notably a rejuvenated Guomindang which, in close alliance with the fledgling Chinese Communist Party (founded in 1921) and with considerable Russian advice and material assistance provided through the Comintern, acquired its own 'National Revolutionary Army', commanded by Chiang Kai-shek, and thereby the possibility of challenging the larger warlord armies still in control of the main areas of economic and political power in central and northern China.

- The suppression, by sending in British and American gunboats, of an attempt in 1923 by Sun Yat-sen to take control of customs collection at Canton, thus disillusioning and helping prompt him to turn to the Russians for assistance.

- Heavy fighting between the major warlord armies in the north during 1924–5, which resulted in the serious weakening of the power of Wu Peifu, the relatively progressive warlord who had seemed the most likely to be capable of establishing a credible national government centred on Beijing; no other warlord emerged as a possible unifier of the country.

- The death early in 1925 of Sun Yat-sen, the definer of the Guomindang's 'Three People Principles' ideology, that is government to promote nationalism, 'tutelage' style democracy and 'people's livelihood' social and economic policies. Sun had gone to Beijing to attempt to negotiate with the victors over the displaced Wu, visiting Japan on the way and speaking there in strong support of Pan-Asian objectives. His death opened the way for the rise of Chiang Kai-shek to political as well as military leadership of the Guomindang.

- Serious and sustained demonstrations, known as the May Thirtieth Movement, provoked by British police and other forces firing on strikers and demonstrators at Shanghai and Canton in 1925.

- The launching in July 1926 of the northern campaign, on the initiative of Chiang, over the doubts of the Communists with whom the Guomindang was still allied, and the rapid advance of their joint forces to the Yangzi valley and control of key cities such as Shanghai,

Nanjing and Hankou. Serious clashes with Westerners occurred at the latter two cities during this advance.

- The open split in 1927 between the Guomindang and the Chinese Communist Party over the spoils of victory, Chiang winning out since he controlled most of the guns. The consequent purging of the Guomindang led to the withdrawal of Russian advisers and the forcing of the Chinese Communist Party underground.

- The consolidation of Guomindang power in central China and the resumption early in 1928 of the northern campaign, in co-operation with the northern 'Christian' warlord Feng Yuxiang, resulting in the occupation of Beijing, by Feng's rather than Guomindang forces, which were obstructed by the Japanese in Shandong. The hostile warlord Zhang Zuolin retreated to Manchuria, but was assassinated en route and was succeeded by his son, known as 'the Young Marshal', Zhang Xueliang. Despite a general recognition by the end of 1928 of the Guomindang as leading a new national government, its power was more nominal than real in much of the north and west of the country, as well as in Manchuria, though it controlled China's most populated and productive central provinces.

Summing up this very packed political survey, it can be said that by the end of 1928 the danger that China might break up indefinitely into rival warlord-led regions seemed to have passed. China survived as a political unity, even if not yet a strong one, with a growing sense of its national identity in a world of nation states, among whom the main threat now came not from the West but from its Asian neighbour, Japan.

The main point needing to be added is that behind and beyond these complex political and military shifts of power occurring within China between 1900 and 1928 a profound intellectual and cultural revolution was taking place, affecting more and more of China's immense population, especially its urban, educated youth. During these years a tide of new thought rose rapidly, carrying many new ideas and values, challenging Confucianism in all its aspects and proclaiming the need for China to develop a new people, a new kind of citizen who would be committed to national aims going beyond the traditional limits of family, clan, region. Thus, for example, nation-wide boycotts were directed at various times against different offending nations – the US in 1905 over its immigration policies; Japan in 1919 over its claims at Versailles; Great Britain in 1925–6 over its severe response to demonstrations in Shanghai and Canton. These boycotts became an increasingly potent weapon in the struggle for equality of status directed against nations still far better armed than China, the 1925–6 boycott against Britain, for example, bringing Hong Kong's trade to a near standstill for over a year. Language reform was another, very different, aspect of this new thought tide, the *bai-hua* or clear speech movement aiming to replace the difficult, arcane writing of the educated elite with a vernacular form more accessible to the people at large. The beginnings of some emancipation for women was another aspect, as evidenced by the decline in the practice of foot binding and an increasing acceptance of women's presence, and even to some degree of their active participation, in public life. There were many, many sides to this great cultural revolution which was far more spontaneous, productive and fundamental than the Mao-inspired movement later given that title.[8]

By the early twentieth century then the West was facing a China undergoing massive political and cultural revolution. Of course the world at large, the West itself not least, was also undergoing great changes, political and cultural, during these pre- and post-World War I years, but surely no major centre of civilization more profoundly than China. One irony is that its political upheaval was directed in large part against the West, against the still substantial fabric of Western imperialism set up in the nineteenth century, whereas the cultural revolution was inspired in great part by the West, and was pursuing essentially modern values and programmes. It was both a confrontation and a confluence of the two great cultures. So, for example, science and democracy, not to mention nationalism, all concepts central to the development of the modern West, were great catchcries for those riding the crest of this new tide of thought and feeling in China. Beijing university, still barely twenty years old, became a powerhouse for the generation of such ideas. One of its professors, Chen Duxiu, who was soon to help found the Chinese Communist Party, proclaimed in his journal *New Youth* in January 1919, that

> To advocate democracy we have to oppose Confucianism, propriety, chastity, old ethics and old politics. To advocate science we have to oppose old art and old religion. To advocate democracy and science we have to oppose the national heritage and old literature.[9]

There were still many who were less radical and who wished to preserve as much as possible of Confucian values and what they saw as the national essence or heritage, and there were those who argued that science and democracy were as much part of China's tradition as the West's. But all, radicals and conservatives alike, were intent upon restoring China's status, independence and dignity within the wider world they now realized could no longer be kept at a distance. By the time the Guomindang rose to effective leadership of this movement of national regeneration the West had come to accept, to some small degree of its own accord but in larger part under pressure from a Chinese people now very evidently growing in strength and national conscious-ness, that the treaty structure it had forced upon China had to be dismantled and China acknowledged fully as a sovereign equal. That process was not formally completed until the 1940s, but the twenties was the decisive decade. To complete this first section of my chapter on the twentieth century, I turn now to summarize briefly the Western experience of, and response to, this rapidly awakening, changing China.

Treaty revision also gathers pace

To review the diplomatic scene first, even among the more liberal of the treaty powers which recognized that the treaty structure imposed on China by the West during the nineteenth century and reinforced by the Boxer settlement would eventually have to be modified, there was still a determination that the West would be the judge of exactly when the legal, commercial and political standards required as pre-conditions for such modifications were being met. Whether and how soon China would meet them, as Japan was recognized as having done, was still very much an open question in Western minds early in the century. Some saw the reform programme launched in its last years of the old dynasty as evidence that it could not be long, but others, especially among the Old China Hands now resident in substantial numbers in one or other of the many treaty ports, were more sceptical. The stereotype of unchan-ging China, 'the land of the eternal standstill', was still strong. Although the Manchu reform programme included some moves towards legal and other institutional changes, the political uncertainty following the revo-lution of 1911 ensured that for some years nothing much changed in the character of Western relations with China. In fact, diplomatically speaking, down to the twenties China was effectively treated very much as it had been since the mid-nineteenth century. Whatever long term good intentions might have existed in certain Western quarters, the practical bias of policy was to maintain the treaty status quo. Thus, although there was no intervention in 1911 to help save the dynasty from its domestic rebels, as there had been against the Taiping fifty years earlier, the West soon threw its weight behind the least radical of these twentieth-century revolutionaries, that is behind Yuan Shikai rather than Sun Yat-sen and the Guomindang, even though the latter had been quick to assure the powers that they would respect the treaties. In the years immediately following the 1911 revolution the weight of Western policy and influence was upon maintaining the status quo as far as possible, even at the cost of a stronger democracy. A national parliament was elected in 1912 – about as close as China has ever come to a free and democratic national election – but Yuan at once sought to exercise autocratic presidential control over it. Western finance helped him bribe his way to success in this endeavour. When the more democratically inclined Guomindang revolted very ineffectually against Yuan, its leaders, including Sun, were forced to flee but gained no support or sympathy from the West. The treaty system remained securely in place.

It was the 1914–18 World War rather than the 1911 revolution that precipitated some real change in China's diplomatic status. By joining, albeit minimally, the ultimately victorious Allies in August 1917 in the war, China gained the opportunity to revoke the extraterritorial and other treaty rights of German and Austrian citizens. Germany, one of the major treaty powers, had been very prominent in the extraction of concessions and of leases from China, and also in imposing tough Boxer settlement terms, so that its loss of treaty rights, confirmed by the post-war settlement, constituted a significant break in the hitherto united front of privilege in China enjoyed by all the major Western powers.[10] China was, however, not successful in regaining full control of the former German leases and concessions in Shandong. These had been seized in September 1914 by the Japanese, who promised 'eventual' restoration to China. But under a secret arrangement made early in 1917 with the British and French (the US not yet in the war) Japan extracted a promise that her seizure of the German concessions would be recognized in the eventual peace terms. This was a price the European Allies were prepared to pay, at China's expense, for Japanese acceptance of their efforts to get China into the war. It was a classic example of treaty power being exercised by the West (and Japan) in an arrogant and insensitive way. The revelation at Versailles of this secret disposal of Chinese resources, without reference to China's rights and interests, prompted the May Fourth student anti-imperialist demonstrations which rapidly spread nation wide, revealing how different the China of 1919 was from that of 1900 or the Opium War years. A wide spectrum of its people, not just its educated elite, was now aroused by what was felt to be betrayal and humiliation at the hands of the great powers. From this point the Chinese drive to overturn the whole treaty system became irresistible.

It was substantially helped by the actions of another major treaty power, Russia – not exactly a Western power, but one which had participated very fully and profitably in the whole nineteenth-century push into China. The October 1917 revolution there brought to power, though not very securely for some years, an avowedly anti-imperialist Bolshevik government. In July 1919, still expecting world revolution and seeking allies wherever it could hope to find them, its deputy Commissar for Foreign Affairs, Karakhan, issued a declaration unreservedly renouncing the gains made by Tsarist governments in Manchuria, including control of the Chinese Eastern Railway, the Russian share of the Boxer rebellion indemnity and all extraterritorial rights.[11] Subsequent negotiations with various Chinese governments were to reveal that the Bolsheviks, once securely in power, were rather less open handed about giving up certain Russian interests, especially control of the railway. But they did remain ready to renounce the substantial Russian share of the Boxer indemnity, in favour of a fund to promote education in China, and showed no desire to preserve extraterritorial rights for the quite large numbers of Russians resident in China, many of whom were anti-Soviet refugees. Whatever the later qualifications made to the 1919 Karakhan declaration, the new Russian government gained great credit in the eyes of most Chinese, including Sun Yat-sen's, for its readiness to renounce the treaties. This was in sharp contrast to a still generally laggard West, which continued to use the excuse of political instability to justify holding on to the full range of its treaty rights in China, excepting only those for the central European powers defeated in its Great War. But by 1920 war and revolution had in fact opened up substantial cracks in the treaty structure created in the previous century. Pressure was coming not only from the forces of Chinese nationalism but also from Soviet-inspired international communism and, more subtly but ultimately most powerfully, from an expansionist Japan. Though it was numbered among the treaty powers, Japan nursed ambitions in China which ran quite counter to the 'open door' rules that the older Western treaty powers had by and large favoured and followed. The system those powers had so confidently created in the mid-nineteenth century was facing the prospect of disintegration by the 1920s.

For the purposes of a survey text such as this the details of the conferences, commissions, demonstrations and declarations which delivered, if not quite the final *coup de grace* at least some further mortal blows to the treaty system during that decade may reasonably be passed over. The major Western powers, while by now acknowledging the principle of treaty revision, continued to stall for time, for example at the Washington Conference in 1921–2 setting up commissions of enquiry into extraterritoriality and tariff autonomy rather than acceding to Chinese pressure for the more or less immediate restoration of rights. But the tide of nationalist feeling in China soon overtook such tactics. Even discredited warlord governments in Beijing were disinclined to await the deliberations of foreign-dominated commissions. When new European governments created by the Versailles settlement, such as Poland and Czecho-Slovakia, negotiated commercial treaties with China they were not accorded extraterritorial rights, and in 1926 long standing treaties made with some of the lesser powers, such as Belgium and Spain, were abrogated by Beijing-based governments.

Meanwhile the strength and confidence of the Guomindang based in the south was growing apace, and the success of its northern campaign meant that by the end of 1928 the excuse that China's political division and instability justified holding on to special treaty rights was becoming less acceptable. Serious clashes with Western, especially British, forces occurred at Hankou (modern Wuhan) and Nanjing in the course of the northern campaign, some foreign lives were lost and troops and gun-boats sent in. But British policy shifted decisively at the end of 1926 by undertaking to no longer insist on the restoration of a strong central government as a precondition for negotiation over treaty rights. It also surrendered administrative control over concession areas in two Yangzi river ports, Hankou and Jiujiang, the beginning of the process of Chinese recovery of Western-controlled enclaves that was to be com-pleted at the end of the century with the return of Macao, Kowloon and Hong Kong. Once in power, after the success of its northern campaign, the Guomindang also quickly asserted tariff control, but did not attempt immediately to take over full control of other major treaty port conces-sion areas, such as the International Settlement in Shanghai, where a foreign resident volunteer defence force was created and substantial military and naval forces were concentrated. In fact, although enjoined by the sacred text of Sun Yat-sen's will to bring about the abolition of the unequal treaties as soon as possible, during the thirties the Guomindang proved ready to temporize over control of the major con-cession areas of Shanghai and Tianjin, hoping that continued Western rights in them would help curb growing Japanese aggression. Thus a sort of remnant half-life remained into the thirties for the Western treaty system, but it was clear by the end of the twenties that its days were numbered.[12]

Summing up the diplomatic story for these crucial years in the history of the Western presence in China the American journalist-historian Nathaniel Peffer wrote in 1931:

> The part of the Western world in determining the future of China has been scaled down almost beyond recognition in the last decade.... Today for all practical purposes China has recovered sovereignty. It is not actually, literally independent, for there are still derogations on its sovereignty to which no independent nation submits. But so much has already been regained and so strongly is the tide running that unless China is torn asunder by its own centrifugal forces it is almost astronomically certain that the whole complex of foreign privilege, special position and entrenchment on domestic concerns will be wiped out.... the whole system of treaties which bound fetters on China for almost a hundred years is being abolished in fact, if not in diplomatic formality.

The title of Peffer's book was *China: the Collapse of a Civilization*, by which he did not mean the collapse of China as a culture and power in the world but simply of the distinctive identity that, as he saw it, had signified China for nearly three thousand years. By the early twentieth century, he argued it was a civilization changing in unprecedented fashion. He concluded his book by asking:

> What happens when two civilizations as widely separated in space and time and content as the Chinese and the Western meet, conflict and merge? Can a race as old as the Chinese violently swerve from a course deeply grooved in the passing of a hundred generations and launch itself on another without losing itself? Can a race, which has lived much and may be spent, have a regeneration? They are the questions. The answers must be given by the event – in fifty years perhaps, more likely a hundred, and maybe two hundred. But by the answers, whenever given, the future of the whole world will be moulded.[13]

Seventy years on from Peffer we can have little doubt that China has 'regenerated', has launched itself on a new course without 'losing itself'. But the question what that means for the future of the world remains.

Western reactions to a changing China

The reform programme initiated by the Manchu dynasty in its last years over the first decade of the twentieth century had prompted many

Westerners before Peffer to speculate what the regeneration of China might mean for the rest of the world. In 1904 the American A.J. Brown expressed a decidedly apprehensive view in his book *New Forces in Old China: An Unwelcome but Inevitable Awakening.* He found:

> something appalling in the spectacle of a nation numbering nearly one-third of the human race slowly and majestically rousing itself from the torpor of the ages under the influence of new and powerful revolutionary forces... Yesterday Chaldea, Egypt, Syria, Babylon, Persia, Greece, Rome! Today England, Germany, Russia, Japan, the United States. Tomorrow what? What indeed, if not some of these now awakening nations! It is by no means impossible that some new Jenghiz Khan or Tamerlane may arise, and with the weapons of modern warfare in his hands and these uncounted millions at his command, gaze about on the pygmies that we call the Powers.[14]

The 'Yellow Peril' syndrome was clearly taking shape in many Western minds by the early twentieth century.

One who took a more positive, less apocalyptic view than Brown was Lord William Gascoyne-Cecil, who visited China in 1907 and again in 1909, on the second occasion as the representative of an Oxford–Cambridge committee set up to help establish a university in China. Yale and Harvard universities in the US undertook similar projects. As one would expect for a man of such title and connections Lord Gascoyne-Cecil met with many highly placed people, both Chinese and Western, whose views, as well as his own, he reported in his book *The Changing Chinese.* In its first chapter he asked 'What has awakened China?' The less appreciated factor he thought was Christianity, the larger and more obvious influence the new national movement. 'China is now progressing', he wrote. 'Young China believes intensely in progress with an optimistic spirit which reminds the onlooker more of the French pre-Revolutionary spirit than of anything else.' Perceptively, he also emphasized the importance for China of the Japanese model. Their recent military success against the Russians clearly demonstrated that there was

> no essential inferiority of the East to the West... With Japan as a successful example and with the threat of national extinction and foreign domination before them the Chinese can never give up the effort, and whatever the result may be I think one may assert without rashness that not only will it fundamentally alter the whole of China, but through China affect the whole world.[15]

A good number of books and articles discussing China became available to the English reading public from this time, many recognizing that great changes were afoot and speculating one way or another as to the outcome.

By no means all these observers of early twentieth-century China were as hopeful as the reverend Lord Gascoyne-Cecil, especially among the by now quite substantial numbers of more or less permanently resident foreigners in the treaty ports, particularly Shanghai. Among Western foreign residents, the British set the predominant social and political tone, and their imperial presumptions flourished well into the twentieth century. Their expectations of China and the Chinese remained generally low. *What's Wrong with China?* and *China: the Pity of It* were the kind of titles such residents published under.[16] A recent fine study of *Britain in China* by Robert Bickers shows that these residents, described by a contemporary as 'the spoilt children of empire', mostly clung as tightly and for as long as they could to their treaty-based privileges. Bickers is also the joint author of an article about a sign stating 'Dogs and Chinese Not Admitted' which was said to have been set up by the British-dominated Municipal Council at the entrances to their parks. The article shows that no such brutally direct phrase ever appeared in any officially sanctioned sign, though the 1903 Regulations did include the following rules:

1 No dogs or bicycles admitted . . .

5 No Chinese are admitted except servants in attendance on foreigners.

The 1917 Regulations laid down similar rules until, reflecting the changed political balance, the park was opened to the fee paying public in June 1928. Thus the sign as commonly quoted, and still firmly believed in by most Chinese, is a myth. But, as so often, myths and legends can override the historical facts and may (though as a historian I wince to admit it) sometimes get closer to the heart of the matter than any strictly accurate factual account. Chinese as well as dogs were generally excluded from Shanghai's parks until 1928, a small but revealing sign of continuing Western racial and cultural presumptions of superiority. As the authors of this article conclude:

> clarifying the empirical facts concerning the infamous notice does not necessarily invalidate basic assumptions about the history of the International Settlement, including a conviction that Chinese residents of this foreign enclave had good reason to feel aggrieved at the treatment they received from the Shanghai Municipal Council.[17]

Real or not, the 'no dogs or Chinese' sign accurately reflected one side, the underside, of a long prevailing Western, and especially Anglo-Saxon, view of China.

The Western racism apparent in the rules that governed entry into Shanghai's parks spread far beyond that city, which for many Westerners symbolized China. A 1984 study of Western views of China during the early Republican period concluded that 'There is little doubt that the dominant popular view of China during the first twenty-five years of this century was influenced by racism and ethnocentrism.'[18] As ever, attitudes varied. Among the favourable writers was the philosopher Bertrand Russell, who lectured in China during 1920 and wrote, in his usual vigorous style, a book entitled *The Problem of China* in which he praised much in China, almost in the manner of Voltaire, while criticizing Western values and policies. 'The Chinese are gentle, urbane, seeking only justice and freedom. They have a civilization superior to ours in all that makes for human happiness', Russell wrote. About the same time H.G. Wells was also writing in his *Outline of History*, that 'no nation in the world today has such a universal tradition of decorum and self restraint.'[19]

But the general Western view of China at this time was shaped less by writers such as Russell and Wells as by Arthur Sarsfield Ward, the real name of Sax Rohmer who began publishing his popular Fu Manchu stories in 1913. The author asked his readers to

> Imagine a person tall, lean and feline, high shouldered, with a brow like Shakespeare and a face like Satan, close shaven skull and long magnetic eyes of true cat green. Invest him with all the cruel cunning of an entire Eastern Race, accumulated in one giant intellect, with all the resources of science past and present, with all the resources of a wealthy government – which however, has already denied all knowledge of his existence. Imagine that awful being and you have a mental picture of the yellow peril incarnate in one man.

Within a few years the reader's mental picture of Fu Manchu would be filled out by film versions of this subtle, sinister figure, who became for many the early twentieth-century embodiment of 'the heathen Chinee'. 'Rohmer's method was to equate evil designs with the Chinese', wrote Jonathan Utley in an essay on American views of China. 'When confronted by a diabolical plan worked out in great detail and much intricacy he would comment on how "oriental" it was. In this way it was not necessary to believe the plot of the novel to absorb the stereotypes of the evil Chinese.'[20] Such images and stereotypes were certainly widespread, though there were also less demonized popular images, such as Earl Biggers' clever Hawaian-Chinese detective Charlie Chan, whose exploits were serialized in *The Saturday Evening Post*. As well there were popular musicals such as *Chu Chin Chow*, which somehow set Chinese among Ali Baba and the forty thieves in Baghdad. A 1927 study on the interpretation of the Far East in modern French literature complained of 'the literary charlatanry' evident in the presentation of Chinese subjects on the French stage, soberly noting that

> Since the Great War pieces of this character still seem popular with the managers of Parisian theatres. It is perhaps quixotic to attack the literary conventions which annexed China years ago to the fairyland of Arabian Nights. However, attention must be drawn to the obstacle which these pseudo-Chinese extravaganzas present to the correct understanding of Chinese civilization ... [21]

The Western image of China during these years seems in fact to have been something of a muddle, reflecting both a long tradition of exoticising the mysterious East and the confusion many felt about the course of contemporary Chinese politics. China was, and is, just too large and complex to be credibly contained within one frame of reference, but a tendency to mix the sinister and evil with the exotic and mysterious has marked much of the Western perception of China.

Missionary ups and downs

To conclude this section on the early decades of the twentieth century something must be said about the fortunes of the Christian missionary during these years. They were mixed. Latourette begins the first of the eight chapters dealing with the years 1901–26 in his history of the missions in China by observing that 'the rising tide of nationalism was to make the close connection of the Christian enterprise with the aggressive imperialism of the Occident a handicap to the missionary and to the Chinese', yet at the same time, 'Never before in the entire history of the Church had so large a body of non-Christians been physically and mentally so accessible to the Gospel.' The number of converts, though still only a tiny percentage of the total population, increased substantially – the numbers of Roman Catholic baptized rose from 720 540 in 1901 to 1 431 258 by 1912 and to 2 244 366 by 1924; Protestant communicants rose from approximately 85 000 in 1900 to 235 303 by 1914 to an estimated total Protestant community by 1922 of 806 926. Missionary numbers also grew substantially – in the case of Protestant missionaries from 3445 (including 1038 wives and 964 single women) in 1905 to 8158 by 1925, and the number of societies in the field from about 60 in 1900 to 130 by 1919.[22] Most promising for the missionary was that early in the century there appeared to be greater interest in the Christian message among educated Chinese than had ever been the case during the nineteenth century. The search for the secret of Western wealth and power led at least some highly educated Chinese to look to Western religion as holding part of the answer. As indicated when quoting from Lord William Gascoyne-Cecil above, graduates from Western universities, such as Cambridge and Oxford, Harvard and Yale, sought to help in this search, as did the YMCA, which entered the Chinese mission educational field strongly during these years. But the scholar-elite and student movement of the new China did not long sustain much interest in Christianity. By the twenties they were influenced more by Marxism, or by the sceptical rationalism of a visiting lecturer such as Bertrand Russell, than by the missionary who, in the midst of the rising tide of nationalism was more and more seen as an agent of imperialism, even though many missionaries had become critical of the unequal treaty system and were far less culturally aggressive than their predecessors had been. The missionary movement in China, though still strongly evangelical, had become more flexible in its approach to its work, putting considerable emphasis on education, medical and other social work designed to do more than simply convert the Chinese. There was also a trend toward the indigenization of the leadership of the Church in China, more within the Protestant than the Roman Catholic missions.

But all this could not protect the Christian church and its agents in China against the nationalist attack on the treaties, so that the exposed missionary, though not subjected to Boxer scale attacks, suffered severely during the advance of the Guomindang and Communist forces northward during 1926 and 1927. The middle of 1927 'found Protestantism in China in the worst plight in its history', wrote Latourette at the end of his great survey account:

> It was indeed much more badly off than was Roman Catholicism. Most of the missionaries were out of the interior and a majority had left the country. Anti-Christian agitation was widespread and actual persecution frequent. The loss of life and property was by no means as great as in 1900 but it was more widespread, and the prospect for an early restoration of orderly government seemed more remote. Nationalist sentiment was such that the missionary could not expect

to recover his former status in the Church, nor his privileged position in the country.[23]

This, broadly, was the way things were to continue to be for the Western missionary in China. Although a Christian church was to survive, grow and gain some prominent converts, such as Chiang Kai-shek in 1928 (in large part as a pre-condition set by her mother for winning the youngest of the Methodist Soong sisters as his bride), the role of the Westerner in leading and directing the fortunes of the Christian church in China, whether Catholic or Protestant, was never to be as great as it had been down to the crisis years of the mid-twenties.

By then Western power and privilege in China was clearly in retreat. The treaty system had not yet quite passed and in a few favoured enclaves, such as the International Settlement in Shanghai, might seem secure still, but its days were clearly passing. The question by the thirties became on what terms the West would henceforth relate to China, terms which it was clear the Chinese rather than the West would determine. But first the Japanese would make a strong bid to take the lead in East Asia, including China, and to greatly reduce, if not utterly destroy, Western power there. In this they were to be ultimately checked by the rising dominant power of the West, the United States.

Together on the Road to Pearl Harbor, and Beyond (1928–49)

The twenty odd years of Guomindang leadership in China saw the US emerge as the major shaper of Western relations with that country as decisively as Great Britain had been in the middle and later decades of the nineteenth century. Indeed, from World War II on the history of Western relations with China becomes basically the history of the efforts of the US to define its role in and attitude towards China. The rest of the West, though still very involved and anxious to share in any potentially profitable development, played less and less of a major role. Yet for all its great power, facing a very different China, the US has never been able to dictate the terms of its relationship to anything like the degree Britain had once been. Not, it should be added, that the approach of the US to China in the mid-twentieth century was of the same order as that of the British in the nineteenth-century heyday of empire. By the twentieth century it was ready (as were the British also by then) to give up rather than extract special rights, and to fight with rather than against the government of China. These were years of co-operation, often strained, rather than of confrontation. But they were also years of apparent failure. Certainly Japan's ambition to dominate China and virtually drive out the West from the whole of East Asia was defeated by 1945, but the China that emerged a few years later seemed hardly more friendly than a Japanese dominated East Asia would have been. *The China Tangle, America's Failure in China, How the Far East Was Lost, Retreat from China* – these are typical titles of books examining Sino-Western relations during these years, and such titles seem to resonate on well beyond mid-century.

But for the long perspective, wide-screen approach adopted in this book words such as 'failure' and 'lost', and metaphors such as 'tangle', may be said to mislead as much as enlighten. The West never possessed China, and about all that could be said to have been lost in 1949, with the collapse of the very flawed and difficult Guomindang government with which the US had by then become closely associated, were unrealistic expectations as to what future relations with a China under that government might be. They would certainly have been very difficult, as of course they were to be under the post-1949 Communist government. Both Guomindang and Communist, Chiang and Mao, were fervent nationalists, determined to see China stand up to its full stature in the post-war world, and to sweep away all vestiges of foreign domination over China. Both were determined, too, that China should not be taken for granted as an ally by any other power, as Russia soon found out from Mao. To its credit the US had long shown itself, even if at times very uncertainly and inadequately, to be the Western power readiest to help China achieve full equality and sovereignty in the world. It failed to keep in power the particular government that it favoured but, by comprehensively defeating Japanese imperialist ambitions, it helped create the conditions in which China, whether under Guomindang or Communist leadership, could indeed stand up as a fully independent sovereign power. Given the basic geopolitical realities of the region and the fundamental strengths of China no doubt that would have eventually come about even had the Japanese empire not been so soon overthrown. But that it happened when and as it did owed much to American power and goodwill. In that larger sense American policy toward China did not fail, even though it did not achieve all it hoped for.

Seeking a new order for East Asia

The main problem facing the West in China during the first decade of Guomindang ascendancy was to determine what sort of internationally recognized system would replace the treaty-based imperialist order which was so clearly on its last legs. A leading historian of twentieth-century diplomacy in East Asia, Akira Iriye, posed the issue thus:

> Granted that the role of the US [for this read Western] in the East Asian crisis was and had to be limited, there still remained the question of what shape the future of Asia should and would take... Would American [Western] interests be best served by a strong Japan dominating the whole of East Asia, or by an Asia made up of equal independent states, or by somehow freezing the status quo? Should stability in Asia, obviously a pre-requisite for economic activities as well as for peaceful relations among peoples, be dependent on the continued existence of Western colonial empires, on a balance of power maintained among them or between some of these on the one hand and Japan on the other, or on Japanese or Chinese hegemony? Basically, how was Asia to be related to the rest of the world?[24]

Relating to Japan became the crucial issue for the West in Asia by the 1930s, and the main determinant of the character of its relationship with China. During the twenties Japanese policies towards both China and the West were relatively moderate and co-operative. For example, at the Washington Conference of 1921–2, and again at the London Naval Conference in 1930, Japan had accepted, not without much internal debate, a proportional limitation on its naval forces. It also negotiated the restoration to China of some of the former German concessions in Shandong and, like the West, showed a readiness to look at treaty revision, including the restoration of tariff autonomy to China. In the mid-twenties its government adopted a more moderate, less alarmist attitude to the advance of Guomindang power in south and central China than did Western governments. Under the influence of the liberal, international-minded foreign minister, Shidehara Kijuro, these were years when it seemed that Japan, while still claiming some special interests and rights in Manchuria, was ready to co-operate with China and the other major treaty powers to establish peaceably a new mutually agreed pattern of relations. Although there were plenty of critics within Japan of Shidehara's policies, and although in July 1927 the doubtfully authentic 'Tanaka memorial', setting out a series of steps for the aggressive expansion of Japan's empire, was published, during the 1920s the settlement and containment of Japan's interests without serious conflict with either China or the West seemed possible.

That, however, was not the way things developed. In the thirties the ultra-nationalists, the militarist minded 'double patriots', set the direction of Japanese policy, at times in defiance of, but as often with the support and encouragement of their governments. Liberals such as Shidehara were more and more eclipsed, if not assassinated. In September 1931 the Japanese armed forces stationed in South Manchuria, the Kwantung army, seized control of the province, driving out the semi-autonomous Manchurian government, which was seen as having become too co-operative towards the Guomindang. When the League of Nations, after a mildly critical commission of enquiry, voted not to recognize their client state of Manchukuo, set up in 1932 with the still surviving last emperor of China, Puyi, as its first and only emperor, the Japanese walked out of the League. Pushing beyond Manchuria into north China and setting up more puppet regimes there, a clash with Chinese forces at the Marco Polo bridge near Beijing in July 1937 was escalated, as much by the government as by the armed forces, into a general war against China. By December the Guomindang was forced to retreat from its capital at Nanjing, first to Hankou and then to Chongqing deep in the western interior, where it held on with US and some British aid until the final victory over Japan in August 1945. Japan, although it talked officially only of a China 'incident', was in truth at war with China from 1937 on, occupying its major cities, including the treaty ports, to the increasing discomfort and insecurity of Westerners residing in them.

In March 1940 a 'Reformed National' puppet government was set up in Nanjing, headed by the high level Guomindang figure Wang Jingwei, who had been at Sun Yat-sen's bedside in 1925 and had transcribed his will. The Japanese hope was that Chiang Kai-shek too would eventually come to terms, though at first they refused to negotiate with him at all. By the late thirties the situation in China had changed dramatically from what it had been in the twenties, when it had seemed reasonable to hope that by negotiation the West, Japan and China could between them establish a stable relationship, an agreed new order in the East Asian region based on one or other of the alternatives spelled out by Iriye as quoted above. A major sticking point to such a peaceably negotiated outcome was Manchuria, a region which raised the question what exactly were the territorial limits of China and of legitimate Chinese sovereignty in much the same way as Taiwan does today. Any attempt to explain the course of events that led China, Japan and the West to protracted war between mid-1937 and August 1945, with Russia entering in its last week, must give considerable attention to the competing aims these powers had for this region, and I do this over the next few pages.

The problem of Manchuria

Today the map of China firmly embraces Manchuria, as well as much of Mongolia, Xinjiang and, somewhat more controversially, Tibet. This map is essentially the creation of the Qing dynasty, which had originated in Manchuria from where, in the mid-seventeenth century, it had advanced to conquer China 'within the wall', subsequently extending its control over the extensive non-Chinese populated regions bordering China proper to the north and west. The Qing dynasty was much the most successful of all Chinese dynasties in establishing firm control over these traditionally difficult Central Asian regions. The Chinese nationalists of the early twentieth century who overthrew this dynasty, though vigorously anti-Manchu, did not hesitate to lay claim to the full extent of its empire, upon which the Qianlong emperor had looked out so complacently when dismissing Macartney. He did so from a tent in the heart of the hunting homeland from which his imperial forefathers had come, and certainly did not think of that homeland as being Chinese, even though it was part of his empire. In fact Chinese migration and settlement into the central and northern reaches of the territory was then forbidden, although there had long been a Chinese 'pale' in its southern parts. The Manchu objective was to keep the extensive pasture and forested regions, which covered most of central and northern Manchuria, as a preserve to which they could periodically retreat, especially in the summer heat, and there keep up their traditional, very un-Chinese hunting and military skills.

By the later nineteenth century several developments had occurred to disrupt this Manchu centred and controlled scenario. One was the steady Sinicization of the whole region. Despite the prohibition against movement northward, the great growth of population going on in China throughout the years of Manchu rule created an irresistible push of settlers into any border areas adaptable to Chinese style settlement, and central Manchuria was such an area. Demographically the whole region became more and more Chinese, so much so that by the early twentieth century Manchu had virtually disappeared as a living language, save in the most remote parts. Further, while the Chinese were moving steadily northwards the Russians were moving rapidly eastwards. They had gained extensive territories by the treaties of 1858–60, enabling them to reach the Pacific and establish an insensitively named naval base, Vladivostok (Lord of the East), to which they began building a railway by 1892. The Russian strategic interest in Manchuria by then was twofold – to gain a more direct route for the railway across its northern expanse, and to gain a warm water port on its southern Liaodong peninsula. In its last years the declining Qing dynasty was obliged to make both these concessions and allow the Russians to build the Chinese Eastern Railway in northern Manchuria and have naval access to Port Arthur in the south. As already noted, the Boxer crisis made the possibility that Manchuria would be totally absorbed into the Russian empire, as Siberia had been, very real.

But Japan, the third main player in this complicated scenario, blocked such an outcome. Japan itself had been a victim of Russian pressure in 1875, when it was obliged to acknowledge Russian sovereignty over the whole of the island of Sakhalin, and again in 1895 when it was obliged, by the intervention of Russia backed by Germany and France, to give up the possession, agreed to by China as part of the treaty settlement of its disastrous war with Japan over Korea, of the Liaodong peninsula in south Manchuria. That triple intervention seared the Japanese consciousness deeply, making it a matter of national pride not to again give way to intervention from any third party in its dealings with China. The US was not directly involved in this 1895 diplomatic pressure on Japan, but it may be counted as an early milestone on the road to Pearl Harbor, helping explain Japan's intransigence in the face of US or other foreign intervention on behalf of China in the thirties. Rapidly modernizing and learning many Western techniques, including forceful imperialist diplomatic methods, Japan was determined to protect and sustain its developing but very vulnerable new economy by securing resources and markets on the mainland of Asia, beginning with Korea and Manchuria, then to China itself. In 1904–5 it went to war with Russia over control of Manchuria, the US then entering the debate significantly as the mediator of the treaty of Portsmouth which concluded that war. This treaty transferred to Japan all Russian leases and rights in south Manchuria while guaranteeing continued formal Chinese sovereignty there. Like the other Western powers, the US had then only minimal trading and investment interests in the region but, aware of its great natural resources, was concerned to maintain the 'open door' principle there as elsewhere in China. The maintenance of an open door for trade and investment and of the administrative sovereignty of China became, more strongly and consistently than for any other outside power, the cornerstones of US policy in China right down to the outbreak of war with Japan in 1941. However worthy in themselves – and there was a great deal of self-interest in the open door policy – they were in the eyes of some American critics, such as the diplomat George Kennan, virtually impossible aims to realize fully in the political context of the time, especially for Manchuria. Pursuit of them guaranteed tension, potential conflict.

To continue this overview of the problems that Manchuria posed in the early twentieth century for the powers interested in its fate – that is Nationalist China, seeking to preserve the full extent of its inherited empire; Japan, claiming special needs and rights in the whole region; Russia, forced to retreat from the south but hovering ominously still in the north; the West, in partial political retreat within China but seeking to preserve as much as possible of its economic stake there, including the potential of Manchuria – the local population should be added to the equation. As noted it had become predominantly Chinese, but a frontier kind of Chinese, exposed to extensive Russian and Japanese influences and seeing their land as to some significant degree distinct from China south of the wall. There were about thirty million of them by the thirties, including a million or so Japanese and Koreans, plus many thousands of Russians in cities such as Harbin. However, though some wished and fought for it, a genuinely independent Manchuria was an unlikely prospect. Incorporation into either the Russian or the Japanese empires, or the creation of a puppet state such as the Manchukuo Japan did set up, were more likely outcomes. But, given that it had long been ruled from Beijing, and given also that it was readily accessible from China and was overwhelmingly settled by Chinese, Manchuria was most likely eventually to be incorporated into modern nationalist China, as it was after 1949. The geopolitics of the region clearly pointed in that direction. During the first half of the century, however, the political fate of the region remained very uncertain. Control of it became a major issue between China, Russia and Japan, with the West an interested onlooker, unsure how far and in what way to become involved. There are parallels here with the still current problem of Taiwan.[25]

With the defeat of Russia in the war of 1904–5 and its international isolation after the Bolshevik revolution, and with the collapse of Manchu rule in 1911–12 and the subsequent decline of China including Manchuria into warlordism, Japan was able during the first decades of the twentieth century to establish itself as clearly the major player in the area. The question was by what rules it would play – its own, or rules agreed upon with the other interested, highly competitive, players? The seizure of Manchuria by units of the Japanese army in 1931, followed by its walk out from the League of Nations in 1933, made it clear that by then Japan was determined to set its own ground rules, not only for Manchuria but for China too. Japan became ready to define and to carve out what it called a Greater East Asia Co-Prosperity Sphere, extending to South East Asia and the islands of the western Pacific, an Asian sphere in which Western activity, as well as Russian, would be severely restricted if not excluded. If the Japanese had been successful in this ambitious project then something like the Chinese-centred hegemony that the West had faced in the pre-opium war years might have been recreated in the mid twentieth century, with Japan rather than China as its controlling power. Because of its size, China would be essential to it, but a China shaped to suit Japanese rather than Western interests.

Could China have joined forces with Japan against the West?

The Guomindang had always had close associations with Japan. Many of its leaders, including Sun Yat-sen and Chiang Kai-shek, had lived, studied and plotted there, first against the Manchus and then against Yuan. Sun, though for many years more strongly influenced by and hopeful of the West, became in his later years greatly disillusioned at Western failure to support him, and so turned more to Russia, but also to Japan, in his struggle to regenerate China. In a lecture given at Kobe just a few months before his death Sun called on Japan, as 'the first nation in Asia to completely master the military civilization of Europe', to lead a united front against the West. He ended by asking, to the cheers of his audience: 'Now the question remains whether Japan will be the hawk of the Western civilization of the rule of Might, or the tower of strength of the Orient. This is the choice which lies before the people of Japan.' In a second lecture Sun, in typically idealistic terms, exhorted Japan, as 'China's younger brother', to help make it free, and urged that the two East Asian nations live as brothers in the same family.[26] Despite the choice Japan actually made in the thirties there always remained within the party Sun had founded a significant number ready to consider collaboration with Japan. These included his close associate and protégé, Wang Jingwei.

But by the 1930s Japan's methods of advancing its claims inevitably aroused strong Chinese resistance and anti-Japanese feeling, so that compromise and collaboration with it, as Wang and a good many others were ready to attempt, came to be seen by most Chinese as traitorous rather than possibly realistic. Nevertheless, had Japan advanced its claims upon China less aggressively and brutally, and not overreached itself in 1941 and brought America decisively into the equation, some kind of Sino-Japanese collaboration might well have eventuated, at least for a time. Then the West which, uninvited and unwanted, had forced its way into the once self-contained world of East Asia might have been again confined to its outer limits. Such an attempt to create a twentieth-century version of a self-sufficient East Asian world was probably impossible to achieve and sustain, given the tensions within it and the global forces pressing in upon it, but one cannot help feeling that there would have been a certain rough justice in Japan and China combining, however uncertainly and temporarily, to throw back the ever insistent West.

In certain conceivable circumstances then, I suggest, China might have co-operated with Japan to overturn the still powerful and privileged position that the West enjoyed throughout most of East Asia, Japan itself only excepted. But those circumstances would have required that Japan cease treating Manchuria as a region detachable from China. Opportunist warlords might be prepared to compromise and accept permanent Japanese domination of the region, but no Chinese government coming to power on a nationalist and anti-imperialist programme, as the Guomindang had done, could be expected to be willing to accept such an outcome. Just as Taiwan was to do for the post-1949 Communist government, Manchuria posed an acute dilemma for the government which had swept to national power by 1928. It still faced considerable challenges to its authority from powerful warlords in various parts of the country, including Manchuria, and in addition was being challenged by its former Communist allies, who were busy reorganising themselves underground in the cities and in some remote parts of the countryside of central China, such as Mao's Jiangxi Soviet. The viability of the new Guomindang government was at first by no means certain. But it survived, defeating Communist attempts to seize an urban base at Changsha and organizing extermination campaigns against their rural bases, while also winning victories over the northern warlords and coming to a working agreement with the warlord still entrenched in Manchuria, the Young Marshal Zhang Xueliang. It was this agreement which prompted the Japanese forces stationed in southern Manchuria under the terms of the Boxer and Portsmouth treaty settlements, to seize control of the province in 1931, to the surprise of their own government and the alarm of the West.

Chiang faced a difficult choice. Given the military weakness of China compared to Japan, to fight back vigorously, as many Chinese wished to do, seemed to him too dangerous a course. So he ordered his forces to avoid clashes with the Japanese, telling the Chinese people:

> If we wish to redress the wrong done to our nation, to avenge our national humiliation, to free China from the oppression of

imperialism and to obtain independence and freedom we must for the present endure disgrace and shoulder responsibility. We must remember what we have suffered and set apart ten years for developing our national strength and ten years for training our people.[27]

There was a good deal of realism in such a message. China was effectively on its own. The Western world, deep in economic depression (as was Japan) and anxious, through such organisations as the League of Nations and declarations such as the 1928 Kellogg–Briand pact, to outlaw war as an instrument of international diplomacy, was ready to condemn the aggression, but not to take any serious action to reverse it. Russia, Japan's great rival in Manchuria, was restructuring itself and, after Chiang's purge of 1927, was not yet willing, even if able, to aid him as it had Sun. From this point of time Western sympathy, though not much more, did swing decisively behind China. This was especially so in 1932 when Chinese forces stationed in Shanghai, eager despite Chiang's orders to show some resistance, clashed heavily with Japanese forces there. Japan, used to easy victories over the Chinese, was taken by surprise and forced to bring in heavy reinforcements, including naval and aerial, indiscriminately shelling and bombing parts of the Chinese city while carefully avoiding the International Settlement area. This was several years before Guernica, and there was no Chinese Picasso to depict graphically the slaughter of civilian innocents in Shanghai. But there were newsreel cameras and many Western observers and reporters there, so that the Western 'civilized' world was fully informed and suitably outraged at such methods, all too soon to become part of the West's own experience of modern warfare.[28] Pearl Buck's best selling novel *The Good Earth* was published about this time, extending Western sympathies and admiration to the hard working Chinese peasant, so it can be said that in the 1930s the long standing popular Western image of the heathen, cruel and inscrutable 'Chinee' was being replaced to a considerable extent by a very human figure of admirable, even heroic, proportions. It would change again soon enough, once Mao replaced Chiang.

But what, one may be excused for wondering, if Chiang had decided to resist in 1931 and had not waited for the still greater crisis of 1937? Another of the minor ironies of our story is that one of the two Japanese officers mainly responsible for planning the unauthorized takeover of Manchuria, Colonel (later General) Ishiwara Kanji, never wished to invade China itself. He recognized the strength of China's new nationalism and became a vehement critic of the trend in Japanese policy after

1931, advanced by many of its civilian leaders as well as by over-confident military figures, to push on aggressively into north China even at the risk of becoming embroiled in a widespread campaign there. A keen student of Western military history, Ishiwara saw such a campaign as madness, as stumbling into a quagmire comparable to Napoleon's disastrous advances into Spain and Russia. He wanted China as an ally, together with a semi-autonomous Manchuria, against the threat of Russia and the spread of Communism.[29] No doubt Chiang and his forces could not have prevented the Japanese take-over of Manchuria in 1931, but had they resisted strongly then they might have persuaded many more Japanese apart from Ishiwara, who needed no persuasion, that aggressive advance beyond Manchuria was likely to be very costly and no mere 'incident'. But Chiang's priorities precluded him from taking at once a firm stand over Manchuria, though he certainly did not intend to abandon it indefinitely. His top priority was to get rid of the Communists. He would negotiate and compromise with warlords, and even with Japanese if need be, but was unwilling (until forced to do so by his own troops when kidnapped at Xian in December 1936) to do so with the Communists. He was intent upon destroying them utterly and, with the help of German military advisers, came very close to doing so in his campaigns against the Jiangxi Soviet. In 1934–5 the Communists were forced to the retreat known as the Long March. For those Communists who survived it that proved to be a victory rather than a rout, creating a legend of survival against the odds and placing them, at its end, in a strategically more advantageous part of China where, far more credibly than in Jiangxi, they were able to establish themselves as defenders of China against Japan, matching and even outbidding the Guomindang as defenders of national integrity. Chiang would have done better to have been content to contain their main body in its southern base, and to have undercut their appeal by developing the democratic and social welfare aspects of the programme sketched out by Sun Yat-sen in his Three People Principles lectures. But such wisdom after the event is easy. There was certainly no well defined path to national security, wealth and power, along which whatever party led China during these years could confidently proceed.

After the seizure of Manchuria China and Japan seemed inexorably locked together on a road which led first to the Marco Polo bridge and beyond that to Pearl Harbor. The caution of Chiang on the Chinese side could not hold back the convictions of many of his compatriots that resistance, whatever the cost, was preferable to continued humiliating retreats before Japanese demands. Nor, on the Japanese side, could the warnings of an Ishiwara weaken the conviction of that country's civilian and military leaders that China, still deeply warlord riven and Communist threatened in their eyes, was too weak to check their drive to establish a new political and economic order in East Asia, a new order into which they unrealistically hoped their great neighbour could be both forced and enticed. First 'annihilate' the Guomindang and then 'regenerate' the central kingdom became the unrealizable programme of the Japanese government of Prince Konoye. Reinforcing this programme was the conviction that the West was morally too weak to be prepared to resist for long the superior 'Japanese Spirit', and indeed many Chinese came to fear that there would be some Western appeasement of Japan, an East Asian Munich.

In a Dark Valley, 1931–41

Increasing popular sympathy within the West for China and its people did not translate automatically into supportive policies by Western governments. Between 1931 and 1941 Western East Asian diplomacy, which is to say essentially US and British diplomacy, may be summed up as a search, uncertain, not always united and ultimately ineffectual, to find a safe path out of what Japanese historians aptly call 'the Dark Valley', those years between the Manchurian crisis and Pearl Harbor. Whether such a path was there to be found is not at all clear. Given, on the one hand, the strength of the Japanese conviction that their national prosperity and even survival depended on their gaining extensive and secure economic and political rights on the Asian mainland, and on the other hand the scarcely less strong conviction of nationalist Chinese that Manchuria must remain within their provenance, and that north China, where Japanese expansionists set up further puppet regimes, should even more certainly be within it, then confrontation between China and Japan was surely inevitable. Had the moderates of the twenties remained in power in Japan during the thirties, that confrontation might have been delayed but, as already suggested, in the long run the lopping off of Manchuria was never likely to be acceptable to a nationalist-minded China, any more than Taiwan is today. In the 1930s the West was more on the sidelines so far as Manchuria was concerned than is the case with Taiwan, but it was never quite off the field altogether. It dithered between being spectator and participant.

In March 1931, that is some months before the Japanese takeover, the newly appointed US ambassador to China, Nelson Johnson, wrote: 'Manchuria becomes more Chinese every day, but if Manchuria is

destined to become part of Japan I do not see why that should necessarily embroil us.'[30] A few months after the take-over, however, the US did
embroil itself to the extent of taking a strong stand on the principle that,
in accordance with the Kellogg–Briand pact of 1928 to which Japan was a
signatory, it would not recognize the legitimacy of a change in political
status brought about through aggression. A year or so later the League
of Nations (of which the US was not a member) did deny recognition
to Manchukuo, prompting the Japanese walkout. However no positive
action, such as imposing sanctions on Japan or substantially increasing
Western forces in the region, was taken by either the British or the
Americans, and within a few years the formal recognition of Manchukuo
was being considered by the British. The US seems never to have got to
that point, but as Warren I. Cohen, has commented, after 1931
Americans had to face the deep dilemma which had been implicit in
their China policy since their Open Door declaration at the beginning of
the century – either to abandon their insistence on equality of economic
opportunity and their concern for Chinese sovereignty, or prepare
to fight a powerful Japan. Cohen went on to note that within the
US Department of State in 1931 there was agreement that American
interests in Manchuria, even within China generally, were relatively
insignificant; that the Secretary of War advised that the American
army and navy were not strong enough to fight, even if the will to do
so existed; and that President Hoover (who was a survivor of the Boxer
siege) was resolutely opposed not only to the use of force but also to
economic sanctions. 'Given this complex of circumstances and attitudes
a decision to appease Japan seemed obvious', Cohen concluded.[31]

   The same may be concluded for the European powers. The European
West certainly had more substantial interests in China than did the US,
but even for Great Britain China was far less of a major area for trade and
investment than were many other parts of the world, including its
colonies and dominions. Why then be prepared to risk war with Japan
in defence of a relatively limited trade and investment stake in China?
The West certainly wished to preserve and expand its existing interests
there, and to ensure that there would be opportunities to develop these
further as China's state and economy modernized. Western objectives
remained essentially the same as they had been at the time of Macartney
and the Opium Wars, though now financial and industrial investment
opportunities and not just direct commodity trade were sought. But
after the trauma of the First World War, and facing an awakened
China, the West no longer had either the capacity or the will to deploy
its navies and armies across the world to force its preferences on the

nations of the region, which now included a modernized and powerful Japan. By the time of the Manchurian crisis of 1931 a new order in East Asia, to be shaped somehow by China, Japan, the West (and possibly Russia) was bound soon to emerge. The Western-created and dominated treaty system, even when relaxed and modified as it was being over the first three decades of the century, was no longer acceptable, insofar as it ever had been, to either of the two powers most vitally involved, China and Japan. The immediate problem was to contain within acceptable limits the demands of Japan. This was a very difficult, probably impossible task given the growing extent of those demands, and given also the strength of Chinese resistance to them. Continuing Western concern to preserve for itself a significant, potentially profitable, place within the East Asian world meant that Manchuria became a focus for all these tensions, which soon exploded into a widespread war, engulfing far more than just that strategic region.

During these years the Western power with the greatest stake in China, Great Britain, was seeking a safe path out of another Dark Valley, one much closer to home. British East Asian policy in the thirties was conducted against the background of both a severe economic depression and a mounting crisis in Europe as the post World War I international order, constructed around the League of Nations, progressively broke down. Japan's 1933 walkout was followed by the rise to power within Germany of a Nazi party which denounced the Versailles settlement, by Italian defiance over its expansionist ambitions in Africa and elsewhere, and by the intervention of both those fascist powers, challenged by Soviet Russia, in the Spanish civil war. As the threat of a general war in Europe loomed Britain was naturally anxious to prevent the situation in Asia also degenerating to such a point. Therefore, although sympathetic to the Chinese facing increasing Japanese pressures and fearful that those pressures, if totally successful, would destroy its own position in China, Britain sought to be as even handed as possible between the two Asian powers. While endeavouring to be conciliatory toward Japan, though not to the extent it was being towards Hitler, it also gradually extended some aid to China, at first only financial advice but later, after the building of the Burma road in 1938, some military supplies. It was a difficult balancing act, its shifting uncertainties shown by the closing of the Burma Road for a time in 1940. This concession to Japanese pressure demonstrated that, in contrast to its position a century earlier, Great Britain could no longer influence decisively the power balance within China. The crucial relationship had become that between the US and Japan. However, China remained somehow the central kingdom of East

Asia, even as it struggled to survive, to renew itself and to find its place in a far more complex world order than it had ever known traditionally.

In 1932 the US had adopted a 'non recognition' position in respect to Japan's actions in Manchuria but, like the European powers in the League of Nations, had not gone beyond that declaration of principle. In fact, despite the strong sentimental attachment of many Americans to China, in the years immediately following the take-over of Manchuria their government's policy was far from supportive, its State Department officials and others expressing strong doubts about the capacity of the Guomindang to unite the country and lead it effectively towards democracy and modernity. Some even expressed the view that an increased measure of Japanese influence, so long as it was not too dominant and monopolistic, might be no bad thing for China, or for Western interests there. Similar opinions were to be found among many Western residents, such as the missionary bishop, 'a rotund and cheerful pro-Franco Spaniard', described by Christopher Isherwood, in his account of the journey he and the poet W.H. Auden made early in 1938 to the war in China, who was 'not displeased at the prospect of a Japanese conquest. The Japanese, said the bishop, would bring law and order to China.'[32] Not a few Western policy makers took a similar view, making many Chinese, Guomindang and Communist alike, fearful that soon they would, like the Czechs, have to pay the price for Western appeasement of aggression. As far as military help went, for some years the Guomindang received more from Nazi Germany, in the shape of military advisers, and from Soviet Russia, in the shape of planes and pilots, than from any democratic Western government. Events were in fact moving the US and Britain towards a point where they would become militarily allied with China against Japan, but throughout the thirties relations between the democratic West and China were often very strained, even though for the time being the Guomindang did not push for the ending of extraterritoriality and the rendition of treaty port concession areas.[33]

The final steps to Pearl Harbor

By 1940–1 relations improved, as much because of Japanese actions as of Western or Chinese. In September 1940, after the fall of France, the Japanese formally allied themselves to Germany and Italy in the Tripartite Pact. By this the Japanese recognized the leadership of Germany and Italy in establishing a 'new order' in Europe, while those two powers in turn recognized Japan as leading East Asia to a similar outcome. Further, each undertook to assist any of the signatories attacked by a power not currently involved in either the European war or the Sino-Japanese conflict. Soviet Russia was, however, excluded from this commitment, so that Japan did not have to become directly involved when, in the following year, Hitler launched his Barbarossa campaign. The prime object of the Tripartite Pact was to warn the US against intervention in either the European or the Chinese conflict. Then, in July 1941, Japan forced the Vichy French to agree to the occupation of Indo-China by Japanese forces, a clear sign that it intended to push further south at the expense of British and Dutch possessions in South East Asia, in effect challenging the West to either resist or be prepared to retreat from the Asian scene. Even more than earlier provocative acts, such as the bombing and sinking of the US gunboat *Panay* in the Yangzi in December 1937, these diplomatic and military moves by Japan in 1940–1 turned US policy decisively away from any appeasement tendency. Intense pressure, by the freezing of Japanese funds in the US and the imposition of embargoes on shipment of oil and other supplies, was applied until Japan would agree to withdraw all its forces from China and Indo-China. Although they talked on with the US for some months, when faced with this kind of choice, requiring retreat without gain from a long campaign in which their armed forces, though not victorious were also not defeated (compare Vietnam later), the Japanese decided to bomb Pearl Harbor and launch a general war in the Pacific.

How far US policy can be held responsible for precipitating that traumatic action is a question many historians have considered but, being strictly a question of US-Japanese rather than of Sino-Western relations, is not one that needs to be pursued here.[34] Of course relations with China were at the heart of that US-Japan confrontation, and if either of those powers had been prepared to change its established approach to that country the conflict between them could probably have been avoided. In that case either America's 'Open Door' principle or Japan's 'Greater East Asia' scheme, or some compromise worked out at China's expense and involving at least the international recognition of Manchukuo, would have prevailed. But probably only for a time. As I have endeavoured to establish, the regenerating China of the mid-twentieth century, whether under Guomindang or Communist leadership, was unlikely to accept for long either a revised Anglo-American order designed to guarantee still, even without the old special treaty-based privileges, fairly free foreign access to the China market and investment field, or a new Japanese-centred hegemony which included the permanent loss to China of Manchuria. Control over north China and Inner

Mongolia, which Japan had been asserting between 1931 and 1937, was also an issue. For an aroused nationalist China any externally devised pattern for the region was not likely to be acceptable very far into the second half of the twentieth century. Even the milder 'Open Door' model, more sensitive though it was to Chinese sovereignty than Japan's 'Greater East Asia' model, was geared to shaping conditions to suit Western interests and objectives. In the long run neither Japan nor the West could determine the manner in which modern China would trade and negotiate with them or the rest of the world. 'Open Door' principles and 'Greater East Asia' constructs were both passing their use-by dates by the 1940s. By the second half of the century China was ready to determine for itself how far and on what terms it would admit Western, Russian or other would-be entrants to the central kingdom of East Asia. Whether under Chiang or Mao that would become very plain.

Wartime promotion of China by the West

But first a war had to be fought – a war begun in China and continued there for eight years, though ultimately decided in campaigns fought by non-Chinese in seas, skies, islands and territories far beyond China itself. The West fought it not primarily to save China from Japanese domination, though that was one of its results, but as part of a wider struggle to ensure that a world political order in which change brought about by unprovoked military aggression would not triumph over the kind of international order the League of Nations had, however inadequately, embodied. Japan's aggression in Manchuria and its walkout from the League marked the beginning of mounting international struggle over this principle, and it was Japan's 1940 alliance with the European powers which most threatened that principle (a real 'axis of evil') that ensured that its ambition to dominate China and the East Asian world would sooner or later be decisively resisted by the West. China's future thus became enmeshed with that of the Western democracies, standing united against the forces of fascist totalitarianism threatening their ideal of a 'free and peace-loving' world.

China under Chiang Kai-shek was now more and more promoted as a to-be-admired and desirable ally for a democratic West facing a deadly challenge, as was Stalin's Russia once it was invaded by Hitler's armies, though neither China nor Russia had any democratic credentials. Japan did have some such credentials, but in wartime the complexities of its internal politics and debates had to be reduced to the evil machinations of a Nazi-like band of conspirators, headed by an emperor on a white horse. China's no less complex and decidedly less democratic politics, in which some later historians would discern strong 'fascist' features,[35] became symbolized by the gallantly cloaked figure of the Generalissimo flanked by his attractive, articulate, American-educated wife. Such images, promoted in *Time-Life* publications and a host of other media outlets, were certainly useful and perhaps necessary to the winning of a life and death global war, but they helped create some real difficulties of adjustment to the Chinese realities that were to emerge in the post war world.

The challenging 1957 book of Harold Isaacs, *Scratches On Our Minds*, recounts how, once China became a wartime ally of the US, the image of Chiang as the heroic defender of his land gained even larger dimensions. He noted that a stream of feature films (*Burma Convoy, A Yank on the Burma Road, The Flying Tigers, God is my Co-Pilot*) provided Chinese backgrounds for American heroes and that, when Mme Chiang Kai-shek addressed Congress, *Time* reported she received a thunderous ovation, reducing some members to the verge of tears. A sympathetic image of the Chinese now rose to a pinnacle in American minds, wrote Isaacs, after years of contempt and benevolence. The image makers had turned China at war into a movie set, and made the Chinese into plaster saints. All this, Isaacs emphasized, was an American not a Chinese experience, feeding a mythology which 'could hardly survive any live experience, and its passing, for many, was quite painful'.[36] This new China myth became part of the complex China tangle that took shape – insofar as tangles can be said to have any shape – during the 1940s and, as Isaac's book indicates, was to go on confusing Western minds, especially American, for many years beyond.

Despite the propaganda build up, during the years of the West's war with Japan, China was not in fact a decisive field of action. China certainly contributed significantly to the ultimate victory by tying down a substantial number of Japanese troops which, if deployed elsewhere, would have made more difficult the Allied efforts to turn back the great sweep of the Japanese advance made in the months immediately after Pearl Harbor. Though Chiang was still capable of using the threat of a separate peace to squeeze more aid and equipment out of his now committed Western allies, they decided, undoubtedly correctly, that the European theatre of this global war had to be the first priority. This made for a good deal of tension, since Chiang was reluctant to accept fully the logic of this strategy, or to commit much of the aid he did receive and the armies under his control to vigorous campaigns against the Japanese, notably in Burma but also in China itself. His primary object was to build up his resources for a post-war showdown with the Communists, who were increasing in strength in north China without any aid from the Americans – beyond, it is said, one pair of binoculars. Some State Department observers who visited them at Yenan thought they deserved more, since they seemed more actively engaged against the Japanese than were Chiang's forces. These observers were to be among the main victims of the McCarthy campaign of the early fifties against alleged Communist collaborators and sympathizers within the American administration.[37]

But in the early forties, whatever the difficulties of dealing with them, Chiang and the Guomindang had still to be recognized and respected as the leaders of an important wartime ally. This was demonstrated by Britain and the US signing, in January 1943, treaties which finally ended their claims to extraterritorial rights, as well as giving up all remaining treaty port concession areas and the right to station their warships in Chinese waters and to have their troops at strategic places on Chinese soil. All the treaty ports where these rights had been operative were of course at that time in Japanese hands, so these new self-denying treaties had little immediate impact. But two days before they were signed the Japanese also signed a 'covenant' with the puppet Wang Jingwei regime whereby they promised to give up their treaty rights, including the 'early abolition' of extraterritoriality. By then, in those extensive parts of China that they occupied, the Japanese exercised powers and privileges far beyond anything the old treaty system had ever conferred on Western powers, but they were nevertheless able to make effective propaganda within China by publicizing the handovers to Wang's regime of areas such as the International Settlement in Shanghai. The treaty system was finally dead, a century after it had begun, a casualty of a combination of Chinese nationalism and Japanese imperialism, mixed with a modicum of Western guilt feelings.

Further signs of the West's, or perhaps more accurately President Roosevelt's, inclination to treat wartime China as more of an equal came later in 1943. The US revised its immigration laws in such a way as to allow a limited number of Chinese to immigrate, and in Cairo in December, Chiang met with Roosevelt and Churchill, who were on their way to confer with Stalin at Teheran. This was not quite a Big Four meeting, Stalin declining on the ground that Russia, though at war with Japan's Axis allies was not at war with Japan itself, so to maintain a facade of neutrality he should not be seen discussing war policy with Chiang. But the Cairo meeting was the first time that China was recognized as being on something like an equal footing with other great powers. This world war, like the first, was precipitating great changes in China's standing in the wider world. The three leaders who met at Cairo agreed that, victory once won, Japan would be stripped of all the territories it had gained at China's expense, especially Manchuria and Taiwan. Although Churchill had considerable reservations about China's war contribution and about its qualifications for the status of a future major power, 1943 marked a high point in the relations between China and the West, especially with America. In July of that year a Guomindang publication enthused over 'two great peoples whose sentiments are in harmony and who have very close ties, because they share similar spiritual foundations for the building of their respective nations.'[38] The wartime making of warm glow myths did not come only from the West.

Another wartime-prompted act of recognition of China's new status came a year or so later, when the post-war replacement of the failed League of Nations, the United Nations, was being planned. This was the decision to add China, as well as defeated France, to the three ultimately victorious great powers to constitute the five permanent, veto-wielding members of the Security Council of the new organisation. Again the prime advocate was Roosevelt, with Churchill less than enthusiastic. But since it was still possible to hope that, after the war's end, Chiang and the Guomindang would reunite China, and perhaps even democratize it, and would, in any case, align with the Western powers who had ultimately fought with it against Japan, China was admitted to this top international power club without much debate. Had there been any suspicion that a Communist rather than Roosevelt's dream of a Guomindang led liberal-democratic and still-open-to-the-West China would emerge within a few years one can guess that, even though the Cold War had not yet started, the West would have been rather more cautious about its new-found recognition and elevation of China.

Post-war attempts to shape China

Soon after these political decisions were taken the war against Japan was won, a victory achieved essentially by vastly superior US naval and air power capped by the use of the atom bomb. It really ended too soon and too quickly to suit Chiang, whose main forces were still confined by the Japanese to the far west and south of China. The Communists were much better placed to move into key areas in the north, especially Manchuria, helped by the Russians, who joined the war against Japan in its last week. The scene was set for a renewal of the internal power struggle between the Guomindang and Communists, a struggle in which the major post-war Western power unwisely decided to take a much less than neutral stance. Having helped defend China against the Japanese the US chose also to involve itself heavily in the post-war internal politics of the country, endeavouring to shape it to fit its own ideals. While the British Foreign Minister, Ernest Bevin, was telling the House of Commons in November 1945 that civil war was an internal problem for the Chinese to resolve the US President Truman was sending General Marshall as his special envoy to attempt to persuade both Chinese parties to agree to the peaceful reunification of the country under, hopefully, some kind of a system of government which would accommodate a range of political views and parties.

It was a mission impossible. Chiang was, if anything, less interested than Mao and the Communists in such a compromise, and was confident that, whatever he did, however much he deceived Marshall, he could count on continued support from within the US. That indeed was the case, and during the civil war, which began in earnest from mid-1946, the US provided the Guomindang with further substantial assistance – financial, military supplies and advice, transport facilities, though not troops. This was more than enough to alienate the Communists, who naturally became virulently anti-American, but was not enough to satisfy the Guomindang. The US had rescued China from Japanese domination as part of a larger global conflict, but there had to be limits to how much further it was prepared to go in attempting to shape China to suit American desires. As Warren Cohen, an historian of US relations with China already quoted, wrote:

> Though willing to use its great wealth and power to protect Western Europe and the Middle East from the Soviet threat – a threat unquestionably perceived in terms of American interests, the United States reluctantly acquiesced in the Communist conquest of China. Whatever American ambitions there were in East Asia – and they were considerable – the Truman administration, like every administration preceding it, did not consider American interests there to be vital. On the scale of American priorities, unlike the scale of American sympathies, China ranked very low indeed.[39]

Yet, for no essential or immediate national interest, during these years the US made a strong commitment to one side in the struggle for power within China and thereby made an enemy of the ultimately victorious party. Although the British, who had a far greater stake to rescue and restore than did the US, endeavoured to hold to a neutral line during the civil war, and were quick to recognize the victorious Communist government, by mid-century the West's position in China had become about as parlous as it would have been had Japan won the war.

Before moving on to review the West's experience of a Communist China during the second half of the twentieth century one further comment about its treatment of China in the forties seems appropriate. That the West, in combination with Russia, still felt it might dispose of Chinese interests without consulting China was made plain at the Yalta Conference in February 1945. There 'the Leaders of the three Great Powers', the Soviet Union, the USA and Great Britain, agreed that Russia would enter the war against Japan a few months after Germany's surrender on condition that, among other things, Outer Mongolia – once, like Manchuria, part of the Qing empire – remained effectively under Russian control, and that in Manchuria all the former Russian rights lost to Japan in 1904 would be restored, including access to Port Arthur as a naval base, to Dairen as a warm water commercial port, and joint control with China over the railways. Piously the agreement went on to state 'that China shall retain full sovereignty in Manchuria' while the agreement concerning Outer Mongolia and the ports and railroads would require the 'concurrence' of Generalissimo Chiang Kai-shek, a concurrence Roosevelt undertook to obtain. But in effect at Yalta the two leading Western powers (Germany and France being by then irrelevant) agreed to hand over substantial Chinese interests to Russia in order to win its participation in the war against Japan.[40] This was done in an agreement that was not officially revealed to the Chinese for some months, although they probably learned of it sooner. They could do nothing but acquiesce. The whole episode is reminiscent of the treatment China received during World War I and at Versailles in 1919, even though by 1945 China was being promoted, at least by Roosevelt, as a major player in world councils. With Japan's ambition to dominate the region soon to be finally crushed, the world of East Asia, and of China in particular, was still being treated by the West as a region in which they had the right, where they had the power, to impose terms to suit their interests whatever the Chinese might feel. Western policy makers, even though they had moved decisively away from the old treaty system and had begun to treat China as an equal in practical ways and not just in legal fiction (as had always been the case), seemed still to find it difficult to cast off old assumptions of a right to make some decisions affecting the country in a manner and to a degree they would never consider extending to China (or Japan) in European or American affairs. One of the Japanese complaints before Pearl Harbor had been that the US would accept no kind of Monroe doctrine for East Asia. Although the analogy was far from perfect it had some force. A revealing comment was made by the British Foreign Minister Anthony Eden when writing to his Prime Minister Neville Chamberlain in January 1938. In his letter he emphasized the importance of still 'effectively asserting white race authority in the Far East',[41] voicing just the kind of sentiment which gave some kind of legitimacy to Japanese plans for a Greater East Asia Co-Prosperity Sphere. 'White race authority in the Far East' had been established on the basis of its capacity to deploy superior power in the region, a capacity the Japanese sought first to match and then to challenge. That challenge certainly weakened Western authority in the region, but did not totally undermine it, as it seemed could happen in 1938, when Eden made his comment. The Yalta Agreement was evidence of the West's (and Russia's) readiness to continue exercising 'white race authority' when it suited, without much concern for Chinese sensibilities. The British determination to hold on to Hong Kong is further evidence of such an attitude.

Hanging on in Hong Kong

Hong Kong was to remain an outpost of Western imperialism and control within the traditional borders of China for another half century, despite the British having had to surrender it to the Japanese from January 1942 to August 1945. The Guomindang government wanted it, when recaptured, surrendered to them rather than to its former colonial rulers, and the Americans were sympathetic, insisting that they were not fighting Japan in order to prop up European colonial empires, British, French or Dutch. (Their own colony of the Phillipines was well on the way to independence before the war with Japan had begun.) When the war ended all Japanese forces within China were ordered to surrender to Guomindang authorities, an order impossible to apply effectively in the north of China, including Manchuria, in view of Communist strength there. In the south the British insisted that, so far as Hong Kong was concerned, they should receive the surrender, thus asserting their right to return to full authority there. Chiang, reluctantly, offered a compromise, suggesting he delegate British officers to receive the surrender with a Guomindang representative also present, but this was rejected by the recently elected Labour government, which seemed as intent on preserving British possession of its colony, without any concession to Chinese claims, as ever Churchill or Eden would have been. With reluctant acquiescence from President Truman (would the anti-colonial Roosevelt, if still alive, have been tougher, one wonders?) the British won the 1945 race back to Hong Kong, to the ongoing discontent of the Chinese, who thought the island, and certainly the leased territory which had been attached to it in 1898, should have been part of the 1943 treaty. The Russians were to retreat from Manchuria by the mid-fifties, but the British remained in control of Hong Kong until finally obliged to sail away in 1997.[42]

Nevertheless by mid century, despite a continuing Russian presence in Manchuria and Mongolia, and Portuguese and British colonies still in Macao and Hong Kong, China was certainly not under the dominance of any outside power, Western, Japanese or Russian. A good many Westerners believed that the victory of the Communist party over the Guomindang in 1949 meant that the Russians would make China their satellite, but in fact despite his statement that, in the rapidly developing Cold War, China under him would 'lean to one side', Mao was no more in thrall to Russia than Chiang had been to the US. Both the Russians and the Americans were to discover soon enough that China was once again the fully independent, sovereign power which, since the Boxer uprising, it had been valiantly struggling to become. Living with that reality was to become a major challenge for both the West and Russia throughout the second half of the twentieth century.

Backwards and Forwards with Mao and his Successors (1949–2001)

The first half of the twentieth century had seen a great shift in the position of the West in China, from one of such dominance at the time of the Boxer settlement that the partitioning of the country by the Western Powers seemed quite possible to one of such uncertainty by the time of the Communist victory over the Guomindang that they faced the prospect of near total exclusion. That near total exclusion in fact eventuated. 'Within just a few years of the Communist victory virtually nothing remained of over a century of Western activity in China,' wrote Beverley Hooper in *China Stands Up: Ending the Western Presence 1948–50.*

> The few remaining representatives of the economic presence were virtual commercial hostages, trying to hand over their firms' assets 'voluntarily' to the Chinese authorities and obtain exit visas to leave the country. The even fewer remnants of the Christian missionary presence were mostly in gaol. Western style education and culture had almost completely disappeared, as had the foreign communities in the former treaty ports, even Shanghai. Virtually the only Westerners who remained voluntarily were a few people who had decided to throw in their lot with the regime.[43]

A few Western countries, Britain chief among them, did retain a minimal diplomatic presence, but for a quarter of a century the West was effectively on the outside looking in, trying to make sense of the often bewildering course of events within China, and fearful of the suspected intent of its Marxist–Maoist government there to promote revolution elsewhere in Asia. During the 1970s, however, the relationship moved gradually, though uncertainly, back towards something like normality – whatever that can be said to be in the always uneasy history of contact between the West and China over the past two centuries. The West has been readmitted to China, but in a controlled and selective way – tourists very welcome; traders and investors also in joint-enterprise ventures; diplomats, so long as the governments they represent acknowledge that Taiwan is part of China and not a separate state; missionaries not at all. The West remains eager to participate in and profit from China's economic modernization, but is also wary of its potential power and disapproving of many of its policies both domestic and foreign. Overall the last half century has shown the West how challenging it is to live with an awakened dragon.

The fact that the dragon continues to flourish a Communist flag, even while following apparently capitalist paths, is part of the explanation for the West's ongoing discomfort in relating to it, but the essential fact is that it remains a Chinese dragon. Even had Guomindang rule continued it is certain that the Western presence in China would have become far more constrained and controlled than had ever been the case during the last years of Manchu or the first years of Republican rule. In the years immediately following the defeat of Japan, when Western diplomats, business men and missionaries returned to China in substantial numbers to renew their activities under the restored Guomindang regime, they experienced a good deal of obstruction, not due just to post-war difficulties. These were not easy years for any of them. This was especially so for the British, still greatly resented as the archetypal oppressors of China. Evan Luard, in his 1962 study of Britain and China emphasized the many problems former British residents and businesses had in recovering their properties, and Aron Shai, in a study of British relations with China between 1941 and 1947, even suggested that Guomindang trade policy was often close to 'the xenophobic autarky of the Manchu period.'[44] Returning missionaries, of whom there were several thousand back in the field by 1948, appear to have faced less government inspired obstruction but nevertheless considerable difficulties at the local level. These included a growing demand from their converts for the indigenization of the church in China. Paul Varg heads his chapter describing these years in his *Missionaries, Chinese and Diplomats* as 'A Brief and Unhappy Respite',[45] and that about sums up the situation generally for the West in China in the years between 1945 and 1949. Much worse was to come, but the strength of Chinese nationalism by mid-century was such that, whether under Guomindang or Communist rule, the Chinese were sure to restrict and control the Westerner in their midst far more stringently than had been the case since before the Opium Wars.

By 1950, with the Communists victorious on the mainland but the Guomindang still holding the large island of Taiwan, (then usually called by Westerners Formosa) the West was at war again with China, this time over Korea. Even without the escalation of hostility that the Korean war involved, Western difficulties with the new regime seem certain to have become acute, despite the readiness of some Western powers to accord it early diplomatic recognition. The British recognized it in January 1950, Winston Churchill expressing strong support, as Leader of the Opposition, for such a move some months before it was actually made by the Labour government. 'Recognizing a person is not necessarily an act of approval', he stated in the House of Commons. 'One has to recognize lots of things and people in this world of sin and woe that one does not like. The reason for having diplomatic relations is not to confer a compliment but to secure a convenience.'[46] But this pragmatic bipartisan British attempt to accept the new regime promptly and maintain relations with it as normally as possible, which differed from the at first wary but soon very confrontational approach of the US, did not work out well in practice. The Cold War was hotting up, and Mao had already indicated the inclination of his government to lean to the Russian side, while the intensity of Chinese Communist nationalist and anti-imperialist ideology, especially strong after US intervention in the civil war, ensured that the West was almost certain to face the kind of exclusion summarized by Hooper above. The British diplomatic initiative of prompt diplomatic recognition was not warmly recipro-cated since, in line with the US policy, the British felt obliged to main-tain some ties with the Guomindang on Taiwan. Then, on 27 June 1950, immediately after the attack on South Korea from the north and several months before direct Chinese involvement in the conflict, President Truman ordered the US Seventh Fleet to prevent any attempt by the Chinese Communists to attack the surviving Guomindang forces on 'Formosa', forces he and his Secretary of State, Dean Acheson, had at first seemed inclined to leave to their fate. The US thus effectively reintervened in the civil war, again on the side of the Guomindang,

now confined to Taiwan but claiming still to be the legitimate government of all China. Since then the status and fate of Taiwan has remained
a major issue between China and the West, most insistently, of course,
between China and the US. The resolution of it is still very uncertain,
and apparently remote. Let us hope it does not require a war to resolve
it, as did Manchuria.

Two decades of confrontation

The early fifties became the nadir years for the West in its relations with
China, and remained so until the early seventies. They began with
China fighting a bitter and inconclusive war with the West (technically
with the UN but mainly with the US), over the status of Korea, while at
the same time appearing to turn to Russia to follow a Stalinist, state-
controlled and heavy-industry-oriented model of development. But
Mao was never enamoured of that model, and never felt that
Communist success in China owed much to the Russians, so, especially
after Stalin's death in 1953, was ready to move China along different,
and he believed quicker, paths towards full Communism. Hence his ill-
fated Great Leap Forward programme, launched in the late fifties, which
aimed at the rapid creation of a distinctively Chinese, rural-oriented and
commune-based Communist society. This ambitious leap precipitated
an ideological split with the Russians which, along with other disputes
over such issues as the sharing of military technology and the demarca-
tion of frontiers, resulted in Russia also being seen as a threat rather than
as a model or an ally. The sixties was the decade in which China seemed
intent on going it alone, neither dependent on nor deferential to either
of the world's super powers.

Mao's Great Leap Forward was overambitious, and after its soon
obviously disastrous failure he was for a time eased by his less visionary
colleagues into virtual retirement. But in the mid-sixties, after swim-
ming the Yangzi to prove to the Chinese masses that he was still far from
moribund and not yet an ancestor, he launched his Great Proletarian
Cultural Revolution, during which many of the leaders of the
Communist party, his long time colleagues in arms, were accused of
leading China away from Communism towards capitalism. After several
years of destructive domestic turmoil, in which many worthy Chinese
suffered most savagely, years complicated by fears of possible war with
Russia, a return to something like normality began in the seventies
under the cautious leadership of surviving moderates such as Zhou
Enlai. Part of that return to a quieter, less Heaven storming life for the
Chinese people was a readiness to open up the country once more to

selected elements from the West – to tourists, to sport ('ping-pong diplomacy'), to Western technology, business investment and trade, but not to missionaries. Trade with some Western countries in non-strategic commodities had in fact continued and even grown throughout the fifties and sixties, though not with the US. After China's entry into the Korean war in November 1950, the US had forbidden its citizens to travel to or trade with China, and sought to persuade others to do likewise. It was calculated by one scholar that during the 19 years following the imposition of these bans the US government sent more Americans to the moon than it gave permission to travel to China. As another scholar commented, to have two major societies so isolated from one another in peacetime as China and the United States were during the fifties and sixties was rare in modern history.[47] The renewal of contacts between them required substantial changes in policy and attitude from the major Western power as much as from China itself.

For two decades American policy, in a near total reversal of its traditional policy, was directed towards isolating and containing China. It was a reaction based less on rational analysis than on an emotional mix, often near paranoid, of fear and disappointment. To quote Harold Isaacs on the subject again:

'Over more than a century an extraordinarily large number of Americans came to think of themselves as the benevolent guardians and benefactors of the Chinese', but after 1949 the Chinese decisively rejected them, ejecting them through the very door the Americans had striven so long to keep open. The Chinese 'were repaying good with evil. They were, in short, ungrateful wretches.'[48]

Not only were they ungrateful; they had become dangerous. In 1964 a Gallup poll in the US showed 58 per cent of respondents judged China to be a greater threat to world peace than was the Soviet Union, which registered only a 27 per cent primary fear vote. Another poll taken two years later showed that, in addition to 'hard working', the favoured adjectives chosen to describe the Chinese were 'ignorant, warlike, sly and treacherous'.[49] The turnaround in popular sentiment from the years when Generalissimo and Madame Chiang Kai-shek had so elegantly presented the public face of China to Americans was indeed striking, though to some degree may be seen as a reversion to older stereotypes, with fear displacing disdain. Official attitudes, especially after the McCarthy purges of the State Department, were comparable. World events where China was involved or suspected of being involved – the

Korean war; the border war with India; the occupation of Tibet; insurgency in Malaya; the war in Vietnam – were regularly interpreted in terms of Chinese Communist aggression and subversion. China was seen as a dangerously unpredictable rogue state, its domestic upheavals in the Great Leap Forward and the Cultural Revolution years serving to confirm it in this character.

Other Westerners, never having been so sentimentally involved with China, and lacking pressure groups with the media and political clout of the US China Lobby, were less extreme in their reactions to China's new Communist regime, and were ready enough to maintain some trade and other connections. But they had also to live with the US as the super power of the West, and so could not take a totally contrary line. The British tried to maintain their formal diplomatic connection with Beijing while at the same time retaining some representation on Taiwan, an in between stance which did not endear them to either the Communist or Nationalist Chinese. In the face of US objections the British and French had supported the inclusion of Chinese Communist representation at the 1954 Geneva Conference, called to attempt to sort out the Indo-China situation and resulting in the division of Vietnam. At that conference the then US Secretary of State, John Foster Dulles, famously refused to shake hands with the moderate, cultivated chief Chinese representative, Zhou Enlai, and was reluctant even to sit at the same table with him. But the 1954 Geneva Conference demonstrated that Communist China was a major power which could, if it chose (which it certainly did not always do) help stabilize developments in Asia. It was also becoming evident that Communist rule in China was not likely to be a passing phase, as Dulles hoped. While the US continued to maintain, well after the passing of Dulles, a sternly hostile stance, promoting the fiction that the surviving, Guomindang regime on Taiwan was still the legitimate government of China and the proper occupant of its Security Council seat at the UN, other Western powers moved as best they could towards normalizing relations, which the regime by no means always made easy. Nevertheless, while the US continued to prohibit any trade with China by its nationals the British steadily relaxed their application of the general trade embargo imposed at the outbreak of the Korean war. Trade delegations were exchanged, and by the early sixties British trade with China was, in terms of value, about three times what it had been before the war, though it should be added that as a proportion of total British trade it remained quite small. The China market still fell far short of what Westerners had long hoped for, but the pragmatic British, the heirs of Macartney, were determined to hold on to, and if possible extend, their access to it, whatever the political colour of its government. The more emotive, judgmental Americans would eventually come round to a similar standpoint. Others also moved a little closer to the regime. In 1964 France, and by 1970 Canada and Italy also, extended formal diplomatic recognition, following Britain, Israel and the Scandinavian countries which had done so back in 1950. By 1970 53 countries world wide recognized China's Communist government while 68 still followed the US line.

It is testimony to the force of the globalization process set in motion by the West back in the fifteenth and sixteenth centuries that, even during this mid-twentieth-century twenty-year stand-off period, during which the once substantial Western presence in China was severely curtailed and what remained of it was often subjected to harsh treatment – missionaries expelled or imprisoned; harried businessmen obliged to 'voluntarily' surrender their assets before being allowed to leave the country; diplomats spurned and, during the Cultural Revolution, besieged and made virtual hostages within their legations – yet significant contact was nevertheless maintained, and in certain respects even grew. The closer coming together of the West and China that had been proceeding since the Portuguese had first made contact by sea was only briefly set back by the events of the mid-twentieth century. There could be no lasting return to the world of the Qianlong emperor, even though, in a confused sort of way, the chronically revolutionary and utopian minded Mao, who took on emperor-like dimensions in his last years, seems at times to have hankered for something like it. But Mao, unlike the Qianlong emperor, could not say he set no value on ingenious articles, being eager for atom bombs and the means to deliver them. He could not totally disengage from the West and its superior technology. But equally the West, however wary and fearful of China, could not disengage, but was bound to continue seeking to develop the economic, diplomatic and cultural links which it had so long sought from China. So by the early seventies of the twentieth century the head of the most powerful nation of the West, a reigning President and no mere ambassador, was ready to come to China and, like Macartney, to negotiate but not to kowtow. He found the modern Chinese, even Mao, more receptive than had Macartney. Though remnants of it remained in the Maoist consciousness the China of the Qianlong emperor had irrevocably passed.

The Nixon visit of 1972 eases tensions

The visit of President Nixon to China in February 1972 was certainly a major turning point in the history of the West's relations with China.

Perhaps it was not quite 'a week that changed the world', as Nixon exuberantly claimed afterwards, but in our particular context it was an event of comparable historical significance to the Macartney embassy, with less delayed positive outcomes. It did not immediately clear every obstacle to closer relations between the West (insofar as there remained a coherent entity that could be so labelled) and the new China, but it shifted the ground decisively, warmed the atmosphere substantially, broke the ice that had formed around Sino-Western, especially Sino-American, relations since 1949. Over the next two decades the West's involvement with and acceptance of – even enjoyment of – a China still calling itself Communist deepened beyond anything that seemed remotely possible through most of the preceding twenty years. The events on Tiananmen Square on 4–5 June 1989, were to chill the atmosphere again, and other ongoing issues – Taiwan, Tibet, trade policies, the proliferation of nuclear weapons, and the treatment of dissidents – meant that throughout the last decade of the century criticisms and tensions returned strongly. But there has so far been no breakdown in relations comparable to that of the mid-century, and despite continuing fears and gloomy prognostications about a possible 'clash of civilizations' China and the West, most importantly China and the US, have remained in reasonably civilized dialogue with one another since the Nixon visit.[50]

Although Richard Nixon had long been a savage critic of Red China, labelling it in 1960 'an outlaw nation' ready to promote a Third World War as a means to spread Communism and consistently advocating full US support for its Taiwan challengers, by the time he was campaigning for the second time to become President he was realist enough to recognize that the Communist regime in China, whatever its internal contortions, was there for the foreseeable future. He concluded therefore that it was desirable for the US to move, as many other Western powers had done, towards recognizing this. So in October 1967 he wrote an article, published in the influential journal *Foreign Affairs*, arguing that:

> Any American policy towards Asia must come urgently to grips with the reality of China. Taking the long view, we simply cannot afford to leave China forever outside the family of nations, there to nurture its fantasies, cherish its hates and threaten its neighbours. There is no place on this small planet for a billion of its potentially most able people to live in angry isolation...

It was easier, though still remarkable, for a Republican politician of impeccable anti-Communist credentials to advocate such a shift of

American policy than for any leader of the Democrat party tainted with the charge of the 'loss' of China to do so. But however urgent Nixon regarded coming to grips with the reality of China to be, it took some years and a good deal of careful manouvering for it to happen. The Chinese as well as the American public had to become receptive to the idea, and shifting leadership factions in China, plus a still vocal pro-Taiwan lobby in the US, meant that much uncertainty remained as to the actual course of developments. The lack of any direct diplomatic link between the two governments also complicated the process. But gradual, sometimes devious, moves, such as ambassadors holding meetings on the more or less neutral ground of Warsaw, half way between the two sides; messages passing via Pakistan or Rumania; relaxation by the US of restrictions on travel to China by scholars and journalists; a US Ping-Pong team competing in Japan in 1971 invited to return home via China and being warmly greeted by Zhou Enlai; a Chinese team then invited to the US; Nixon's chief foreign policy adviser, Henry Kissinger, making first a secret journey to Beijing via Pakistan and then a second public one to discuss details of a possible visit by the President – all these and other moves helped prepare the ground for a visit in February 1972. Altogether it was quite a performance, as was the week long visit, soon the subject of an opera. Nixon had been concerned at possible adverse public reaction, hence the secrecy surrounding many of the preliminaries, but in the event won general approval for his diplomatic break-through.

That breakthrough came not only because of his recognition, expressed in his 1967 article, of the long term realities but also because more immediate considerations helped draw China and the US cautiously towards some common ground. A major one was a heightened shared fear of Russian intentions. The suppression of hopes for 'socialism with a human face' in the Prague Spring of 1968 and the subsequent promulgation of the Brezhnev doctrine, which asserted the right of the USSR to ensure that there were stable, pro-Soviet regimes in power in Communist bloc countries, alarmed the Chinese as much as it outraged Westerners. By 1969 China was facing a greatly increased concentration of Soviet forces on its northern borders, where some serious clashes occurred. However, the Nixon visit was not made to set up a Sino-US common front against the USSR. The US, heavily involved in Vietnam, was seeking detente rather than confrontation with both Russia and China, and although China had moved well away from its 'lean to one side' stance of the early Cold War years it was far from wishing to commit itself completely to the other side. In the global balance of power a kind of strategic triangle was taking shape by 1970, with the super powers providing still by far the two strongest sides, but with China emerging as a crucial link which might tilt the balance either way. From the American standpoint it now seemed possible, despite the domestic excesses of Maoism (which in any case were receding by the early seventies) to work with rather than against China on a number of important issues. A significant sign of this calmer attitude was evident in 1971, when the US did not oppose the resolution of the majority of UN members to admit mainland rather than Taiwan-based delegates to China's seat in the Assembly and on the Security Council. The possibility of easing tensions was strengthened by the personal rapport that built up between Zhou Enlai and Henry Kissinger, which created an atmosphere very different from that at Geneva in 1954, when China and the US had last come together at the negotiating table. Personalities can help move history along (or slow it down), and have a place in helping explain the easing of tensions between China and the US at this time.

The Nixon visit, if it did not exactly change the world, certainly changed the course Western relations with China had taken after 1949, though, as I have suggested, some of the lesser Western powers were trying to do that even before the US began to move away from its once consistently hostile stance. But the visit did not result in anything like complete normalization of relations. At its conclusion a joint communiqué was issued which carefully spelled out, in balancing paragraphs, the different standpoints of the two sides on a number of sensitive issues within Asia – Korea, Vietnam, Kashmir and especially Taiwan – and recognized that there were 'essential differences between China and the United States in their social systems and foreign policies.'[51] However it was agreed that, regardless of these differences, relations should be conducted on the basis of mutual respect, and that disputes should be resolved without resorting to the use or threat of force. Neither would seek 'hegemony', that is dominance, in the Asia-Pacific region, and each would oppose any other country that might attempt it, as Japan had once done. Formal diplomatic relations were not set up, but the two sides agreed that they would 'stay in contact through various channels, including the sending of a senior US representative to Beijing from time to time for concrete consultations to further the normalization of relations between the two countries', and both would facilitate trading and people-to-people contacts in such fields as science, technology, culture, sports and journalism. It was altogether a 'feel good', far from formal, stiff diplomatic document, ending with a quite personal expression of appreciation from the

President, his wife and the American party for 'the gracious hospitality shown them by the Government and people of the People's Republic of China'.

Taiwan remained the major sticking point, 'the crucial question obstructing the normalization of relations' as the Chinese paragraph on the issue put it. The Chinese statement went on to insist that 'Taiwan is a province of China which has long been returned to the motherland; the liberation of Taiwan is China's internal affair in which no other country has a right to interfere; and all US forces and military installations must be withdrawn from Taiwan.' Any activity aiming at the creation of two Chinas or an independent Taiwan was firmly opposed. The US paragraph acknowledged that 'all Chinese on either side of the Taiwan strait maintain there is but one China and that Taiwan is a part of China', and reaffirmed its interest in achieving a peaceful settlement of the question of its status by the Chinese themselves. 'With this prospect in mind it (the US) affirms the ultimate objective of the withdrawal of all US forces and military installations on Taiwan as the tension in the area diminishes.' But for the time being the Chinese were ready to allow the Taiwan issue to be pushed on to a back burner, where it could be allowed to simmer away quietly. In his memoir *The White House Years* Kissinger reported Mao as showing no impatience over the issue, quoting him as saying 'We can do without them for the time being and let it come after 100 years... This issue is not an important one... the big issue is the world.' Kissinger added that such thoughts were shared by Zhou Enlai and Deng Xiao-ping, and that in their talks with the Americans these Chinese leaders spent very little time on this issue.[52] However, as the Shanghai Communiqué made plain, it remained a sleeper, even while the prospect of much warmer, mutually beneficial relations between Communist China and the US, and by extension with the West generally, was being opened up.

Truly closer encounters

Leadership uncertainties following the forced resignation of Nixon in 1974 and the death of Mao in 1976, as well as continuing shifts in the international power balance after the US withdrawal from Vietnam in 1975, meant that it was a few years before the prospective benefits envisaged in the Shanghai Communiqué began to be realized and for the West to move really closer to China once again. But by late 1978, with the pragmatic Deng Xiao-ping reasonably secure in his succession to power in China, and with an insecure and uncertain President in the US needing to buttress his credibility with some foreign policy achievement, the conditions for a further advance towards normalization of relations were present on both sides.

Thus it was that in December 1978 President Carter, not having made plain his intentions by consulting beyond the circle of his close advisers, announced that the US was now ready to recognize the government of the Peoples Republic as the sole legal government of China, and to establish formal diplomatic relations with it, adding rather vaguely that 'within this context the people of the US will maintain cultural, commercial and other unofficial relations with the people of Taiwan'.[53] This move beyond the 1972 Shanghai Communiqué to formal recognition was logical enough, one that Nixon himself would probably have attempted had he not been overtaken by Watergate. But Carter's handling of it was subject to much complaint, if not quite to outright opposition and rejection. It was said that he had eradicated the myth that Communist China did not exist, but had created another – that Taiwan did not exist. Certainly the status of Taiwan and the degree of US future commitment was left very indeterminate by his brief announcement. The US Congress was quick to unite on a bipartisan basis in defining how it believed the question should be resolved by passing the Taiwan Relations Act of April 1979. This made it clear that US recognition of the Communist government rested 'upon the expectation that the future of Taiwan will be determined by peaceful means', and to this end guaranteed to continue to provide Taiwan with arms of a defensive character and to maintain US capacity to resist any resort to force in the region. The Act went on to establish mechanisms whereby close relations, even if 'unofficial', could be maintained between the US and Taiwan. It also reaffirmed as an objective 'the preservation and enhancement of the human rights of all the people on Taiwan.'[54] Thus President Carter's move to at last formalize US relations with the Communist government of China resulted in the reaffirmation and closer definition of US commitment to the government and people of Taiwan. At one level the scenario between China and the West was being simplified and clarified, on another made more complicated and uncertain.

To clinch the normalization agreement Deng Xiao-ping visited the US early in 1979 and was enthusiastically received, especially in Texas when he attended a rodeo and rode round the arena in a stage coach wearing and waving a ten gallon hat. Public opinion polls showed a swing in US popular perceptions of China from only 21 per cent favourable in 1978 as against 67 per cent then unfavourable, to 65 per cent against 25 per cent in 1979, and similar figures in 1980. By 1991 the figures had swung back to 35 per cent favourable against 53 per cent unfavourable.[55]

At least the volatility of US feelings about China remained consistent! While Deng was in the US the Taiwan Relations Act came under consideration by Congress. Even when specifically asked to do so Deng refused to endorse the expectation expressed in the Act that the Taiwan issue should be settled peaceably, a clear sign that sooner or later the sleeper would awake, or be awakened.

But for the next ten years Sino-Western relations, with Sino-American relations at their core, moved into an expansive, promising phase, in marked contrast to the hostilities of the fifties and sixties, and to the tentative uncertainties of the seventies and the tensions that were to come in the nineties. The eighties indeed may be said to be the years in which China really opened up to the West, far more extensively than had happened after those mid-nineteenth century Opium War years credited in older textbooks as marking 'the opening of China'. China, the Chinese people, joined the world decisively in these post-Mao years, to an extent that makes it difficult to believe that any Qianlong like dismissals, any Boxer 'exterminate the foreign' manifestos, or any Maoist self-propelled Great Leaps Forward will figure again in its complex history. One can never be sure of future developments of course, and historians should be as wary as anyone else of predicting them, although perhaps better qualified to attempt to do so. But the central kingdom is now irrevocably out in the wider world, and is crucial to the well-being of that world to a degree it never was even in its proud self-contained, self-centred past. Present day and future China may aim to reassert its primacy in the region of its traditional dominance, but will not again retreat behind any Great Wall of indifference towards the world beyond.

Our main focus, however, is upon the West, upon its experience of and reaction to China. The eighties may be said to be also the years in which the West became aware of and involved with China far more extensively than ever before, when not just a relatively few traders, diplomats and missionaries, and not many others, came to know something of China directly. Over the past 20 years or so millions of Western tourists have visited China for a few weeks or months, while many thousands of students, teachers and business people have lived and worked there for substantial periods of time, none of them enjoying extraterritorial rights. Conversely great numbers of Chinese have gone to Western countries for study or other purposes, and it seems probable that within a few years affluent Chinese will be prominent in the ranks of international tourists. Thus there has been far more direct contact, more intermingling of Westerners and Chinese as equals pursuing shared objectives, than ever before. These personal contacts have been reinforced by best-selling Chinese accounts of life under Mao such as in *Wild Swans*, which for a time set off a surge of interest and sympathy for ordinary Chinese comparable to the impact of *The Good Earth* on an earlier generation, and also by films such as *From Mao to Mozart*, far removed from the Fu Manchu genre. Such books and films have helped immensely to humanize the Chinese for Westerners and to destroy negative stereotypes. Some of those older stereotypes had returned during the hostile years of the fifties and sixties, when the prevailing Western image of Chinese became for a time one of blue-suited automatons marching *en masse* waving little red books and mindlessly chanting slogans. Chinese were seen as Blue Ants, the English title given to a 1957 account of Mao's China written by the French journalist Robert Guillain, who had had previous experience of China. Guillain was both greatly impressed and horrified by what he saw as happening to the country. Although there were also many books which gave very favourable accounts of developments, with titles such as *Daybreak in China*, the predominant Western view, especially during the Cultural Revolution years, was in the blue ant mould.[56] Such negative images seem now to have dissolved, and Fu Manchu is surely no more. With the marked swing away from Maoist austerities and regimentation achieved under Deng and his successors, as well as because of far wider tourist and other contacts, Westerners generally have come to view the Chinese people in a more balanced, less stereotyped way than ever before. Their suspicions now focus upon the government, on the still very authoritarian political system, not on any supposed malevolent characteristics of the people at large.

That, surely, is progress, though it would be unwise to exaggerate its extent. The political analyst David Shambaugh has warned that:

> while extensive contact and interaction between Chinese and American societies has facilitated many tangible gains and increased mutual understanding for both sides, at the same time it must be recognised that a great 'perception gap' remains. This factor has lurked not far beneath the surface of the relationship since 1972, and over time has become more important in affecting the bi-lateral relationship. The conflict of values is very apparent in terms of human rights, but it has also underlain differences in business practices, scholarly exchange and press reporting. Thus ... it can be concluded that contact between the two societies has both increased mutual understanding and accentuated misconception.[57]

That comment was made in 1994 but remains true for the West in general and not just for Sino-American perceptions. Significant, possibly dangerous, gaps in perception and understanding remain on both sides.

Missionary uncertainties

One group formerly very active in China but not permitted to share in this late twentieth-century reopening of China to the West has been the missionaries. All Western missionaries in the country at the time of the Communist take-over were soon forced to leave, if they were not accused of spying, imprisoned and in some cases executed. The Christian church in China, both Protestant and Catholic, was forced to cut all foreign ties, and to follow the 'Three Self' principles of self-propagation, self-administration and self-support. A Religious Affairs Bureau was set up to supervise all recognized religious organisations – Buddhist, Islamic and Daoist as well as Christian – and, although freedom of religious belief was promised under the new Constitution, the exercise of it often became very difficult, especially when local party cadres were particularly zealous. Churches were forbidden to pursue other than strictly religious activities, such as educational or social welfare work, and during the Cultural Revolution years even religious activities were proscribed and church buildings taken over. During the first 30 years of Communist rule all religious groups in China were subjected to close government supervision, amounting at times to severe repression and persecution, with the partial exception, for local political reasons, of Islam in the Western regions of China. Probably no group was more closely watched than the Christian since it was the least indigenous, the most institutionally organized and the most closely identified with foreign power. But like the others it has survived, even without the Western missionary, and now seems reasonably securely established, in both its Protestant and Catholic forms, within the Chinese religious scene.

Self-reliance, if adequate to enable the church in China to sustain itself and grow in strength, is surely a development very welcome to the wider Christian community. Maintaining some effective communion with the church in the West is, however, a problem. The recognition of papal authority, including the consecration of bishops, remains a particularly serious issue for the Catholic body in China, which is divided between an 'open' Church led by the Catholic Patriotic Association not in communion with Rome, and a possibly larger group which rejects government control and generally follows old ways, even to the use of the Latin mass. The government resolutely opposes any deferment to Rome, and in 1999 refused permission for a papal visit to Hong Kong because of the Vatican's continuing recognition of and relations with Taiwan. Among the Protestants denominational differences appear to have been subsumed in the Chinese Christian Three-Self Movement, but there are also many so-called 'house Christians' worshipping in groups outside the approved bodies under Religious Affairs Bureau supervision. There are, then, still significant variations within the Chinese Christian community and this, plus its now very tenuous links with the West and the eclectic nature of the Chinese religious tradition, makes one wonder about its possible future development. It seems certain to become Christianity with Chinese characteristics, though whether as radical as the Taiping form was, only time will tell.

For the present, however, it is clear that Christianity in China has survived and continues to grow. It has done so through a century of very variable fortunes. After the Boxer trauma it recovered strongly for a couple of decades, then retreated in face of a surge of post-World War I anti-imperialist nationalism which made a particular target of the foreign missions. Those attacks were followed by the disruption and destruction of the war against Japan. For a few years after the end of that war Western missionaries were able to return to the field, but their hopes of full resurgence and renewed expansion were soon dashed by the Communist victory in the civil war. The foreign missionary became one of the chief targets of the very virulent anti-imperialist, and especially anti-American, nationalism of the new regime. To this nation-alism had now to be added an atheistic Marxist philosophy promoted by a Communist state which, although it promised its citizens the right to enjoy freedom of religious belief also saw it as its duty to educate them 'to deal with the world and our fellowmen from a conscious scientific viewpoint and no longer have any need for recourse to an illusory world of gods to seek spiritual solace.' That quotation is from what is known as Document 19, a statement circulated within the party in 1982 in an effort to define, as its title put it, the Party's 'Basic Viewpoint and Policy on the Religious Question During Our Country's Socialist Period.'[58] The Document is critical of the 'leftist' excesses of the Cultural Revolution years and accepts the need, at the present stage of China's social development, for the State to acknowledge and even help (for example in the restoration of places of worship) those of its citizens with religious beliefs, provided they are patriotic and ready to share in 'the common effort for Socialist modernization'. Their organisations, however, must be open, ready to subject themselves to supervision by the Religious

Affairs Bureau, and not dependent on foreign support or control. The return of the foreign Christian missionary to any significant role in China therefore seems unlikely, but the seed that was planted there 400 years ago by Ricci and his successors has not died, and may yet flourish.

It is difficult to say just how well it is flourishing at present. The proportion of those who may reasonably be called Christian in China today is still small relative to the total population, but is probably as high as it has ever been. Official Chinese sources in 1998 gave the figures of 6.5 million Protestants and four million Catholics, but these are almost certainly too low, covering only those associated with the government recognized churches. The numbers of 'house Christians' and those that may be called, depending on one's viewpoint, either faithful or recalcitrant Catholics can only be guessed at. Some optimists put the total Christian community in China as high as 80 or 100 million. That seems excessive, but there can be no doubt that the following for Christianity, along with other religious movements, has grown considerably in recent years. The credibility of the official Marxist–Maoist ideology has faded and, despite the earnest intent of Document 19 to wean the Chinese populace away from religious beliefs and practices, the diffuse and basically fairly tolerant religious tradition of China seems to be reasserting itself.

The recently developed Falun Gong movement, the leader of which denies it is a religion, seems to be part of this revival. It is certainly subject to severe persecution within China, but this is for its feared political and social influence rather than for any quasi-religious char-acteristics it may have. Its proven capacity to organize mass demonstra-tions which, if it turned political (as happened with the Taiping and the Boxers) could make it a threat to the regime; its considerable following in the West (mainly, but not entirely among overseas Chinese) which is contrary to the Three Self principles; and its alleged cultic practices, which the government claims endanger the health and well-being of its practitioners – all these aspects of the movement make the govern-ment determined to suppress it. But so long as other religious move-ments within China avoid suspicion of such tendencies they will continue to be recognized and tolerated, though not promoted, by the present regime. This includes Christianity as was the case under the Kangxi emperor until the Rites controversy soured the relationship. For the present, within the limits set by the State, the prospects for Christianity in China are reasonably promising. The Western missionary may be excluded, but not his central religious message, which is now presented by Chinese to Chinese without any overtones of cultural imperialism or of direct Western control.[59]

China's acceptance of western style trade and diplomacy

Whatever the ultimate fate of the Christian missionary's message to China proves to be, the messages brought by the other two main agents of the Western push into China, the diplomat and the trader, appear to have been very thoroughly accepted by both government and people. China seems now well integrated into the diplomatic and economic world created by the expansion of Europe since the sixteenth century, a world in which all major states relate to one another on the basis of theoretically equal status, (within the General Assembly of the United Nations, for example) and in which all recognize the importance of participating in international trade (by making trade agreements and seeking membership of bodies such as the World Trade Organization, for example). Had either the UN or the WTO then existed, neither organization would have attracted the rulers of China that Macartney faced 200 years ago, but they are certainly important to its present day rulers. Over the past two centuries the West has part forced, part persuaded China that the messages on trade and diplomacy that Macartney and those who followed him brought had to be listened to and acted upon.

In diplomatic and political terms it has been in the second half of the twentieth century that China has succeeded in decisively redefining itself as a modern nation state, one determined and, within some limits, able to assert its perceived rights and status effectively. As we have seen, it struggled to achieve such a position throughout the first half of the century and, during World War II especially, made considerable progress towards it. When they seized power in 1949, Mao and his followers were the heirs as well as the rivals of Chiang Kai-shek and the Guomindang. During the first twenty years of their half century in power so far the Communist rulers of China seemed in Western eyes to be a destabilizing force in world affairs. They were viewed at first as a Cold War satellite of a Russia seriously threatening 'the free world' and then, once their split with Russia was accepted as real, as a rogue state intent on creating its own peculiar order in Asia by, among other means, helping subversive movements in neighbouring states. The so-called domino theory, widely accepted in the West, ignored the fact that as a revolutionary Mao was a firm believer in self-help, and never felt that the success of the movement he had led to power owed much to revolution exporting organizations such as the Comintern. Although justified in Western eyes by such Chinese actions as intervention against the UN forces in Korea, by the invasion of Tibet, the encouragement to the Communist led forces challenging the existing regimes in Vietnam and Malaya, the frontier war with India, the determination to acquire the atom bomb, plus the constant strident denunciation of alleged Western imperialism, the long held Western perception of Communist China as an aggressively expansionist and revolution-promoting power was seriously flawed. Basically China was asserting its determination to round out its national frontiers, as defined by both the Communist party and the Guomindang to include Tibet and Taiwan, and to acquire the means to defend those frontiers effectively in an atomic-powered world. Although some actions, such as the rough treatment of British diplomats during the Cultural Revolution, suggested indifference to the norms of international relations, other actions, such as its co-operative participation in the 1954 Geneva Conference, indicated a capacity and readiness to work with other powers realistically. Earlier recognition of its claim to occupy China's seat within the United Nations might have made such co-operation more frequent, but the West itself did not explore that possibility much until just before the Nixon visit of 1972.

Since that visit, and since taking its place within the UN, China's relations with the world beyond its borders, with the US in particular, have 'normalized', to use a word favoured by many China watchers. It remains 'a fragile relationship', the title of a major study on relations between US and China since 1972.[60] But despite many points of serious friction, some to be noted further below, the choice has been to maintain dialogue, both through regular diplomatic channels and through fairly frequent high level contacts, rather than to return to any pattern of rejection and confrontation. Communist China is now accepted by the West, including a still wary US, as a fully equal member of 'the family of nations', and in turn is prepared, for the most part, to accept the rules of behaviour supposed to regulate relations within that family. There are some areas, such as in international copyright and in the arbitrary legal treatment of visiting former nationals accused of commercial or political misdemeanours, where apparent indifference to the norms of international law is shown, but China is not altogether alone in indulging in such behaviour. No doubt China's rulers, conscious of its great imperial past, aspire to see it become again the dominant central kingdom of at least the East Asian world. But for the present and for the foreseeable future, China seems ready to function as a nation state, the most populous and potentially one of the most powerful, within a world which, however 'global', remains still a world of nation states. Popular

Chinese reaction to some recent perceived affronts to their national status, such as the NATO bombing of an embassy in Belgrade and the surveillance flights of American spy planes, as well as the degree of effort and emotion invested into winning the right to stage the Olympic games, provides evidence, if any is needed, of the strength of the sense of national identity and pride within China today.

Even more fully than in the area of foreign relations China has entered into the economic world of trade and investment created by the West. At the beginning of the twentieth century the China trade was described as the miserablest in the world relative to its large population. 'China accounted for approximately one-fifth of world population, and yet its recorded foreign trade never exceeded 1.5 per cent of the total value of world trade, and exceeded 1 per cent only briefly', claimed Rhoads Murphey in his study of the treaty ports, *The Outsiders*, published in 1977, that is just on the eve of the great turn around in the Chinese economy launched by Deng Xiao-ping.[61] Since then China has achieved what has been called 'stellar' economic growth, at an average annual rate of nearly ten per cent. This was from a low per capita base, and is spread very unevenly through the whole society, but many parts of the country have now been drawn very actively into the circle of world trade and investment. Though still well below its proportion on a total population basis, China's share in the world economy has grown apace, and seems set to continue to do so. Still categorized as a developing economy it is, among such economies, now far and away the largest recipient of foreign investment, and its share of total world trade, both imports and exports, is four or five times what it was in 1977. The US has been a major participant in that growing trade, though worried by the fact that the balance has moved strongly in China's favour. In its trade with the US China exported four times as much as it was importing during much of the nineties. Britain's share, though much smaller by then than that of the US, showed a similar imbalance, demonstrating that doing business with a thoroughly awakened Chinese dragon poses some considerable challenges for the Western trader and investor. This should occasion no surprise for, as Macartney observed back in 1792, whatever the restrictive economic inclinations of their rulers, the Chinese lower orders have always been 'of a trafficking turn'. Their restrictively inclined rulers, whether Confucians or Maoists, have been replaced by pragmatists who recognize that for China to get really strong in the modern world it needs also to get rich. Towards that basic end foreign trade and investment can help substantially, so at present, in contrast to the missionary, the Western trader and investor faces a reasonably open door into China. But it is a door to which the Chinese firmly hold the key.[62]

The human rights problem

One issue which has cast a shadow for the West over its path through this more open door into a share in a rapidly growing Chinese economy has been the Chinese record on human rights. This has been a concern of several recent US administrations, especially since the events on Tiananmen Square in June 1989, causing them to become for some years reluctant to grant China most favoured nation status on a permanent basis within the World Trade Organization. This stand upon moral principle irritated the Chinese deeply – as well as some large American corporations, which complained that they were losing profitable business (for example in the sale of commercial aircraft) to other Western suppliers whose governments were less vocal about human rights. Although taking a strong rhetorical stand on moral grounds is a long term characteristic of US foreign policy, US administrations in fact did not make a big issue of human rights during the decade following the reopening of contacts with China. In 1972 President Nixon had said to Mao 'What is important is not a nation's internal political philosophy. What is important is its policy towards the rest of the world and towards us.' Harry Harding, after quoting this hard-headed statement in his study *A Fragile Relationship*, comments that the Chinese seem to have regarded it, as well as the American willingness to include the principle of non-interference in the internal affairs of other states in the Shanghai Communiqué issued at the end of Nixon's visit, as a tacit commitment that the US would refrain from official criticism of China's human rights record.[63] After Nixon the Carter administration, even though it made human rights one of the cornerstones of its foreign policy, also did not make a big issue of it with China, offering only mild criticism of the imprisonment of the Democracy Wall activist Wei Jingsheng and granting, with Congress approval, most favoured nation status to China in a bilateral trade agreement made in 1980. By the mid-eighties, as relations with and knowledge of China expanded rapidly, and even before the trauma of Tiananmen Square, more concern came to be expressed in the US, not only about the treatment of political dissidents but also about the treatment of Tibet and policies of family limitation. By the nineties human rights became a major issue, seriously and fairly consistently clouding the relationship of the major power of the West with China. From the point of view of China's present rulers, there has been a shift in the US stance on this question since 1972. But the Western, especially the US, commitment to individual rights, including the democratic right to peaceable political dissent, has always been very strong, even if often imperfectly maintained. There is a deep, perhaps unbridgeable gulf in basic values here, with China by no means alone on its side of the gulf. Although it can be argued that the Confucian tradition was not, and is not, indifferent to individual rights, the authoritarian, legalist element within the Chinese tradition is also very strong.[64] One must expect ongoing tensions if the West makes human rights, as they have emerged from within the Western post-Enlightenment tradition, a touchstone of relations with China even though they may have universal appeal and perhaps validity. This is a very complex, emotive issue, where for some time yet it is likely the West will have to compromise more than China's present rulers are likely to feel obliged to do. 'The truth, and it is a bitter truth for those who care about China's imprisoned dissenters, is that the average person in China is rather apathetic about human rights, the way they are defined in the West.' That is the sober judgment of Richard Bernstein and Ross H. Munro in their troubled and troubling book *The Coming Conflict with China,* to which they add

> The indications are that the people, gratefully released from the terrible intrusions of the past, are happy with their government; and this happiness depends more, as it does in other countries, on its economic performance and its ability to maintain law and order than on its respect for civil liberties.[65]

Certainly we should not expect greater economic openness to the West to advance political freedom and diversity within China for some time yet.

The Taiwan problem

The other main, and potentially more dangerous, irritant issue between the West and China is Taiwan. Over more than half century since the defeated Guomindang took refuge there and was given the protection of the US fleet against any attempt by the Communist forces victorious on the mainland to drive them out, the question of the ultimate fate of this part of the traditional Chinese empire has remained unanswered. Taiwan has become what Manchuria was during the first half of the twentieth century, a strategic frontier region where foreign intervention has frustrated Chinese attempts to incorporate it into their modern nation state. There are contrasts as well as parallels between the course of developments in the two regions, including the role played by the West, but before pursuing them some account of the history of the island and its relation to mainland China, as was given earlier for Manchuria, may help the reader assess what the answer to the Taiwan problem should or is likely to be.[66]

As with Manchuria, Taiwan did not become part of the Chinese empire until the seventeenth century, when the Manchus, victorious like their Communist successors on the mainland but facing some continued resistance from forces based on the island, eventually occupied it, some forty years after their initial success. Earlier inland-oriented dynasties had shown little interest in the island which, though sometimes a base for troublesome pirates, had only a small aboriginal population and posed no threat to China's security. In early Ming times Zheng He, returning from one of his voyages, stopped there briefly and reported on the miracle powers of aboriginal herbal medicines, but there was no follow up. Westerners, once arrived on the China coast, showed more interest, the Portuguese naming the island Formosa, the Spanish and Dutch competing for control in the early seventeenth century. The Dutch drove out the Spaniards, and for several decades developed bases there vigorously, the Dutch East India Company even claiming sovereignty over the island for Holland. But by 1663 the Dutch in turn were forced out by the Ming loyalist forces led by Zheng Chenggong, generally known as Koxinga. His successors surrendered to invading Manchu forces in 1683, when Taiwan was for the first time brought within the administrative bounds of the empire as a prefectural outpost of the province of Fukien. As an island frontier it was viewed by the new rulers of China very differently from their Manchurian homeland, being largely neglected, especially its eastern side, where the aboriginal population, no friends to shipwrecked sailors, remained in control. Some Chinese migration occurred, but not on the scale of that into Manchuria. By the end of the nineteenth century, when the island passed into Japanese control, the total population was only a few million, not much more than half of it Chinese. A few years before the Japanese take-over in 1895 the island was upgraded to provincial status by the Qing, and a relatively progressive governor was appointed, but for most of its years under Qing rule the island was 'noticed by high imperial statesmen only when it exploded in rebellion'.[67]

It was noticed by the nineteenth-century Western treaty powers, but they were for a time rather uncertain about what view to take of it, what use to attempt to make of it. Although they had doubts as to the reality of China's control over the eastern half of the island, the British discouraged suggestions that China's sovereignty there might be challenged. In the mid-1850s Commodore Perry, on his famous expedition to Japan, showed some interest in the island's commercial and coaling possibilities, and recommended that the US take the initiative in developing this 'magnificent island', which he considered to be only nominally a province of China and 'practically independent'. The American consul in Japan, Townsend Harris, suggested that the US should seek to purchase the island, as it had Louisiana from the French in 1803, and was to do again in Alaska from the Russians in 1867, but his government was not then interested in such distant acquisitions. After the second Opium War two treaty ports were opened there, and some limited trade developed, camphor being one of the main items. Inevitably there were shipwrecks, raising the problem of controlling the responses of the 'raw aborigines' of the southern and eastern regions to the victims of such events. Some of those shipwrecked came from the Ryukyu islands, over which a rapidly modernizing and incipiently expanding Japan was asserting its sovereignty. In early 1874, encouraged by some American advisers who saw Taiwan as a virtual no-man's-land, Japan sent a sizeable expedition to the eastern side of the island, without first advising the Chinese, whom they claimed had admitted that the aborigines were beyond the reach of their government and culture. If Japan had received support from the Western treaty powers it might well have annexed at least the eastern half of the island then, but in fact was obliged to enter into protracted negotiations with the Qing government, which insisted on its sovereignty over the whole island. It was following this crisis that Taiwan was upgraded to provincial status, but 20 years later China did have to hand the whole island over to Japan as part of the settlement of the war of 1894–5.

In general the island can be said to have had a somewhat tenuous connection to mainland China during the Qing period, and by 1895 it had passed altogether out of Chinese control. For 50 years Japan ruled the island, not bringing in large numbers of Japanese colonists but exploiting the resources of the island vigorously. An infrastructure of roads, ports and railways was developed which helped its economy develop well beyond that of mainland China, and the island became a base from which Japanese penetration of South China and South East Asia was advanced. Over the first half of the twentieth century it seemed that Taiwan was lost to China. Thus Mao, in talking to Edgar Snow in July 1936 could say:

It is the immediate task of China to regain all our lost territories, not merely to defend our sovereignty south of the Great Wall. This means that Manchuria must be regained. We do not however include

Korea...and if the Koreans wish to break away from the chains of Japanese imperialism we will extend to them our enthusiastic help in their struggle for independence. The same thing applies for Taiwan.[68]

At that point in time, when still apparently far from victory and national power, Mao it seems could envisage an independent Taiwan. But Chiang Kai-shek seems never to have shared that idea, and at his Cairo meeting with Roosevelt and Churchill in December 1943 he made sure that Taiwan was listed among the territories to be restored to China after Japan's defeat. Since then both major Chinese parties have held to the line that Taiwan is an integral part of China, and have opposed any suggestion that it become independent, as a growing proportion of its population seem now to prefer. The longer the current de facto separation of the island from mainland rule continues the stronger that preference is likely to become.

Western intervention has been a major factor in creating the current impasse, since it may fairly be assumed that without it Communist forces would sooner or later have occupied the island to ensure that it did not become a base for continued opposition, as the Manchus had done three centuries earlier. While Chiang Kai-shek remained alive the Guomindang opposition kept up the fiction that it would return to rule the mainland again, but with the passage of time that fantasy faded. US policy was directed toward helping preserve the Guomindang on Taiwan while not encouraging it to take the initiative by attacking the mainland – in short to stabilize and neutralize the situation across the straits in the hope that somehow, sometime, a peaceful resolution would be reached by the Chinese interests involved, the US meanwhile holding the ring. But with the further passage of time that hope for a peacefully agreed Chinese settlement also seems to be, if not quite disappearing, not coming any nearer to realization. The ambiguity inherent in the US relationship to Taiwan, present since the Truman decision of June 1950, remains acute, and seriously complicates its relationship to China itself.

The crucial uncertainty is whether the US will intervene actively if mainland China attempts to invade Taiwan. The successors of Chiang Kai-shek have stated that they will not attempt to use their forces to reunify China, and have acknowledged the sovereignty of the Communist regime on the mainland, while at the same time asserting the sovereignty of their own regime on Taiwan. The mainland successors of Mao Zedong on the other hand have all so far refused to renounce the possibility of their using force to regain control of the island, and periodically give signs of actually preparing to do so. They also deny any sovereign status to the Taiwan government, and condemn any hint of international recognition to it, such as admission to the UN General Assembly. Indeed the present rulers of mainland China seem more vehement over Taiwan than Mao and his colleagues ever were, perhaps because, lacking any Long March type credentials, they see it as an issue around which they must establish their own revolutionary nationalist legitimacy. They have, following Deng rather than Mao, offered the kind of compromise worked out with the British over Hong Kong, that is on a 'one-country two-systems' basis which would allow Taiwan to retain a significant degree of economic and political autonomy for a period of time. But the evidence of Hong Kong since 1997 suggests that the present rulers in Beijing are rather heavy-handed in their interpretation of the 'two systems' principle, while in recent years Taiwan has moved towards a degree of democratization which the mainland regime shows no signs of even beginning to match. Economically Taiwan enjoys a degree of prosperity far outstripping the mainland, while the personal ties of the populace with the mainland, though still significant for many, are steadily weakening. It is difficult to see that the population of Taiwan, now numbering about 25 million, is likely to be willing in the foreseeable future to support the possibility of the island becoming a province of greater China once again. The wishes of the local population are a far more potent element in the total Taiwan equation than was the case in Manchuria. Also, whereas in Manchuria Japanese ambitions were under challenge from both Russia and the West, as well as from China, there is only one external power exercising any effective influence in Taiwan. There, in terms of international relations, the basic confrontation is between China and the US, with the Taiwanese government and people playing an important, perhaps ultimately decisive role.

Thus, over the course of the twentieth century Western, most notably US, policy has shifted from upholding China's claims to sovereignty in the case of Manchuria to frustrating them in the case of Taiwan. The policy is ambiguous insofar as, while it does not actually deny that the island of Taiwan is an integral part of China (a position about which, as we have seen, the historical record leaves some room for debate) its effective thrust, or rather drift, has been towards establishing Taiwan's separateness and political independence. After 20 years of maintaining the fantasy that Taiwan had become the base for the legitimate government of all China, the 1972 Nixon visit, and especially the Taiwan Relations Act of 1979, placed the island and its population in a kind of diplomatic shadow land. It has continued to be supported and protected by the US, but has ceased to be formally recognized by it, as well as by many other powers. Those other powers, unable to influence the course of events, have simply tagged along behind the US, awaiting developments. The indecisiveness that characterized Western policy in the 1930s toward Manchuria has been repeated, over an extended time span, to the understandable frustration of Chinese on both sides of the straits which separate the island from the mainland. So far the West, having created the dilemma, has been able and willing to guarantee protection against any forced return to mainland control, but given the inevitable shifts in priorities that history brings, plus the geopolitical realities of the region, one must assume that sooner or later this will change, probably within the hundred years Mao was prepared to wait.

How long the US will be willing to sustain its protective wall around Taiwan, to provide 'whatever it takes' as George W. Bush has promised, is a question which poses itself, especially given its new commitment to a war against international terrorism. China has indicated a willingness to help in that anti-terrorist war, but may expect some quid pro quo, perhaps over Taiwan, in return. It is difficult to envisage any US administration being ready to abandon Taiwan, but the present stand-off cannot remain fixed in a volatile world. Ultimately a Chinese formulated resolution of the Taiwan dilemma will surely assert itself, whatever the West thinks or prefers. Whether that will be by force, or by some 'one-country two-systems' agreement such as was reached over Hong Kong, remains uncertain. The ideal solution would be for mainland China to accept an independent but non-aligned Taiwan which, without becoming an appendage, would retain close cultural and other ties with a modernizing, and hopefully liberalizing, central kingdom. But history rarely works so neatly.

The limits of Western power

In protecting Taiwan the West has been able to continue to assert some control over China, but that appears to be about the last remnant of Pannikar's model of Western dominance. Many Westerners would like to be able to assert comparable control on behalf of Tibet, but that seems now to be a region beyond the capacity of the West to influence decisively. As with Taiwan, the maintenance of the human rights of the Tibetan populace, in particular of their religious freedom, is a concern for the West, but it has virtually no capacity to advance the cause of Tibetan autonomy, much less its independence. Tibet seems to be undergoing, in a more rapid, open and painful way, the process of full absorption into the polity of modern nationalist China that Manchuria experienced during the nineteenth and early twentieth centuries. The West, no longer having any firm political or military base within China proper, is having to recognize the limits of its power in respect of Tibet, which in Chinese eyes is as much part of their sovereign state as Manchuria or Taiwan.

As the survival of Taiwan demonstrates, the West is still able to exert some effective pressure on China from the sea, the highway by which 500 years ago it began to come regularly to China, and with modern technology it can also exert some additional pressure by air and from outer space. But the century or so of considerable power it enjoyed within China itself has passed and, strategically speaking, it has been forced back to the oceans which, save for a short-lived Japanese challenge, it has consistently controlled, indeed dominated. How long that control of the seas around China, including those around the island of Taiwan, can be maintained is a question the present century may see raised more acutely. Will a modernized equivalent of the great Ming fleets emerge, and the West be at last obliged to retreat on the China seas as it has been on its mainland? That is a development which, if it comes at all, is certainly a little way off, and control of its air space and approaches may be a higher priority for China. But whatever the military technology of the future, the West, meaning especially but not only the US, must expect the always shifting balance of power in the East Asian region to move further towards restoring China's status and influence there, albeit a China now fully open to the world at large. That observant, patient, rational man, Macartney, would have been well satisfied with such a balance, as the modern West should be.

Conclusion: Peering ahead, Uncertainly

Five hundred years of sustained contact has seen the West learn much from China, gain much from it and impose much upon it. While in the earlier centuries of the relationship it was China that set the terms, from the mid-nineteenth to the mid-twentieth centuries the West was dominant, often very aggressive. In recent decades, however, the two great traditions have edged cautiously, if uncertainly, towards a more even balance of power and interests than at any point in the past. Maintaining and securing that balance is a challenge for both traditions, but especially for the West, which over the centuries has been responsible for creating and for insisting on sustaining and extending the contact.

From one perspective that contact may fairly be described as a clash of civilizations, with the West the main troublemaker. Some fear it may continue in that mode, with China now more likely to be the main troublemaker. But the contact may equally well be seen as having been a process of coming together, very painfully and unevenly for China, to the enrichment of both traditions – enrichment, that is, unless one wishes to mourn the passing of the less affluent, less technologically advanced, and more contained worlds we have long lost. Given mutual good sense and goodwill the chances for still greater enrichment seem as real as the chances that there will be ongoing confrontations and yet more serious clashes. Despite continuing important points of difference – over Taiwan, human rights, trade practices, the balance of military power, the sale of arms, and so on – China appears better able to adapt to the secular, humanist, nation-based and capitalist world the modern West has sought to universalize than do some other great traditions, such as that of Islam. China's eclectic, this-world-centred intellectual tradition seems better attuned, though by no means perfectly so, to that of the post-Enlightenment West than are some other alternative traditions. This may be a good basis for future co-existence – so long, that is, as the West itself does not aggressively assert presumptions of superior authority and righteousness, as it has been prone to do.

Whatever the degree of future co-operation or confrontation between the West and China, the twenty-first century is sure to see, as the nineteenth and twentieth centuries did, great changes in the global balance of forces. Western power dominated those centuries, though it was seriously challenged for a time in East Asia by Japan. How far China may develop as an effective countervailing force, as some suggest it could have been back in the sixteenth century if it had retained its naval power, is a question impossible to answer at present. But overall there seem to be reasonable grounds to hope that the West and China can establish a comfortable enough future pattern of fruitful co-existence. Such a desirable outcome requires, among other things, that 'the West' does not come to mean simply an over-mighty, often well-meaning but as often self-righteous and go-it-alone, US. The total Western experience and understanding of and involvement with China needs to be sustained and drawn upon. The British diplomat, Sir Percy Cradock, concluding his most interesting memoir of 30 years experience of China, years which included the peak of Mao's Cultural Revolution and the negotiations with Mao's successors over Hong Kong, reflected that, looking back over both the shorter and longer term vistas of Sino-British (for which we may here fairly read Western) relations, 'Both sides have enjoyed at best partial vision. To us they were the inscrutable Chinese; to them we were the unfathomable barbarians.' Partial vision remains a problem, but entering the sixth century of sustained contact the West does seem to have gained a clearer, more balanced view of China, its people, their needs and interests, than was the norm in the past. A clear eyed view of that past and of the West's role in it, such as this survey has endeavoured to convey, is a desirable, perhaps necessary, condition for future peacable and profitable relations with China. Who was it said that those who ignore the past condemn themselves to repeating it?

Notes

1 A Wide World Apart, with Differing Views of Heaven and Earth

1 Frances Wood, *Did Marco Polo Go to China?* (London, Secker and Warburg, 1995); but compare John Larner, *Marco Polo and the Discovery of the World* (Yale, 1999) pp. 58–63.

2 P.N. Stears et al., *World Civilizations: the Global Experience* (New York, Harper Collins, 1992) p. 648, also 476–7. For the 'countervailing' argument note also C.P. Fitzgerald, *China: A Short Cultural History* (New York, Praeger, 1954) pp. 473–4: 'Had the Chinese sustained the work so well began by Cheng Ho [Zheng He], established permanent bases, maintained their sea power and founded an overseas empire, it is at least possible that the course of history would have been profoundly different . . . China in later centuries was to pay dearly for missing this opportunity'. J.K. Fairbank in *China Watch* (Harvard, 1987) p. 132 also suggests 'If they had wanted to the Chinese could have made all of S.E.Asia their colony long before the Europeans did so.' Basic articles on the Ming voyages are by Paul Pelliot and J.L. Duyvendak in *T'oung Pao* vols 30 (1933) and 34 (1938). Note also J. Needham, *Science and Civilization in China* (Cambridge, 1954–99) vol. 4, Section 29, and Louise Levathes, *When China Ruled the Seas* (New York, Simon and Schuster, 1994).

3 Needham, op.cit., pp. 484, 525.

4 J.H. Parry, *The Age of Reconnaissance* (Mentor, 1964) p. 141; also his *Europe and a Wider World* (Hutchinson, 1949) Ch. 1.

5 C.M. Cipolla, *Guns and Sails in the Early Phase of European Expansion 1400–1700* (London, Collins, 1965) pp. 122–3.

6 Louise Levathes, op.cit., Ch. 4. On the size of these ships in his article 'Paul Pelliot and the State-of-the-Art in Research on Fifteenth Century Ming Navigations' in *Varietés Sinologiques (N.S. No. 78) Actes du VIme Colloque International de Sinologie* (Sept. 1989) Shi-shan Tsai gives the following table for the total built for the seven expeditions:

	Masts	Length (ft)	Width (ft)	Numbers
Treasure Ship	9	444	180	36
Horse Ship	8	370	150	700
Grain Ship	7	280	120	240
Billet Ship	6	240	94	300
Fighting Ship	5	180	68	180

7 E. Schafer, *The Golden Peaches of Samarkand* (University of California Press, 1963) p. 35.

8 C.K. Yang, *Religion in Chinese Society* (Berkeley, 1961) p. 21: 'Buddhism is of foreign origin, but it has been so assimilated into Chinese culture that the untutored common man in China is no longer aware that it was introduced from India.'
9 P.D. Curtin, *Cross Cultural Trade in World History* (Cambridge, 1984) Ch. 6.
10 Robert Hart, *These From the Land of Sinim* (London, Chapman Hall, 1901) p. 61.
11 D.F. Lach, *Asia in the Making of Europe* (Chicago, 1993) vol. III, p. 1892.
12 K.N. Chaudhuri, *Trade and Civilization in the Indian Ocean* (Cambridge, 1985) p. 122; also F. Braudel, *Civilization and Capitalism 15th to 18th Century* (London, Fontana Press, 1985) pp. 484ff, 528–9.
13 Joanna Waley-Cohen, *The Sextants of Beijing: Global Currents in Chinese History* (New York, W.W. Norton, 1999) passim. Two other recent works which challenge excessive Euro-centred emphasis on global economic development are Andre Gunder Frank, *Re Orient: Global Economy in the Asian Age* (Berkeley, 1998) and K. Pomeranz, *The Great Divergence Europe, China and the Making of the Modern World Economy* (Princeton, 2000). Note also E.L. Jones, *Growth Recurring: Economic Change in World History* (Oxford, 1989).
14 C.P. Fitzgerald, *Europe and China: an Historical Comparison* (Canberra, 1969) pp. 8–10.
15 G. Cressey, *China's Geographic Foundation* (New York, McGraw Hill, 1934) Ch. 1, and R.J. Smith, *China's Cultural Heritage* (Boulder, Westview Press, 2nd edn, 1994) p. 23.
16 D. Bodde, *Chinese Thought, Society and Science* (Honolulu, 1991) Ch. 4. On China's religious tradition see C.K. Yang op.cit., and the essay by T.H. Barrett in (ed.) P.S. Ropp, *Heritage of China* (Berkeley, 1990) which gives further references.
17 J.K. Fairbank, *China: a New History* (Harvard, 1992) pp. 183–6, also 257–9.

2 Coming Together, Rather Slowly and on China's Terms (1500–1800)

1 K.M. Pannikar, *Asia and Western Dominance* (1st edn, London, Allen & Unwin, 1953) pp. 11–13; compare 2nd edn, 1959, p. 14.
2 B.B. Kling and M.N. Pearson, *The Age of Partnership* (University of Hawaii Press, 1979) Introduction.
3 Quoted. D.F. Lach, *Asia in the Making of Europe*, vol. 1 (Chicago, 1965) p. 731.
4 On the Pires embassy see J.E. Wills in *The Cambridge History of China*, vol. 8 (1998) pp. 333–41, and T.T. Chang, *Sino-Portuguese Trade from 1514 to 1644* (Leiden, E.J. Brill, 1933) Ch. 2.
5 J.K. Fairbank, *Trade and Diplomacy on the China Coast* (Harvard, 1953) p. 46.
6 L. Dermigny, *La Chine et l'Occident: Le Commerce a Canton du 18me siècle 1719–1833* (Paris, 1963) Ch. 1, pp. 74–5. For detailed statistics of Western trade to China, including numbers of ships coming to Canton, see the many Tables in Earl H. Pritchard, *Anglo-Chinese Relations During the Seventeenth and Eighteenth Centuries* (New York, Octagon Books, 1970, reprint of 1929 edn).
7 On Anson's stay at Canton see L.A. Wilcox, *Anson's Voyage* (London, Bell, 1969) Ch. 17, 19, and Glynn Williams, *The Prize of All the Oceans* (London, Harper Collins, 1999) Ch. 7.

8   Quoted in Select Committee Report on Trade with China, in the House of
    Lords Sessional Papers 1840, vol. 24, p. 172.
9   From his *The Law of Nations* (c. 1765) as quoted by J.L. Hevia in *Cherishing
    Men From Afar* (Duke, 1995) p. 80; note also Vattel quoted in H.B. Morse
    The International Relations of the Chinese Empire, vol. I (1910) p. 138, n. 2:
    'Men are therefore under an obligation to carry on that commerce with each
    other, if they wish not to depart from the view of nature; and this obligation
    extends also to whole nations or states...'
10 S.A.M. Adshead, *China in World History* (London, Macmillan, 1988) pp. 240–2.
11 L.J. Gallacher (tr) *China in the 16th Century: the Journals of Matthew Ricci
    1583–1610* (New York, Random House, 1953) pp. 97–8.
12 P.A. Rule, *K'ung-tzu or Confucius? The Jesuit Interpretation of Confucianism*
    (Sydney, Allen & Unwin, 1986) p. 26; also V. Cronin, *The Wise Man from
    the West* (Readers Union edn 1956) p. 255.
13 Père de Premare in *Lettres Edifiantes et Curieuses* (Toulouse, 1810 edn) t. 16, p. 338.
    For the text of the 1692 Edict of Toleration see Fu Lo-shu, *A Documentary
    Chronicle of Sino-Western Relations 1644–1820* (Tucson, 1966) vol. I, pp. 105–6.
14 Quoted in A.H. Rowbotham, *Missionary and Mandarin* (University of
    California Press, 1942) pp. 145–6.
15 Quoted in Rule, op.cit., p. 145.
16 Père Amiot, quoted in Hope Danby, *The Garden of Perfect Brightness* (London,
    1949) pp. 131–2; note also Rule, pp. 183–5.
17 Rule, op.cit., p. 149; note also Fairbank, *Trade and Diplomacy*, p. 14, and
    Rowbotham, op.cit., pp. 207–11.
18 C.R. Boxer, 'European Missionaries and Chinese Clergy 1654–1810' in
    B. Kling and M.N. Pearson, op.cit., pp. 97–121; also R. Entenmann,
    who examines the survival of Christian groups in Szechuan in the late
    18th century in (ed.) Daniel Bays, *Christianity in China* (Stanford, 1996).
19 J. Needham, *Science and Civilization in China*, vol. I (Cambridge, 1954) p. 149.
20 P. Hazard, *The European Mind* (Pelican Books, 1964) p. 36.
21 D.F. Lach, *The Preface to Leibniz Novissima Sinica* (1957).
22 Voltaire, *The Age of Louis XIV*, Ch. 39. Voltaire's writings on China included
    Chs 1, 2 and 195 of his *Essai sur les moeurs*, *Entretiens Chinois* and the play
    L'Orphelin de Chine. On Voltaire's views of China note A.H. Rowbotham,
    Voltaire: Sinophile (in Modern Languages Association of America Publications
    XLVII, 1932, pp. 1050–65) and J.H. Brumfitt, *Voltaire: Historian* (Oxford,
    1958), pp. 78–80.
23 John Webb, 'An Historical Essay Endeavouring a Probability that
    the Language of China is the Primitive Language' (1668) quoted by
    G.A. Kennedy, 'The Monosyllabic Myth', in *Journal of the American Oriental
    Society*, vol. 71 (1951) p. 161.
24 James Boswell, *Life of Johnson* (Oxford University Edn, 1980) p. 984; also
    p. 1211, n. 2.
25 Robert Lloyd The Cit's [sic] Country Box (1756), quoted in W.W. Appleton,
    A Cycle of Cathay (New York, Columbia University Press, 1951) p. 109. Better
    known is John Cawthorne's verse 'Of Taste' (1751):
    'Of late, 'tis true, quite sick of Rome and Greece
    We fetch our models from the wise Chinese;
    European artists are too cool and chaste,

For Mand' rin is the only man of taste' etc.
Quoted by A.O. Lovejoy in 'The Chinese Origin of a Romanticism', in his *Essays in the History of Ideas* (Capricorn Books edn, 1960) pp. 121–2.

26 A.O. Lovejoy, op.cit., p. 135.
27 Quoted ibid., p. 123.
28 S.A.M. Adshead, op.cit., pp. 279–80; also pp. 244–6.
29 See J.E. Wills, *Embassies and Illusions: Dutch and Portuguese Embassies to K'ang Hsi 1666–87* (Harvard University Press, 1984); also Fu Lo-shu, 'The Two Portuguese Embassies to China During the K'ang Hsi Period', in *T'oung Pao* 43 (1954) pp. 75–94.
30 J.K. Fairbank, *Trade and Diplomacy*, p. 14.
31 J.E. Wills, op.cit., p. 3; also his *Pepper, Guns and Parley: The Dutch East India Company and China 1662–81* (Harvard, 1974) p. 202.
32 On the kowtow ritual see J.L. Hevia, *Cherishing Men from Afar* (Duke, 1995) Ch. 5, and his essay 'Sovereignty and Subject: Constituting Relations of Power in Qing Guest Ritual', pp. 181–200 in (ed.) A. Zito and T. Barlow, *Body, Subject and Power in China* (University of Chicago Press, 1994), where he challenges the 'abject servitude' view of this ritual found in the writings of Anglo-American historians. The essay by Andrew Kipnis, pp. 201–223 in this collection, also emphasizes the function of the kowtow in maintaining social relations rather than expressing subordination. See also C.K. Yang *Religion in Chinese Society* (Berkeley, 1961) Ch. 6 and, for kowtowing before the tomb of Confucius, J. Spence, *Emperor of China* (Penguin Books, 1974) p. 71.
33 H.B. Morse, op.cit., vol. I, p. 53.
34 J. Boswell, *Life of Johnson*, pp. 296, 732, etc.; on Macartney's career and personality, see Alain Peyrefitte, *The Collision of Two Civilisations* (London, Harper-Collins, 1992) pp. 20–24.
35 For Macartney's Instructions see H.B. Morse, *Chronicles of the East India Company Trading to China 1635–1834* (5 vols, Oxford, 1925) vol. II, pp. 232–42. All subsequent quotes from the Instructions are to be found in these pages.
36 On the gifts see H.L. Hevia op.cit., see Index under 'Gifts' esp. p. 110; also Aubrey Singer, *The Lion and the Dragon* (London, Barrie & Jenkins, 1992) see Index Under 'Presents' esp. pp. 88, 92–3, and J. Barrow, *Travels in China* (London, 1806) p. 113, who reported that he was sneeringly asked whether he supposed the emperor would suffer any man to sit higher than himself.
37 The source of this saying is uncertain. In a letter to me in response to my query about it Alain Peyrefitte replied: 'I am sorry to admit that I am unable to give you a proper reference as to the famous warning attributed to Napoleon ... I had made thorough researches in the books recording Napoleon's words (Saint Helena's Chronicles; Las Cases Memoirs; Montholon, etc.) but in vain. It is simply the oral tradition that has transmitted this expression to us.'
38 See Hevia, Singer, Peyrefitte as in refs 32, 34 and 36 above; also Christopher Hibbert *The Dragon Wakes* (Longman, 1970) and esp. (ed.) J.L. Cranmer-Byng, *An Embassy to China, Being the Journal kept by Lord Macartney during his embassy to the Emperor Ch'ien Lung 1793–1794* (London, Longmans Green & Co., 1962).
39 On the Amherst embassy see H.B. Morse, *Chronicles of the East India Company*, vol. III, pp. 256–306, esp. 300–2 for the Edict of the Jiaqing emperor in very similar terms to the Qianlong emperors of 1793.

40 J.L. Hevia, op.cit., Chs 6, 7.
41 For full text see J.L. Cranmer-Byng, *An Embassy to China*, pp. 336–41.
42 Bertrand Russell, *The Problem of China* (Allen & Unwin; 1st edn 1922; 1966 reprint) pp. 49–51.
43 See Cranmer-Byng, op.cit., pp. 166–7.
44 Ibid. p. 164.
45 Ibid. p. 153. Not only 'the lower orders' were of 'a trafficking turn'. When the central government limited trade too severely, or proposed to cut it off altogether as a means of punishing unruly barbarians, there were generally strong protests from merchants, gentry and local officials in the ports affected. See T.T. Chang, *Sino-Portuguese Trade* Ch. 4, esp. pp. 81–4.
46 Ibid. p. 213.
47 On the Dutch embassy of 1795 see J.L. Duyvendak, 'The Last Dutch Embassy to the Chinese Court', in *T'oung Pao* XXXIV (1938).
48 N. Peffer, *The Far East* (Ann Arbor, University of Michigan Press, 1958) pp. 53–4 for a discussion of this principle.

3 Closer Encounters, on the West's Terms (1800–1900)

1 Quoted in M.E. Cameron, *The Reform Movement in China 1898–1912* (New York, Octagon Books, 1963) pp. 36–7.
2 J.K. Fairbank in *New York Times Book Review*, 11 January 1976, reviewing Peter Fay's *The Opium War 1840–42* (Chapel Hill, 1975). See Fay's article 'Was the Opium War of 1840–42 a Just War?' in *Ch'ing-shih wen-t'i*, vol. 3, Supplement 1, 1977. For other comments by Fairbank on the opium trade see *Cambridge History of China*, vol. X, Part 1(1978) pp. 213–216, and his *China Watch* (Harvard University Press, 1987) pp. 13–14.
3 J.K. Fairbank and S.Y. Teng, *China's Response to the West* (Harvard, 1954) pp. 24–7.
4 V. Berridge and G. Edwards, *Opium and the People, Opiate Use in 19th century England* (London, Allen Lane, St Martins Press, 1981) pp. 30–1. See also Martin Booth, *Opium: a History* (New York, Simon and Schuster, 1996) Ch. 4.
5 Quoted, M. Greenberg, *British Trade and the Opening of China* (Cambridge, 1951) p. 105.
6 The French observer is quoted by J. Spence in his essay on opium in his collection *Chinese Roundabout* (New York, W.W. Norton & Co., 1992) p. 233. The estimate of one per cent, which would amount to 3–4 million consumers, is in Martin Booth, op.cit., p. 128, but Fairbank, in *Trade and Diplomacy*, p. 64, states that, judging by the quantity available, the total number of smokers in the 1840s 'can hardly have exceeded one million, and was probably less.' Estimating the total number of consumers and smokers in China at any point of time is largely guesswork, but there can be no question that it became substantial.
7 Greenberg, op.cit., p. 104.
8 Carl A. Trocki in *Opium, Empire and the Political Economy* (Routledge, 1999) argues that the opium trade was crucial to the development of the European empire of trade – 'Though difficult to prove beyond question, it seems likely that without opium there would have been no empire. Opium, both in the case of capitalist development as well as in the case of colonial finance,

served to tighten up those key areas of "slack" in European systems, and facilitated the global connections that in effect were the empire.' (p. 59). See also J.W. Wong, *Deadly Dreams* (Cambridge, 1998), Part VI, and K. Pomeranz and S. Topik, *The World That Trade Created* (New York, 1999) pp. 102–5.

9   Quoted in Greenberg, op.cit., p. 215. For Bowring see Fairbank, op.cit., pp. 73, 277–9. J.W. Wong argues strongly that for the British such free trade principles did not extend to their trade in Opium – see *Deadly Dreams*, p. 416ff.

10   On Lord Napier in China see H.B. Morse, *International Relations of the Chinese Empire* (Longmans, 1910) vol. I Ch. 6; W.C. Costin, *Great Britain and China* (Oxford, 1937) pp. 21–5 and Priscilla Napier, *Barbarian Eye: Lord Napier in China 1834, The Prelude to Hong Kong* (London, 1995).

11   J. Polachek, *The Inner Opium War* (Harvard, 1992) p. 102.

12   On Commissioner Lin see Hsin-pao Chang, *Commissioner Lin and the Opium War* (Harvard, 1964) and Polachek, op.cit., p. 127ff.

13   Quoted in Morse, *International Relations*, vol. I, p. 622.

14   Quoted in Costin, *Great Britain and China*, p. 74.

15   Hudson Taylor, quoted in M. Booth, *Opium*, pp. 148–9; compare S.A.M. Adshead, *Material Culture in Europe and China 1400–1800* (Macmillan, 1997) pp. 234–8.

16   See M. Booth, *Opium*, p. 151ff.

17   See Berridge and Edwards, op.cit., Ch. 14, esp. pp. 185–8 and K. Lodwick, *Crusaders Against Opium* (University Press of Kentucky, 1996) Chs. 3, 4. See also Gregory Blue in T. Brook and B.T. Wakabayashi (eds), *Opium Regimes* (Berkeley, 2000), pp. 31–47.

18   Mary Wright, *China in Revolution: the First Phase 1900–1913* (Yale, 1968) pp. 14–15.

19   For the texts of these treaties see W.F. Mayers, *Treaties Between the Empire of China and Foreign Powers* (Taipei, Ch'eng wen Co., 1966) pp. 1–20. All following quotes from the treaties are to be found there.

20   I.C.Y. Hsu, *China's Entry into the Family of Nations* (Harvard, 1960) p. 140.

21   P.A. Cohen in *The Cambridge History of China*, vol. X, Part 1, Ch. 11, esp. pp. 550–2, 571–2.

22   See E. Swisher, *China's Management of the American Barbarian 1841–61* (Yale, 1953) p. 137.

23   J.K. Fairbank, *Trade and Diplomacy*, p. 198.

24   G.W. Keeton, *The Development of Extraterritoriality in China* (London, Longmans Green, 1928), vol. II, p. 155.

25   *Cambridge History of China*, vol. X, Part 1, pp. 375–85.

26   Teng Ssu-yu, *Chang Hsi and the Treaty of Nanking* (University of Chicago Press, 1944) pp. 93–4 and 176, n. 339.

27   See B.A. Ellemann, *Modern Chinese Warfare 1795–1989* (London, Routledge, 2001) Ch. 2; also P. Fay, *The Opium War 1840–42* (Chapel Hill, University of North Carolina Press, 1975) Chs 24, 25.

28   Quoted Fairbank, *Trade and Diplomacy*, p. 129.

29   See Fairbank, op.cit., pp. 57, 114, 466–7; also *Cambridge History of China*, vol. XI (1980) pp. 20–21. Compare Li Chien-nung, *The Political History of China 1840–1928* (Princeton-van Nostrand, 1956) p. 42.

30   T. Walrond (ed.), *Letters and Journals of James, 8th Earl of Elgin* (London, 1872) p. 251. On Elgin's distaste for the task he had to do in China note I.C.Y. Hsu, op.cit., Ch. 5.

31   For Elgin's admonition see *Correspondence Relative to the Earl of Elgin's Special Mission to China and Japan 1857–59*, pp. 240–1 (pp. 660–1 in vol. 33 of the Dublin University Press reprint of British Parliamentary Papers).

32   Quoted in I.C.Y. Hsu, op.cit., pp. 96–7.

33   For this Proclamation see W.F. Mayers, op.cit., p. 7.

34   On the attempted co-operative policy see Mary Wright, *The Last Stand of Chinese Conservatism* (Stanford, 1957) Ch. 3. Note also J.W. Wong, op.cit., Ch. 9, on 'the Liberal conscience' toward China in the British parliament. For a German historian's recognition of this aspect of the situation see Wolfgang Franke, *China and the West* (Oxford, 1967) pp. 88–9.

35   See the letter of Sir Frederick Bruce, dated Peking 12 January 1864, reprinted in *Ch'ing-shih wen-t'i*, vol. 1, no. 5 (April 1967) pp. 11–14. For Bruce's worry about the principle of extraterritoriality, which he warned 'would become a source of disorganization and prejudicial to all interests unless exercised with great caution and confined within the narrowest limits', see S.F. Wright, *China's Struggle for Tariff Autonomy* (Shanghai, 1938; Taipei reprint, 1966) p. 165.

36   See N. Pelcovits, *Old China Hands and the Foreign Office* (New York, Kings Crown Press for the Institute of Pacific Relations, 1948).

37   Quoted in Morse, *International Relations*, vol. II, p. 220.

38   K.S. Latourette, *A History of the Christian Missions in China* (London, 1929; Taipei reprint 1966) pp. 181 and 196.

39   J. Spence, *God's Chinese Son* (Harper Collins, 1996) pp. 107–8. On the Chinese-ness of Taiping Christianity see Jordan Paper, *The Spirits are Dark* (State University of New York Press, 1995).

40   See F. Michael, *The Taiping Rebellion* (Seattle, University of Washington Press, 1966) vol. I, Part VI.

41   E. Stock, *History of the Church Missionary Society* (London, 1899) vol. II, p. 312, and C.P. Fitzgerald, op.cit., pp. 582, 584.

42   J.K. Fairbank and Merle Goldman, *China: a New History* (Harvard, 1998) p. 211.

43   For statistics see Latourette, op.cit., pp. 181, 196; also *Cambridge History of China*, vol. X, Part I, pp. 546, 557.

44   Ibid. p. 543.

45   Ibid. p. 560.

46   J. Gernet, *China and the Christian Impact* (Cambridge, 1985) p. 247.

47   See Jessie Lutz, *Christian Missions in China: Evangelists of What?* (Boston, Heath, 1965) pp. 11–12.

48   From *The Missionary Magazine and Chronicle*, vol. 7 (1843) p. 20. For another example note the Inaugural Address by the American missionary E.C. Bridgman to the Shanghai Literary and Scientific Society, in their Journal no. 1 (June 1858) – 'In almost every sphere of learning the ground is to be cleared; mountains of superstition are to be leveled; and old foundations, laid deep in error are to be broken up, so that new structures, beautiful and substantial, may be erected in their stead' etc. (p. 4).

49   For these reports see *Occasional Papers of the China Inland Mission 1872–75* (London, 1875) pp. 47–9. Doolittle, op.cit., Ch. 18.

50 E. Zurcher, *The Buddhist Conquest of China* (Leiden, Brill, 1959).
51 J.L. Cranmer-Byng, op.cit., pp. 161, 212–213.
52 John Barrow, *Travels in China* (London, 1806, Taipei reprint, 1972) p. 355.
53 Quoted in G.A. Kennedy, 'The Monosyllabic Myth' in *Journal of the American Oriental Society*, vol. 71 (1951) pp. 161–6.
54 Quoted in P.A. Cohen, *Discovering History in China* (Columbia, 1984) p. 59.
55 Quoted in W.L. Schwartz, *The Imaginative Interpretation of the Far East in Modern French Literature 1800–1925* (Paris, 1927) pp. 17–18.
56 G.W.F. Hegel, *The Philosophy of History* (New York, Dover Publications edn, 1956) pp. 116, 136–7.
57 *Karl Marx on Colonialism and Modernization*, Shlomo Avineri (ed.) (New York, Anchor Books, Doubleday, 1969) pp. 49–50.
58 *The Times*, 29 Dec 1856, p. 10.
59 See Raymond Dawson, *The Chinese Chameleon* (London, Oxford, 1967) Ch. 7.
60 J.H. Bridges, et al., *International Policy: Essays on the Foreign Relations of England* (London, Chapman & Hall, 1866) pp. 431–42.
61 *Church Missionary Society Record*, vol. 21 (Nov 1850).
62 Quoted by J.G. Utley pp. 115–16 in J. Goldstein et al. (ed.) *America Views China* (Bethlehem Pa., Lehigh University Press, 1991). On Bret Harte note J. Spence *The Chan's Great Continent* (London, Penguin Press, 1998) pp. 126–9.
63 Robert Fortune, *Three Years Wandering in the Northern Provinces of China* (London, John Murray, 1847) Ch. 1.
64 Quoted in R. Dawson, op.cit., p. 139; see also Legge's comments in his Introduction to *The Chinese Classics* (Hong Kong University Press edn, 1960) vol. I, pp. 90–111.
65 See *British Documents on the Origin of the War 1898–1914*, ed. G.P. Gooch & H. Temperley (London, HMSO, 1926–1938) vol. I.
66 K. Pannikar, op.cit., pp. 173, 190.
67 Rhoads Murphey, *The Outsiders: the Western Experience in India and China* (Ann Arbor, 1977) p. 204.

4 Hither and Thither, in Search of Comfortable Common Ground (1900–2001)

1 C.C. Tan, *The Boxer Catastrophe* (New York, Octagon Books, 1967).
2 Mary Wright (ed.) *China in Revolution: the First Phase 1900–1913* (Yale, 1968) p. 1.
3 For this edict see H.F. MacNair, *Modern Chinese History: Selected Readings* (Shanghai, Commercial Press, 1927) pp. 610–14.
4 There is a very extensive literature on the Boxers. In addition to C.C. Tan noted above see especially P.A. Cohen, *History in Three Keys: the Boxers as Event Experience and Myth* (New York, Columbia University Press, 1997) and J. Esherick, *The Origin of the Boxer Movement* (University of California Press, 1987); Jerome Ch'en, 'The Nature and Characteristics of the Boxer Movement', in *Bulletin of the School of Oriental and African Studies* (1960) pp. 287–308 (p. 295, n. 2 for the Taiyuan placard and Cohen, pp. 83–7, 320).
5 Quoted in W.L. Langer, *The Diplomacy of Imperialism* (New York, Alfred A. Knopf, 2nd edn 1960) p. 699.

6 Ibid. p. 704; also Esherick, op.cit., pp. 309–11.
7 For negotiations over this treaty of 1902 see S.F. Wright, *China's Struggle for Tariff Autonomy 1843–1938* (Shanghai, 1938) pp. 371–5; G.E. Hubbard, *British Far Eastern Policy* (Institute of Pacific Relations, 1943) pp. 29–30; F. Whyte, *China and the Foreign Powers* (Oxford University Press – R.I.I.A 1928) pp. 12–13. For the treaty see *Treaties, Conventions etc. between China and Foreign States* (Shanghai, Imperial Maritime Customs, 1907–8).
8 The basic study is T.T. Chow, *The May Fourth Movement* (Harvard, 1960).
9 On Chen Duxiu see Chow, op.cit., pp. 45–7, 275–6, 302–3, etc. and Lee Feigon, *Chen Duxiu. Founder of the Chinese Communist Party* (Princeton University Press, 1983).
10 W.R. Fishel, *The End of Extraterritoriality in China* (University of California Press, 1952) pp. 40–50.
11 For the Karakhan Declaration of 25 July 1919 see J. Degras (ed.), *Soviet Documents on Foreign Policy* (Oxford University Press – R.I.I.A, 1951) vol. I 1917–24, pp. 158–61.
12 On the diplomacy between China and the Western powers during the 1920s see R.T. Pollard, *China's Foreign Relations 1917–31* (New York, Macmillan, 1933). Akira Iriye, *After Imperialism* (Harvard, 1965). E.S. Fung, *The Diplomacy of Imperial Retreat* (Hong Kong, 1991); D. Borg, *American Policy and the Chinese Revolution 1925–28* (New York, Octagon Press, 1968); W.R. Louis, *British Strategy in the Far East 1919–39* (Oxford, 1971).
13 N. Peffer, *China: the Collapse of a Civilization* (London, Routledge, 1931) pp. 260–1, 289.
14 Quoted in S.J.G. Utley, 'American Views of China 1900–1915' in (ed.) J. Goldstein et al., *America Views China* (Lehigh, 1991) pp. 119–20.
15 Lord William Gascoyne-Cecil, *Changing China* (London, 1910) Ch. 1.
16 Rodney Gilbert, *What's Wrong With China?* (London, J. Murray, 1926); J.O.P. Bland, *China, the Pity of It* (London, Heinemann, 1932).
17 R.A. Bickers and J.N. Wasserstrom, 'Shanghai's "Dogs and Chinese Not Admitted" Sign: History and Contemporary Symbol', in *China Quarterly* 142 (1995) pp. 444–9. R. Bickers, *Britain in China* (Manchester, 1999).
18 Kay Knickrehm, 'The Early Republican Period in China 1900–1925: Western Actions and Reactions', in R.L. Lembright (ed.), *Western Views of China and the Far East* (Hong Kong, 1984) II, p. 103.
19 Bertrand Russell and H.G. Wells as quoted in ibid. p. 102.
20 S.J.G. Utley (Note 14 above) pp. 126–30.
21 W.L. Schwartz, *The Imaginative Interpretation of the Far East in Modern French Literature* (Paris, 1927) pp. 181–2.
22 K.S. Latourette, op.cit., pp. 533, 537, 567, 740, 779–80.
23 Ibid. p. 821; also Ka-che Yip, *Religion, Nationalism and Chinese Students: the Anti Christian Movement of 1922–27* (Bellingham Center for East Asian Studies, Western Washington University, 1986).
24 Akira Iriye, *Across the Pacific* (New York, Harcourt Brace, 1967) p. 186.
25 On Manchuria, see F. Michael, *The Origin of Manchu Rule* (New York, Octagon Books, 1965); Sara R. Smith, *The Manchurian Crisis 1931–2* (New York, Columbia, 1948); Hsu Shuhsi, *Essays On the Manchurian Problem* (Shanghai, Institute of Pacific Relations, 1932); K. Mitter, *The Manchurian Myth* (Berkeley, 2000); I. Nish, *Japan's Struggle with Internationalism*

(London, Kegan Paul, 1993); Louise Young, *Japan's Total Empire: Manchuria and the Culture of Wartime Imperialism* (Berkeley, 1998); Christopher Thorne, *The Limits of Foreign Policy: the West, the League and the Far Eastern Crisis 1931–33* (New York, 1973).

26 Quoted in H. Schiffrin, *Sun Yat-sen: Reluctant Revolutionary* (Boston, Lisle Brown & Co., 1980) p. 265 and Akira Iriye, *After Imperialism* (New York, 1969) p. 57. On KMT threats to collaborate with Japan note M.R. Clifford, *Retreat from China* (London, Longmans, 1967) pp. 85–7, and on 'the highly ambivalent' sentiments of many Chinese towards the Japanese during the war Lloyd Eastman's essay 'Facets of an Ambivalent Relationship' in A. Iriye (ed.), *The Chinese and the Japanese: Essays in Political and Cultural Interaction* (Princeton, 1980).

27 Quoted in F.F. Liu, *A Military History of Modern China* (Princeton, 1956) p. 60.

28 See Stella Dong, *Shanghai: The Rise and Fall of a Decadent City* (New York, Harper Collins, 2000) pp. 212–17.

29 On Ishiwara see J.H. Boyle, *China and Japan at War 1937–45* (Stanford, 1972) Ch. 3.

30 Quoted in W.I. Cohen, *America's Response to China* (Columbia, 3rd edn, 1990) p. 104.

31 Ibid. pp. 107–8.

32 W.H. Auden and C. Isherwood, *Journey to a War* (London, 1938) p. 86.

33 On Sino-Western relations during the 1930s see B.A. Lee, *Britain and the Sino-Japanese War 1937–39* (Stanford, 1973); D. Borg, *The United States and the Far Eastern Crisis of 1933–38* (Harvard, 1964); W.R. Louis, *British Strategy in the Far East 1919–39* (Oxford, 1971); A. Iriye, *Across the Pacific* (Harcourt Brace, 1967) Chs 7, 8.

34 See for example *Pearl Harbor as History: Japanese American Relations 1931–41*, Dorothy Borg and Shumpei Okamoto (eds), (Columbia, 1973); note also A. Ben-Zvi, *The Illusion of Deterrence* (Westview Press, 1987).

35 For example L. Eastman, *The Abortive Revolution: China under Nationalist Rule 1927–37* (Harvard, 1974).

36 Harold Isaacs, *Scratches on Our Minds* (New York, John Day & Co. 1958; reprint by Greenwood Press, 1973) pp. 174–6.

37 On Sino-Western relations in the 1940s see H. Feis, *The China Tangle* (Princeton, 1953); Tang Tsou, *America's Failure in China 1941–50* (Chicago, 1963); D. Borg and W. Heinrichs (eds), *Uncertain Years: Chinese American Relations 1947–50* (New York, Columbia, 1980); Xiang Lanxin, *Re-casting the Imperial Far East* (New York, M.E. Sharpe East Gate Book, 1995); Aron Shai, *Britain and China 1941–47* (Macmillan, 1984); B. Porter, *Britain and the Rise of Communist China* (London, Oxford, 1975).

38 Quoted A. Iriye, *Across the Pacific*, p. 235.

39 W.I. Cohen, op.cit., pp. 175–6.

40 For the Yalta text see Cohen, p. 144.

41 Quoted in B.A. Lee, op.cit., p. 94.

42 On the return of Hong Kong to British rule in 1945 see E. Luard, *Britain and China* (London, Chatto & Windus, 1962) pp. 180–4 and L. Allen, *The End of the War in Asia* (London, Hart Davis, 1976) pp. 251–3.

43 Beverley Hooper, *China Stands Up* (Sydney, Allen & Unwin, 1986) pp. 1–2.

44   E. Luard, op.cit., Ch. 7 and Aron Shai, op.cit., pp. 148–52: 'The foreigner was expected to assist in the launching of an independent Chinese economy on the road to modernisation and to withdraw when requested, to help and not be helped.'
45   P.A. Varg, *Missionaries, Chinese and Diplomats* (Princeton, 1958) Ch. 17; also Luard, op.cit., Ch. 6.
46   Quoted B. Porter, op.cit., Ch. 2.
47   See Harry Harding, *A Fragile Relationship: the US and China Since 1972* (Washington, the Brookings Institute, 1992) p. 33, quoting M. Oksenberg and Doak Barnett.
48   H. Isaacs, op.cit., p. 190.
49   See Table A and p. 372 in H. Harding, op.cit.; also Steven Mosher, *China Misperceived* (Harper Collins, 1990) pp. 16, 118, 172–3, 210.
50   See E. Economy & M. Oksenberg (eds) *China Joins the World: Progress and Prospects* (New York, Council of Foreign Relations, 1999); H. Harding, op.cit., and R. Moorsteen and M. Abramovitz, *Re-Making China Policy* (Harvard, 1971).
51   For text of the Shanghai Communiqué see Harding, op.cit., pp. 373–9.
52   Henry Kissinger, *The White House Years* (Boston, Little Brown, 1979) p. 1062.
53   For President Carter's statement of 15 December 1978 see *The China Factor: Sino American Relations and the Global Scene* (The American Assembly and Council on Foreign Relations, 1981) p. 300ff.
54   For the Taiwan Relations Act of 10 April 1979 see *The China Factor*, p. 304ff.
55   H. Harding, op.cit., Table A (see Note 49 above).
56   Robert Guillain, *The Blue Ants*, H. Savill (tr), (London, Secker and Warburg, 1957).
57   T. Robinson and D. Shambaugh (eds), *Chinese Foreign Policy: Theory and Practice* (Oxford, 1994) p. 212.
58   For Document 19 see D.E. MacInnis, *Religion in China Today: Policy and Practice* (New York, Orbis Books, 1989) pp. 8–26.
59   On the acceptance of religious organizations including the Christian church within a 'united front' framework see P.L. Wickeri, *Seeking the Common Ground* (New York, Orbis Books, 1988). A good short study of the Falun Gong is that of J. Wong and W.T. Liu, *The Mystery of China's Falun Gong* (Singapore, 1999).
60   Harry Harding, op.cit., (see Note 47 above).
61   Rhoads Murphey, *The Outsiders: the Western Experience in China and India* (University of Michigan Press, 1977).
62   See E. Economy and M. Oksenberg (eds), *China Joins the World: Progress and Prospects* (New York, 1999). For a study of a particular aspect of this process see Xiaohong Liu, *Chinese Ambassadors: the Rise of Diplomatic Professionalism Since 1949* (Seattle, University of Washington Press, 2001).
63   Quoted H. Harding, op.cit., p. 198.
64   On the issue of human rights within the Chinese tradition see W.T. de Bary, *Asian Values and Human Rights: a Confucian Communitarian Perspective* (Harvard, 1998) and R. Weatherley, *The Discourse of Human Rights in China* (London, Macmillan, 1999).
65   R. Bernstein and R.H. Munro, *The Coming Conflict with China* (New York, Alfred A. Knopf, 1997) p. 89.

66 The comments on Taiwan which follow are based on a selection of texts, including M.A. Rubinstein (ed.), *Taiwan: a New History* (Armonk, New York, M.E. Sharpe, 1999); John F. Copper, *Taiwan: Nation State or Province?* (Westview Press, 1996); Simon Long, *Taiwan: China's Last Frontier* (London, Macmillan, 1991); J.R. Shepherd, *Statecraft and Political Economy on the Taiwan Frontier* (Stanford, 1993); Sophia Su-fei Yen, *Taiwan in China's Foreign Relations 1836–74* (Conn., Shoestring Press, 1965); L.H.D. Gordon (ed.), *Studies in Chinese Local History* (Columbia, 1970).

67 J.E. Wills, 'From Wild Coast to Prefecture: the Transformation of Taiwan in the 17th century', in E.K.Y. Chan et al. (ed.), *Taiwan: Economy, Society and History* (Hong Kong, 1991) pp. 382–3.

68 Edgar Snow, *Red Star Over China* (London, Victor Gollancz, 1937) p. 102.

Bibliography

Note: There are many excellent survey histories of China and East Asia not listed here but to be found on the shelves of any major library at the Dewey numbers 950–1. The most substantial is the multi-volumed *Cambridge History of China*. The chapters I have looked at in that work are listed below under the individual authors.

Adshead, S.A.M., *China in World History*, London, Macmillan, 1988.
  Material Culture in Europe and China 1400–1800: The Rise of Consumerism, London, Macmillan Press, 1997.
Allen, Louis, *The End of the War in Asia*, London, Hart Davis, 1976.
Anderson, Benedict, *Imagined Communities: Reflections on The Origin and Spread of Nationalism*, London, Verso, 1991.
Appleton, W.W., *A Cycle of Cathay: The Chinese Vogue in England During the Seventeenth and Eighteenth Centuries*, New York, Columbia University Press, 1951.
Barrett, T.H., *Singular Listlessness: a Short History of Chinese Books and British Scholars*, London, Wellsweep Press, 1989.
Barrow, J., *Travels in China*, London, Cadell and Davies, 1806.
Bays, Daniel, H. (ed.), *Christianity in China: From the Eighteenth century to the present*, Stanford University Press, 1996.
Ben-Zvi, Abraham, *The Illusion of Deterrence: The Roosevelt Presidency and the Origins of the Pacific War*, Boulder & London, Westview Press, 1987.
Bernstein, R. and Munro, R.H., *The Coming Conflict with China*, New York, Alfred A. Knopf, 1997.
Berridge, V. and Edwards, G., *Opium and the People: Opiate Use in 19th Century England*, London, Allen Lane, St Martin's Press, 1981.
Bickers, R.A., *Britain in China: Community, Culture and Colonialism 1900–1949*, Manchester University Press, 1999.
Bickers, R.A. and Seton, Rosemary, *Missionary Encounters: Sources & Issues*, Curzon Press, Richmond, Surrey, 1996.
Boardman, Robert, *Britain and the People's Republic of China 1949–74*, London, Macmillan, 1976.
Bodde, D., *Chinese Thought, Society and Science*, Honolulu, University of Hawaii Press, 1991
  China's Gifts to the West, Washington, American Council On Education, 1942.
Booth, Martin, *Opium: a History*, New York, Simon and Schuster, 1996.
Borg, D., *American Policy and the Chinese Revolution 1925–28*, New York, The Macmillan Co, American IPR, 1947.
  The United States and the Far Eastern Crisis of 1933–38, Harvard University Press, 1964.
Boyle, John, H., *China and Japan at War 1937–1945. The Politics of Collaboration*, Stanford University Press, 1972.
Bridges, J.H. et al., *International Policy: Essays on the Foreign Relations of England*, London, Chapman & Hall, 1866.

Brook, Timothy and Wakabayashi, Bob, T. (eds), *Opium Regimes: China, Britain and Japan 1839–1952*, Berkeley, University of California Press, 2000.

Brumfitt, J.H., *Voltaire: Historian*, Oxford University Press, 1958.

Chang, Hsin-pao, *Commissioner Lin and the Opium War*, Harvard University Press, 1964.

Chang, T.C., 'Maritime Trade at Canton During the Ming Dynasty', in *Chinese Social and Political Science Review*, XVII. 2, 1933, 264–79.

Chang, T'ien-tse, *Sino Portuguese Trade from 1514 to 1644*, Leiden, E.J. Brill, 1933.

Chaudhuri, K.N., *Trade and Civilization in the Indian Ocean*, Cambridge University Press, 1985.

Ch'en, Jerome, *China and the West: Society and Culture 1815–1937*, London, Hutchinson, 1979.

'The Nature and Characteristics of the Boxer Movement' in *Bulletin of the School of Oriental and African Studies*, XXIII. 2, 1960, 287–308.

Ch'en, Shou-yi, 'Sino-European Cultural Contacts Since the Discovery of the Sea Route' in *Nankai Social and Economic Quarterly*, VIII-I, April 1935, 44–74.

'Daniel Defoe: China's Severe Critic' in ibid. VIII. 3, October 1935, 511–59.

Ch'u, T'ung-tsu, *Law and Society in Traditional China*, The Hague, Mouton & Co., 1961.

Ci, Jiwei, *Dialectic of the Chinese Revolution: From Utopianism to Hedonism*, Stanford University Press, 1994.

Clayton, David, *Imperialism Revisited: Political and Economic Relations between Britain and China 1950–54*, London, Macmillan, 1997.

Clifford, Nicholas, R., *Retreat from China. British Policy in the Far East 1937–1941*, London, Longmans Green & Co., 1967.

Spoilt Children of Empire. Westerners in Shanghai and the Chinese Revolution of the 1920s, Middleburg College Press, Hanover, 1991.

Cohen, P.A., *China and Christianity: the Missionary Movement And the Growth of Anti-Foreignism 1839–1939*, Harvard University Press, 1963.

'Christian Missions and their Impact to 1900', in *Cambridge History of China*, vol. X, Ch. 11.

Discovering History in China: American Historial Writing on the Recent Past, New York, Columbia University Press, 1984.

History in Three Keys: the Boxers as Event, Experience And Myth, New York, Columbia University Press, 1997.

Cohen, Warren, I., *America's Response to China: An Interpretive History of Sino-American Relations*, New York, Columbia University Press, 3rd edn 1990.

Costin, W.C., *Great Britain and China 1833–1860*, Oxford University Press, 1937.

Cradock, Sir Percy, *Experiences of China*, London, John Murray, 1994.

Cranmer-Byng, J.L. (ed.), *An Embassy to China: Being the journal kept by Lord Macartney during his embassy to the Emperor Ch'ien-Lung 1793–1794*, London, Longmans Green & Co., 1962.

Cressey, G., *China's Geographic Foundation*, New York, McGraw Hill, 1934.

Crowley, J.B., *Japan's Quest for Autonomy*, Princeton University Press, 1962.

Curtin, P.D., *Cross Cultural Trade in World History*, Cambridge University Press, 1984.

Danby, Hope, *The Garden of Perfect Brightness*, London, Williams & Norgate, 1950.

Davidson, Basil, *Daybreak in China*, London, Jonathan Cape, 1953.

Dawson, Raymond, *The Chinese Chameleon: an Analysis of European Conceptions of Chinese Civilization*, Oxford University Press, 1967.

'Western Conceptions of Chinese Civilization', in R. Dawson (ed.), *The Legacy of China*, Oxford University Press, 1964.

de Bary, W.T., *Asian Values and Human Rights: a Confucian Communitarian Perspective*, Harvard University Press, 1998.

Dermigny, Louis, *La Chine et l'Occident: Le Commerce á Canton au XVIIIme siècle 1719–1833*, 3 vols, Paris, 1964.

Dong, Stella, *Shanghai: the Rise and Fall of a Decadent City*, New York, Harper Collins, 2000.

Duyvendak, J.J.L., *China's Discovery of Africa*, London, A. Probsthain, 1949.

Economy, E. and Oksenberg, M., *China Joins the World*, New York, Council on Foreign Relations Press, 1999.

Elleman, Bruce, A., *Modern Chinese Warfare 1795–1989*, London, Routledge, 2001.

Esherick, J., *The Origin of the Boxer Movement*, University of California Press, 1987.

Eto, Shinkichi, 'China's International Relations 1911–31', in *Cambridge History of China*, vol. XIII, Ch. 2.

Fairbank, J.K., *Trade and Diplomacy on the China Coast: The Opening of the Treaty Ports 1842–1854*, Harvard University Press, 1953.

China Watch, Harvard University Press, 1987.

China: a New History, Harvard University Press, 1992.

The Chinese World Order (ed.), Harvard University Press, 1968.

Chinese Thought and Institutions (ed.), University of Chicago Press, 1957.

'The Creation of the Treaty System', in *Cambridge History of China*, vol. X, Ch. 5.

'Maritime and Continental in Chinese History', in *Cambridge History of China*, vol. XII, Ch. 1.

Fay, Peter, *The Opium War 1840–42*, Chapel Hill, University of North Carolina Press, 1975.

'Was the Opium War of 1840–42 a Just War?' in *Ch'ing-shih wen-t'i*, vol. 3.1, Dec 1977, pp. 17–31.

Feis, Herbert, *The Road to Pearl Harbor*, Princeton University Press, 1950.

The China Tangle: the American Effort in China from Pearl Harbor to the Marshall Mission, Princeton University Press, 1953.

Feuerwerker, A., 'The Foreign Presence in China', in *Cambridge History of China*, vol. XII, Ch. 3.

Fishel, W.R., *The End of Extraterritoriality in China*, University of California Press, 1952.

Fitzgerald, C.P., *China: A Short Cultural History*, London, Cresset Press, 1935; rev.edn New York, Praeger, 1954.

The Chinese View of their Place in the World, Oxford University Press, 1964; *Europe and China: an Historical Comparison*, Canberra, Australian Humanities Research Council, 1969.

Fletcher, J., 'The Heyday of Ch'ing Order in Mongolia, Sinkiang and Tibet', in *Cambridge History of China*, vol. X, Ch. 8.

Frank, Andre, G., *Re Orient: Global Economy in the Asian Age*, Berkeley, University of California Press, 1998.

Franke, Wolfgang (tr R. Wilson), *China and the West*, Oxford University Press, 1967.

Fu, Lo-shu, *A Documentary Chronicle of Sino Western Relations 1644–1820*, (2 vols) University of Arizona Press, 1966.

Fung, S., *The Diplomacy of Imperial Retreat: Britain's South China Policy 1924–31*, Hong Kong, Oxford University Press, 1991.

Gernet, J. (tr Janet Lloyd), *China and the Christian Impact*, Cambridge University Press, 1985.

Goldstein, J., Israel, J. and Conroy, H. (eds), *America Views China: American Images of China Then and Now*, Bethlehem Pa., Lehigh University Press, 1991.

Gray, Jack, *Rebellions and Revolutions: China from the 1800s to the 1980s*, Oxford, 1990.

Greenberg, Michael, *British Trade and the Opening of China*, Cambridge, 1951.

Gregory, J.S., *Jiang Jieshi (Chiang Kai-shek)*, St. Lucia, University of Queensland Press, 1982.

'British Missionary Reactions to the Taiping Movement in China', in *Journal of Religious History*, II. 3, 1963, 204–17.

Great Britain and the Taipings, London, Routledge Kegan Paul, 1969.

Harding, Harry, *A Fragile Relationship: the U.S. and China Since 1972*, Washington, The Brookings Institute, 1992.

Hevia, J.L., *Cherishing Men From Afar: Qing Guest Ritual and The Macartney Embassy of 1793*, Durham, Duke University Press, 1995.

Honour, Hugh, *Chinoiserie: the Vision of Cathay*, London, John Murray, 1961.

Hooper, Beverley, *China Stands Up: Ending the Western Presence 1948–1950*, Sydney, Allen & Unwin, 1986.

Hsu, I.C.Y., *China's Entry into the Family of Nations*, Harvard University Press, 1960.

'Late Ch'ing Foreign Relations 1866–1905', in *Cambridge History of China*, XI, Ch. 2.

Hu, Weixing, Chan, Gerald and Zha, Daojiang, *China's International Relations in the 21st Century: Dynamics of Paradigm Shift*, Lanham & New York University Press of America, 2000.

Hudson, G.F., *Europe and China: a Survey of their relations from the earliest times to 1800*, London, E. Arnold, 1931.

'China and the World', Ch. 7 in R. Dawson (ed.), *The Legacy of China*, Oxford University Press, 1964.

Hughes, E.R., *The Invasion of China by the Western World*, Oxford, 1937.

Huntington, S.P., *The Clash of Civilizations: Re-making of World Order*, New York, Simon & Schuster, 1997.

Iriye, Akira, *After Imperialism: the Search for a New Order in the Far East 1921–31*, New York, Atheneum Books, 1969; original edn Harvard University Press, 1965.

Across the Pacific, New York, Harcourt Brace, Harbinger Book, 1967.

(ed.), *The Chinese and the Japanese: Essays in Political and Cultural Interaction*, Princeton University Press, 1980.

'Japan's Aggression and China's International Position 1931–49', in *Cambridge History of China*, vol. XIII, Ch. 10.

The Cold War in Asia, New Jersey, Prentice Hall, 1974.

Isaacs, Harold, *Scratches on Our Minds: American Images of China and India*, New York, John Day & Co., 1958.

Jones, E.L., *Growth Recurring: Economic Change in World History*, Oxford University Press, 1988.

Keeton, G.W., *The Development of Extraterritoriality in China*, London, Longmans Green, 1928.

Kennan, G.F., *American Diplomacy 1900–1950*, University of Chicago, 1951. Mentor edn 1952.

Kennedy, G.A., 'The Monosyllabic Myth', in *Journal of the American Oriental Society*, 71 (1951), 161–6.

Kirby, W.C., 'The Internationalization of China: Foreign Relations at Home and Abroad in the Republican Era', in *China Quarterly*, 150, June 1997.

Kling, B.B. and Pearson, M.N., *The Age of Partnership: Europeans in Asia Before Dominion*, Honolulu, University of Hawaii Press, 1979.

Lach, D.F., *Asia in the Making of Europe*, University of Chicago Press, 3 vols., 1965, 1970 and 1993.

The Preface to Leibniz Novissima Sinica, Honolulu, University of Hawaii Press, 1957.

'China and the Era of the Enlightenment', in *Journal of Modern History*, 1942, pp. 209–23.

'Leibniz and China', in *Journal of the History of Ideas*, 1945, pp. 436–55.

Langer, W.L., *The Diplomacy of Imperialism*, New York, Alfred A. Knopf, 1935; 2nd edn 1960.

Latourette, K.S., *A History of the Christian Missions in China*, London, SPCK, 1929.

Lee, B.A., *Britain & the Sino Japanese War, 1937–1939: A Study in the Dilemmas of British Decline*, Stanford University Press, 1973.

Lembright, R.L. et al., H.A. Myers, (ed.), *Western Views of China and the Far East*, Hong Kong, Asian Monograph Series, 1984.

Levathes, Louise, *When China Ruled the Seas*, New York, Simon & Schuster, 1994.

Li, H.H., *The Garden Flowers of China*, New York, Ronald Press, 1959.

Liu, Xiaohong, *Chinese Ambassadors: the Rise of Diplomatic Professionalism Since 1949*, Seattle, University of Washington Press, 2001.

Lodwick, Kathleen, L., *Crusaders Against Opium: Protestant Missionaries in China, 1874–1917*, University Press of Kentucky, 1996.

Long, Simon, *Taiwan: China's Last Frontier*, London, Macmillan, 1991.

Louis, W.R., *British Strategy in the Far East 1919–39*, Oxford, 1971.

Lovejoy, Arthur, O., *Essays in the History of Ideas*, New York, Putnam, Capricorn Book, 1960; original edn John Hopkins Press, 1948.

Lu, Aiguo, *China and the Global Economy Since 1840*, Houndmills, Basingstoke, Palgrave, 2000.

Lu, David, J., *From the Marco Polo Bridge to Pearl Harbor: Japan's Entry into World War II*, Washington, Public Affairs Press, 1961.

Luard, Evan, *Britain and China*, London, Chatto & Windus, 1962.

MacFarquhar, R., *Sino-American Relations 1949–71*, London, R.I.I.A., 1972.

MacInnis, Donald E., *Religion in China Today: Policy and Practice*, Maryknoll New York, Orbis Books, 1989.

Mackerras, Colin, *Western Images of China*, Oxford University Press, 1991.

Mancall, M., *China at the Centre*, New York, Free Press, 1984.

Mason, Mary, G., *Western Concepts of China and the Chinese*, New York, Columbia University Press, 1939.

Maverick, L.A., *China: a Model for Europe*, San Antonio, P. Anderson, 1946.

Michael, F., *The Origin of Manchu Rule in China: Frontier and Bureaucracy as Interacting Forces in the Chinese Empire*, Baltimore, John Hopkins Press, 1942.

Mitter, K., *The Manchurian Myth*, Berkeley, University of California Press, 2000.

Moorsteen, R. and Abramowitz, M., *Re-Making Chinese Policy*, Harvard University Press, a Rand Corporation Study, 1971.

Morley, J.W. (ed.), *The China Quagmire: Japan's Expansion on the Asian Continent 1933–41*, New York, Columbia UP, 1983.

Morse, H.B., *The International Relations of the Chinese Empire*, 3 vols, London, Longmans, 1910–18.

The Chronicles of the East India Company Trading to China 1635–1834, 5 vols, Oxford, 1925.

Mosher, Steven, W., *China Misperceived: American Illusions and Chinese Reality*, Harper Collins, 1990.

Mungello, David. E., *The Great Encounter of China and the West 1500–1800*, Rowman and Littlefield, 1999.

Curious Land: Jesuit Missionaries and the Origin of Sinology, University of Hawaii Press, 1985.

Leibniz and Confucianism: the Search for Accord, Honolulu, University of Hawaii Press, 1977.

Murphey, Rhoads, *The Outsiders: the Western Experience in India and China*, Ann Arbor, University of Michigan Press, 1977.

Napier, Priscilla, *Barbarian Eye: Lord Napier in China 1834, Prelude to Hong Kong*, London, Washington Brassey's, 1995.

Nish, Ian, *Japan's Struggle with Internationalism*, London, Kegan Paul, 1993.

Owen, D.E., *British Opium Policy in China and India*, Yale University Press, 1934.

Pak, Hyobom, *China and the West: Myths and Realities in History*, Leiden, E.J. Brill, 1974.

Pannikar, K., *Asia and Western Dominance*, London, Allen & Unwin, 1953; 2nd edn 1959.

Pelcovits, Nathan, *Old China Hands and the Foreign Office*, New York, Kings Crown Press, 1948.

Petersen, W., 'Learning from Heaven: the Introduction of Christianity and Other Western Ideas in Late Ming China', in *Cambridge History of China*, VIII, Ch. 12.

Peyrefitte, Alain (tr J. Rothschild), *The Collision of Two Civilisations: The British Expedition to China in 1792–4*, London, Harper Collins, 1993.

Polachek, J., *The Inner Opium War*, Harvard University Press, 1992.

Pollard, R.T., *China's Foreign Relations 1917–31*, New York, Macmillan Co., 1933.

Pomeranz, K., *The Great Divergence: Europe, China and the Making of the Modern World Economy*, Princeton University Press, 2000.

Pomeranz, K., and Topik, S. *The World that Trade Created: Society, Culture and the World Economy, 1400–the Present*, Armonk, New York, M.E. Sharpe, 1999.

Porter, Brian, *Britain and the Rise of Communist China: a Study of British Attitudes 1945–54*, London, Oxford University Press, 1967.

Pritchard, Earl, H., *The Crucial Years of Anglo-Chinese Relations*, reprint, New York, Octagon Books, 1970.

Anglo-Chinese Relations During the Seventeenth and Eighteenth Centuries, reprint, New York, Octagon Books, 1970.

Reichwein, A., *China and Europe: Intellectual and Artistic Currents in the 18th Century*, London, Kegan Paul, 1925.

Ricci, M., *China in the 16th Century: the Journals of Matthew Ricci 1583–1610*, tr L.Gallacher from the Latin of N.Trigault, New York, Random House, 1953.

Roberts, J.A.G., *China Through Western Eyes: the 19th Century*, Phoenix Mill: Sutton, 1991.

Robinson, T. and Shambaugh, D. (eds), *Chinese Foreign Policy: Theory and Practice*, Oxford University Press, 1994.

Rowbotham, A.H., *Missionary and Mandarin: the Jesuits at The Court of China*, University of California Press, 1942.

'China in the Age of Enlightenment in Europe', in *Chinese Social and Political Science Review*, XIX. 2, July 1935, 176–99.

'Voltaire: Sinophile', in *Modern Languages Association of America Publications*, XLVII, 1932, 1050–65.

'The Impact of Confucianism on Seventeenth Century Europe', in *Far Eastern Quarterly*, IV. 3, May 1945.

Rule, P.A., *K'ung-tzu or Confucius? The Jesuit Interpretation of Confucianism*, Sydney, Allen & Unwin, 1986.

Sargent, A.J., *Anglo-Chinese Commerce and Diplomacy*, Oxford University Press, 1907.

Schafer, E.H., *The Golden Peaches of Samarkand*, University of California Press, 1963.

Schaller, Michael, *The United States and China in the Twentieth Century*, Oxford University Press, 1990.

Schiffrin, Harold, Z., *Sun Yat-sen: Reluctant Revolutionary*, Boston, Little, Brown and Co., 1980.

Schwartz, W.L., *The Imaginative Interpretation of the Far East in Modern French Literature 1800–1925*, Paris, H. Champion, 1927.

Shai, Aron, *Britain and China 1941–47: Imperial Momentum*, London, Macmillan, 1984.

Shao, Wenguang, *China, Britain and Businessmen: Political and Commercial Relations 1949–57*, London, Macmillan, 1991.

Singer, Aubrey, *The Lion and the Dragon: The Story of the First British Embassy to the Court of the Emperor Qianlong in Peking 1792–1794*, London, Barrie & Jenkins, 1992.

Smith, R.J., *China's Cultural Heritage: the Qing Dynasty 1644–1912*, Boulder, Westview Press, 2nd edn, 1994.

Smith, Sara, R., *The Manchurian Crisis 1931–2*, New York, Columbia University Press, 1948.

Spence, Jonathan, *The Chan's Great Continent: China in Western Minds*, London, Allen Lane Penguin Press, 1998.

'Western Perceptions of China from the Late Sixteenth Century to the Present', in Paul S. Ropp (ed.), *Heritage of China*, Berkeley, 1990.

To Change China: Western Advisers in China 1620–1960, Boston, Little Brown, 1969.

Chinese Roundabout, New York, W.W. Norton & Co., 1992.

'Opium Smoking in Ch'ing China', in (ed.), F. Wakeman and Carolyn Grant, *Conflict and Control in Late Imperial China*, Berkeley, 1975, 143–73.

God's Chinese Son: the Taiping Heavenly Kingdom of Hong Xinquan, New York, W.W. Norton & Co., 1996.

The Search for Modern China, New York, W.W. Norton & Co.,1990.

Stears, P., Adars, M. and Schwartz, S.B., *World Civilisations: the Global Experience*, New York, Harper Collins, 1992.

Storry, R., *Japan and the Decline of the West in Asia*, London, Macmillan, 1979.

Sullivan, Michael, *The Meeting of Eastern and Western Art*, Berkeley, University of California Press, 1989.

Thompson, J.C., *Sentimental Imperialists: American Experience in East Asia*, New York, Harper & Row, 1981.

Trocki, Carl, A., *Opium, Empire and the Political Economy, A Study of the Asian Opium Trade 1750–1950*, London, Routledge, 1999.

Tung, W.L., *China and the Foreign Powers*, New York, Oceana Publications, 1970.

Turner, F.S., *British Opium Policy and its Results in India and China*, London, 1876.

Valder, P., *The Garden Plants of China*, Rozelle, N.S.W. Florilegium, 1999.

Varg, P.A., *Missionaries, Chinese and Diplomats*, Princeton University Press, 1958.

Wakeman, F., 'The Canton Trade and the Opium War', in *Cambridge History of China*, X, Ch. 4.

Waldron, Arthur, *From War to Nationalism: China's Turning Point 1924–1925*, New York, Cambridge University Press, 1995.

Waley-Cohen, Joanna, *The Sextants of Beijing: Global Currents in Chinese History*, New York, W.W. Norton, 1999.

'China and Western Technology in the late 18th Century', in *American Historical Review*, 98.5, 1993, 1525–1544.

Wang, Gungwu, *China and the World Since 1949: The Impact of Independence, Modernity and Revolution*, London, Macmillan, 1977.

'Ming Foreign Relations: South East Asia', in *Cambridge History of China*, vol. VIII, Ch. 6.

Weatherley, R., *The Discourse of Human Rights in China*, London, Macmillan, 1999.

Wickeri, Philip, L., *Seeking the Common Ground: Protestant Christianity, the Three-Self Movement and China's United Front*, Orbis Books, Maryknoll, New York, 1988.

Wills, J.E., *Embassies and Illusions: Dutch and Portuguese Embassies*, Harvard University Press, 1984.

Pepper, Guns and Parley: the Dutch East India Company and China 1622–1681, Harvard University Press, 1974.

'Relations with Maritime Europeans 1514–1662', in *Cambridge History of China*, VIII, Ch. 7.

Woetzel, J.R., *China's Economic Opening to the Outside World: The Politics of Empowerment*, New York, Praeger, 1989.

Wong, J. and Liu, W.T., *The Mystery of China's Falun Gong*, Singapore, East Asia Institute of the National University, 1999.

Wong, John, W., *Deadly Dreams: Opium and the Arrow War (1856–60) in China*, Cambridge University Press, 1998.

Wood, Frances, *No Dogs and Not Many Chinese: Treaty Port Life in China 1843–1943*, London, John Murray, 1998.

Did Marco Polo Go To China?, London, Secker & Warburg, 1995.

Wright, Mary, *The Last Stand of Chinese Conservatism*, Stanford University Press, 1957.

China in Revolution: the First Phase 1900–1913, Yale University Press, 1968.

Wright, S.F., *China's Struggle for Tariff Autonomy 1843–1938*, Shanghai, Kelly & Walsh, 1938; Taipei reprint 1966.

Yang, C.K., *Religion in Chinese Society*, Berkeley, University of California Press, 1961.

Young, J.D., *Confucianism and Christianity: The First Encounter*, Hong Kong University Press, 1983.

Young, Louise, *Total Empire: Manchuria and the Culture of Wartime Imperialism*, Berkeley, University of California Press, 1998.

Index